THE STORY OF MY LIFE

An Autobiography
1888—1922

BOOKS BY ERNEST RAYMOND

NOVELS

A London Gallery *comprising:*

We, the Accused	*Was There Love Once?*
The Marsh	*The Corporal of the Guard*
Gentle Greaves	*A Song of the Tide*
The Witness of Canon Welcome	*The Chalice and the Sword*
A Chorus Ending	*To the Wood No More*
The Kilburn Tale	*The Lord of Wensley*
Child of Norman's End	*The Old June Weather*
For Them That Trespass	*The City and the Dream*

Other Novels

The Bethany Road	*Mary Leith*
The Mountain Farm	*Morris in the Dance*
The Tree of Heaven	*The Old Tree Blossomed*
One of Our Brethren	*Don John's Mountain Home*
Late in the Day	*The Five Sons of Le Faber*
Mr. Olim	*The Last to Rest*
The Chatelaine	*Newtimber Lane*
The Visit of Brother Ives	*The Miracle of Brean*
The Quiet Shore	*Rossenal*
The Nameless Places	*Damascus Gate*
Tell England	*Wanderlight*
A Family that Was	*Daphne Bruno I*
The Jesting Army	*Daphne Bruno II*

BIOGRAPHIES, ETC.

Paris, City of Enchantment	*In the Steps of St. Francis*
Two Gentlemen of Rome	*In the Steps of the Brontës*
(The Story of Keats and Shelley)	

ESSAYS, ETC.

Through Literature to Life	*Back to Humanity*
The Shout of the King	(with Patrick Raymond)

PLAYS

The Berg　*The Multabello Road*

'Dum'

ERNEST RAYMOND

The Story of My Days

An Autobiography 1888-1922

Time . . . in the dark and silent grave,
When we have wandered all our ways,
Shuts up the story of our days. . . .

Sir Walter Raleigh

CASSELL · LONDON

CASSELL & COMPANY LTD
35 Red Lion Square, London WC1
Melbourne, Sydney, Toronto
Johannesburg, Auckland

FAR

S.B.N. *304 93174 8*

0304931748

Printed in England by
Cox & Wyman Ltd
London, Fakenham and Reading
F. 568

CONTENTS

ILLUSTRATIONS

1

DUNSANY ROAD

There is a little road off Brook Green, London, called Dunsany Road, and a more complete reminder of Victorian days it would be hard to find. Its little two-storeyed homes are of red brick with ornate white dressings around door and bay windows. Each house has a shallow garden behind a dwarf wall and privet hedge, and a tiled pathway to the front door. I have called it a little road, for it always seemed so to me; there are but eleven red-and-white houses terraced along one side, and six along the other. To my surprise, however, I learned, when after seventy years I went to look at it again, that Dunsany Road wanders shyly on, over two crossings and past the heedless side-walls of other houses, till it is brought sharply to an end by the brusque and busy faces of Blythe Road and Addison Gardens.

No. 5 Dunsany Road was our home, and it is the first that memory shows me. I went to look at it yesterday before I sat down to write, and it seemed little different, though seventy years, the span of a life, had gone by: a little worn, perhaps, and obviously the creature of an age long lost, but still playing its part as a small well-tended home. Of a sudden I felt sad to think that no one behind those curtained windows knew anything of us who were living there as the last century died: two little children, Ernest Raymond and Dorothy Makepeace ('Dots'), our 'Auntie' who was a Miss Emily Calder, and, most imposing denizen of all, the General: Major-General George Frederic Blake, late of the Royal Marine Light Infantry.

You will have observed, I suspect, that all our surnames were different.

It was out of No. 5, that little red-and-white home that, in this my first clear memory, I see myself, a child of four emerging in a white sailor-suit and long brown stockings on to the pavement of Dunsany Road.

It is a memory as clear as the daylight on to which I stepped, and often in memory it almost assumes the character of someone issuing from the darkness of a womb into the light of life.

Dots came behind me, and my impression is that she was in white broderie anglaise and a large floppy hat; then came Auntie in a tailored dress with constricted waist, leg-of-mutton sleeves, and a fashionable 'boater' above. It was a summer afternoon, so there would be no muff slung before her; probably she carried a white parasol against the sun.

'Auntie' we always called her, but since the repetition of that word after a while becomes, beyond tolerance, farcical, she shall be 'Aunt' henceforward.

Where we were going I do not know, for my memory stops with us walking beneath the plane trees and wych elms, the lindens and syca-mores, that mounted a processional guard around the long grass plats of Brook Green. The only significant moment of that walk was our meeting on the pavement under the trees with a pleasant gentleman who wore mutton-chop whiskers joined by a moustache, and whom we knew as Mr Reay. Mr Reay stayed talking with Aunt. He was a friend who came frequently to visit her—but only when the General was not in residence. Aunt was thirty-seven then, but that was nearer middle age than it would be today. She was becoming stout, and sought to conceal this enlargement with the armour of a 'cuirass corset' which enforced a waist and flattened a stomach by means of a hidden plate.

And there, with us leaving Mr Reay, and walking on beneath the trees, ends my first truly clear memory. But there are a few dim memories of things that must have happened within the walls of that house before this clear and sunlit hour. From the earliest I had no love for Aunt Emily, but much fear. She had a violent temper and was quick with her slaps, and among these twilit pre-dawn memories there is a quaking fear of these slaps. I can see myself in a high-railed cot beside the big brass bed in the front bay-windowed room, crying to myself—crying about what I no longer know; probably it was some native and nameless fear such as only little children know, when nothing but the night-light in its basin spreads its halo in the darkness of a bedroom and lays a bright nimbus on the ceiling.

Aunt comes up at last and demands impatiently, 'What are you crying for?'

No answer from me. I knew no answer.

'Howling like that! Are you thirsty?'

'No.'

'Hungry or something?'

'No.'

'Do you want to go Somewhere?'

'No.'

'Have you any pain?'

'No.'

'Well, stop it, will you, or I'll give you something to cry for.'

And sometimes, in her quick irritation, she stamps a foot at me and gives me that something: a smarting slap on the cheek. 'Now perhaps you'll stop.'

But this is not the whole picture of Aunt Emily. She was not always hot with temper or ready with a slap; she could be lively with both of us children; she could tell us stories, comic or extremely sentimental, the latter her favourites; she could play the piano for us to sing with her; she could be pleasant with me when her mood was calm; but I cannot recall, as I sit here, one caress from Aunt Emily, nor, even in that dark womb, can I hear her call me 'dear'. But I can see Dots caressed and hear her called 'darling'.

There was no slapping of me once Dummy was back home from his unknown occupations in town. 'Dummy'? Yes, Major-General George Frederic Blake. 'Dum' or 'Dummy' was our name for that dear figure. And because I had no love for Aunt Emily all my childhood love poured towards him. Was I not safe from slaps once his latch-key had clicked in the door? Would I not stand by the bay window of the dining-room, looking along Dunsany Road towards Brook Green in the hope of seeing him return home in his top-hat from Hammersmith station? And did he not always call me 'Mr Koko' or 'Mr Koko-man', even as he called Dots 'Queenie', and addressed Aunt (though I only overheard this once) as 'Beauty'? And did he not say that he liked to have Mr Koko-man in that cot beside his big brass bed?

What a figure he was for a child's admiration: erect as a Royal Marine should be (the Royal Marines being beyond denial or argument the first of all regiments); with pointed grey beard and long straight moustaches of a brown tint; and perhaps wearing his fur-lined coat with the deep astrakhan collar. You should have seen him in full-dress uniform, as I did once when he went to some military ceremony: scarlet tunic, gold shoulder-cords, gold oak leaves on cuffs and collar, sash, sword, and plumed cocked hat.

As I see him now, so tall and imposing, he seems out of scale with that little house in a little road. Not so then, of course, since to me, as a child, whatever was, was right. How came he there, another dweller in the road might have asked; what was he doing in Dunsany Road; and what was his relationship with that Miss Calder? 'Lodger' was no word to associate with a man of sixty, so impressive in figure and of such rank.

It seems to me that I slept in that railed cot beside his bed till I was four at least. Dots slept with Aunt in the smaller bedroom behind. When I was five or six I joined Dots in the back room, and then it was often our morning custom to rush into Dum's room and to climb into his big bed, one on either side of him, for a game we called 'When I say Kipper'. Each in turn would begin a story into which sooner or later would be introduced the word 'kipper', whereupon Dum instantly assaulted the narrator with a violent tickling while he or she screamed and giggled and yelled, 'Oh, *stop.*' Apparently Dum enjoyed this game as much as either of us, and Aunt would have to come in and put an end to it, saying, 'You're all three equally silly. And for heaven's sake, child, stop that screaming. What will the neighbours think?'

For a time there was another general in 5 Dunsany Road: Annie Olden, our general servant. I can no longer see her face but remember her as a kind creature with roughened hands, and I have a story to tell of Dum's kindness to her. Aunt told it to us when we were old enough to understand; and because she loved a sentimental story her mouth worked and trembled with tears, her speech was tripped by them, as she approached its moving climax.

So dim is the figure of Annie Olden that she comes to life for me only in a business not usually discussed in a book: my infantile micturition. In my railed cot I was at first only interested by certain uncontrolled eliminations, and it came as a surprise to learn that Aunt and Annie did not view them with the same interest. After a time I got my slaps from Aunt for them. 'Perhaps that'll teach you. Doing that sort of thing at your age!' And thereafter I would lie in the cot hoping the place would dry enough during the night to escape observation in the morning. I can remember scraping with a finger-nail at a stain so as to undo the prospect of a slap.

There was a frequent performance on the landing of that house, just outside the bathroom. I am perhaps four years old, standing there with a lifted nightgown, and Aunt or Annie are holding a chamber-pot in place that I may be an empty vessel before being put to bed. Sometimes they are both there, taking it in turns to hold the chamber and wait. '*Will* you get on with it,' Aunt demands, stamping an impatient foot. But the more she raises her voice and stamps a foot, the less can I oblige. The more I try to oblige, the less I can. I just stand there in the promising position, fearing a slap. Then comes from Aunt the dreadful word, 'wuncenfraw!' Its only meaning for me is that Aunt's wrath is now near the boil. '*Wuncenfraw*, will you do it. How many times am I to tell you? It's not much to ask.'

There are times today when I think, 'If only I could have done it for them once and for all, how much easier life would have been for me on later occasions.'

'Ernest, *will* you stop biting those nails, wuncenfraw.' Poor Aunt often used phrases like a parrot, never giving thought to what they really implied. Another alarming word of hers was 'fragesendages'. 'Haven't I been telling you fragesendages?' I couldn't translate this for a year or two but I arrived at its essence quicker than that of the mysterious and terrible 'wuncenfraw'. I didn't come abreast of that one fragesendages.

Whether Dum or our doctor told Aunt that her impatient and imperious methods would be worse than useless in this matter of micturition I cannot say, but they ceased, and all that would happen was that Annie, before putting me to bed, would ask, "Ev you used your Potty? No? Well, then, 'ev you paid a Visit?"

'What?' I might reply, being an inattentive child.

"Ev you bin to You-know-where?"

'Yes.'

'You 'ev? And you did your dooty?'

'What?'

'Come on. Tell me. S'already hah parse six. And I gommy work to do. You done your dooties?'

'Yes.'

'What? Number one *and* Number two?'

I shudder from my next sentences, but let them stand. For years afterwards these three syllables of Annie's, 'number two', at first hearing, meant only one thing—what Don Quixote's Sancho Panza called 'the major operation'—and if anyone said something like 'Commander Breakthorn was Number Two in that ship' I had to correct my first childish connotation. (Though it is possible, of course, that, if the Commander was unpopular, this first connotation would have been accepted by some of the ratings on the lower deck.)

Enough of that. Annie, kind-hearted, would conclude her inquiries and exhortations with a pat on the shoulder and the gentle reminder of a first Law of Life, 'You see you *got* to be reglar.'

She could have been with us for only a few months, but we children saw much of her in that time. Nursemaid as well as general servant, she would take us on walks to a happy green playground, Ravenscourt Park—a name which, from her lips, I always heard as Ravens caught a park. That was how she pronounced it. 'Come, Master Ernie; come, Miss Dots. We'll go s'arternoon for a nice walk to ravens caught a park.' In the gracious park, with the peacocks screeching around she would sit with her sewing while we two played or squabbled. Her main anxiety was to stop us from sitting on wet grass or wet seats lest we 'got piles'.

'What are piles, Annie?' Dots would ask.

'Never you mind. Not nice things to talk about. But you get them on your sit-upons.'

Objection from Dots. 'Auntie doesn't call them sit-upons. She calls them b-t-m's.'

'What say?'

Dots explains again.

'Eh? B-t-m's? Well, there! But never mind what anyone calls them. Just do what Annie tells you. Never sit on cold or wet stones if you don't want piles.'

Then Annie Olden went. Suddenly. It had become obvious to Aunt's small black peering eyes that she must have been pregnant before she came into our service. Aunt did not in the fashion of those days tell her roughly to 'pack up and go'—indeed I believe she had sympathy for her—but it was impossible to keep her in the house. 'Annie, who is the father?'—and how she enjoyed the comedy here as she was about to enjoy the tears when she came to the pathos at her story's end. 'Who is he?'

'I don't know, 'm.'

'You don't *know*?'

'No'm. I don't really know if it was the young master or the old one.'

But soon after Aunt's laugh as she told us this, the quivering of her lips began, and the catches and gulping in her voice, for she was telling us now of Dum's response to the fascinating news. He went out to the Hammersmith Road, she said, and found a four-wheeler and came back in it to the house. He helped the weeping Annie put her rope-bound tin trunk into it and got in with her. In Dum there was always a strange lonely indifference to what people around him might say or think. Together he and Annie drove to—but here my memory fails. Where was he taking her? To some railway station that she might return to her family? But that was not likely in these stern Victorian times.

Perhaps to the Female Philanthropic Society in Great Church Lane nearby, or to the Asylum for Penitent Women kept by Sisters of the Good Shepherd in Fulham Palace Road. But wherever it was that he parted from Annie, he held her rough hand and said, 'Keep a stout heart, my dear.'

This was the point in the story when Aunt was in tears and could proceed no further. Nor was there any further she could go. Annie had withdrawn into a dark and was lost to us.

§

In these last years of the century Sigmund Freud, away in Vienna, had written some of his books, but he had not yet appeared in Dunsany Road or knocked at any of its little doors. None of us knew that, according to him, the dragon's teeth are sewn in a child's nervous system during his first five years and the armed warriors will later arise from these seeds to plague him through life. These twilit years in Dunsany Road were my first five years, and though in the theories of Freud the teeth of the dragon lie in the unconscious, deeply forgotten, and may take years of skilled analysis to unearth, I yet feel sure in my conscious mind, without benefit of deep analysis, that the facile slappings from Aunt Emily's hand (though she meant no serious harm) and my lively fear of her when she was in the house were the root causes of a nameless and irrational fear that can leap out and grip me for brief minutes, even though my brain is telling me that there's no warrant for it and it's idiotic. I am naturally a sanguine person who hopes always, and half-believes, that the best will happen one day, yet this tendency to a nameless semi-panic can fling its black and heavy cloak around me while my brain despises and disowns it. Inevitably it is the small hours and the dark that provide its best opportunity. Then while my brain is ridiculing it as a mild lunacy it can start a rapid and irregular sick beating of the heart and even get the sweat running, so that I have to turn out of bed (out of that cot?), switch on the light for comfort, and towel the sweat away, while I call up my sense and bid it take command. Three minutes, four, and sense is in command. Bed and the dark are tolerable again. In the morning I can laugh at the memory.

This thorn in the flesh, this messenger of Satan sent to buffet me, can find any peg from which to take down the black cloak and wrap it round me: how awful to be drowning, to go down for the last time, to wake up in a coffin and find oneself buried alive, to be bricked up in a prison cell as in a safe, to be totally paralysed and have no hand to rub an eye or soothe some other itching place—I experience one of these things—for seconds I *am* bricked up, I *am* beneath the surface drowning—and the heart beats fast while the sweat beads run.

This meaningless attack (I call it 'the horrors') occurs too rarely and is too easily overcome, to have upset seriously a long and happy span of years. So I often wonder, do most people walk through their days, happy and successful enough, though every now and then feeling a shadow of unwarrantable fear all around them. The eyes of some of my friends, if I describe these brief lapses into neurosis, light up with instant recognition.

Unless I misjudge her, an insecurity was planted deep in me, all unwillingly, by Aunt's stinging hand. And this companionable insecurity causes me to over-insure against every possible mishap: I keep too much money in the bank ready in case of need; I hold too much in my pocket-book, I pack for a holiday an excessive supply of shirts and socks, and if I sew a button on a shirt, then one thing is sure, it will never in its strength part from the material; they will go to the waste together, for the stitches are three times too many.

§

A quality in Aunt Emily which I now, with an adult's more forgiving eyes, find endearing was her restless hunger to witness all that Life—or Death—in our London could display before her. Aunt missed no spectacle anywhere. Let London stage some coloured pageantry, and she was away early to see it properly and well—the Jubilee of 1887, the State Visit of a foreign monarch, the Trooping the Colour, a State Funeral, a Lying-in-State—especially did she enjoy any of these occasions that stirred the sweetness of tears.

Recently we discovered two diaries of Aunt's, jotted down in rapid fragments: one written mostly before we were born, the other addressed to Dots at this time. It opens:

'*April 24th, 1893.* 10.55 p.m.

'My sweet little Dots, I have been thinking that as you are now five years old it may interest you some day when you are grown up to read all that you said and did when you were a little child. . . .

'*Tuesday, May 9th, 1893:*

'There was a drawing room at Buckingham Palace today and I promised I would take you to see the people going to attend it. Such a lovely day it has been, you and Ernest went on top of the Bus to the Park and walked through it and then down Constitution Hill to the Mall where we waited and saw all those lovely carriages and ladies and flowers. It was very crowded and when a splendid scarlet and gold carriage passed you called out Oh Auntie, there goes the cart to fetch the Princess of Wales, which made everyone around us laugh. I held you up in my arms for a long while. Presently some kind ladies made room for you both and you went there and saw everything well but poor Auntie was very anxious for she could no longer see you and she was afraid you would get pushed away in the crowd. You saw the Prince of Wales and his son and the Princess May who is soon to be married to the son, and after that you went to the Army and Navy Stores and had a nice little tea and wash, and then we went by train to South Kensington and walked past the Institute and saw all the preparations for tomorrow, for tomorrow is to be a grand day in London, the Queen is going to open the Institute built with the money given to her for a present on her Jubilee which was before you were born, little Dots, and was a very gay time too.

'And then when you had seen all the flags and masts and crimson-covered stands we walked on into the Park and there presently we saw all the carriages stop and the Royal footmen came along and then the Queen drove by and bowed to everyone. . . .

'*Wednesday, May — 1893*

'Today we got up and dressed ourselves and went off to see the procession. All the buses were so full that we had to walk a long way to get on to one and come back to Hammersmith and remain on it for the return journey. When we got into the park we found everyone hurrying along too. We stood opposite the Queen's Gate. There was a great crowd so we could only see by standing on tip-toe, and then only the heads of the coachmen, but I expect you and Ernest saw more for we lifted you up well. It was so hot. Ernest sat in a very lumpy way on my arm and it is now so shaky I can hardly write. There was a great deal of cheering as the processions went by, the Prince of Wales, his son, his intended bride and her mother in one carriage. There were soldiers from Australia and India and elsewhere and plenty of our own beautiful soldiers and guards, and presently there was a cry of here she comes, and the outriders came in sight and the lovely cream-coloured horses and then the Queen bowing and the people cheering. All the little babies in the crowd were held up and everyone stood on tip-toe. Do you not think you are a lucky little girl to go and see all these lovely sights?'

Westminster Cathedral was not yet built, and the Roman Catholic Pro-Cathedral was then a Gothic church not ten minutes' walk along the Kensington Road from our Brook Green. You can be sure that Aunt went quickly and early to the Pro-Cathedral after she'd read that a famous Jesuit father, Father Bernard Vaughan, was going to preach a series of sermons there, denouncing the Sins of Society. (This was their title.) She was in her place for the whole series; and since the good father's denunciations were sensational and violent, I have no doubt that there was one in his packed audience who enjoyed every word of them.

§

Aunt Emily was one of five Calder sisters, daughters of the late Colonel Calder, once of the 8th Foot. Three of these aunts I saw but seldom; they were dispersed over the country. Very different it was with the fourth, Aunt Ida. She lived in Margravine Gardens at no great distance across the District Railway, with her second husband, a plump little German professor, Dr Franz Broenner, whom she loved and bullied and kept in subservience. She appeared with regularity at Dunsany Road—but only when 'the General' was not there. Ten years older than Emily, she was on the brink of fifty and getting stout like Emily, but as neat-waisted a figure as the whalebones, hooks and eyes of her corsets could make her. Her great pride was her figure. I once heard her say angrily to Percy, her hugely tall ten-year-old son, 'Few people have a figure like mine,' after he had complained that it was 'all in here and out there'. If Aunt Ida bullied her kindly German husband, her son, Percy, so tall, was soon to bully both her and this new German stepfather, whom he called 'the Deutscher'.

Aunt Emily used to say, 'It's dear Ida's nature either to domineer or to be dominated. She lords it over Franz, and now Percy is lording it over her.' Let me point out that Percy introduces another surname into our galaxy. He was Percy Wilkinson, Ida's first husband having been (to parody a famous parody of Wordsworth) 'a Mr Wilkinson, a civil servant'.

When we first saw this new 'Uncle Franz', and learned that Aunt Ida had now become 'Mrs Broenner', Dots offered to Aunt Emily the astonishing comment, whose genesis at her age I cannot hope to explain, 'When *I* buy my babies I'm going to have them made in Germany.'

The Calders are a recognized sept of the Clan Campbell of Cawdor, and whether this inheritance from so many unruly and bullying fellows (remember Macbeth) accounts for a domineering quality in four of these Calder sisters, is probably no more than an amusing query. But these four, Aunts Clara, Ida, Emily and Mary were certainly dynamic creatures, the exception being Aunt Sophie who lived placidly, within a figure of massive fatness, far away in Dover.

Aunt Ida's so-valued figure was always attired as exquisitely as she thought it deserved. She gave most of the forenoon between breakfast and luncheon to dressing and embellishing it, and to arranging her beautiful auburn hair and her soft-featured, pretty face as the culmination of a picture for the public view in the afternoon. When she embraced me I was embraced also, and all round, by the fragrance of her favourite scent; what it was I don't know; parma violet, perhaps, or patchouli or attar of roses.

Embrace me? Yes. Here was the remarkable fact of this aunt who appeared so frequently (later when I was a schoolboy ever 'trying to be funny', I used to call Aunt Emily 'my permanent aunt' and Aunt Ida 'the intermittent one'.) Yes, there was no lack of caresses from Aunt Ida. She gushed over me as surely as Aunt Emily did not. She called me her 'little sweetheart' and somehow induced me to address her as 'Sweetheart'; I was never clear why, but at five years old, accepting all the facts around me as normal and beyond question, I produced the behaviour that seemed required of me. Willing to oblige, I said my 'Good-bye, sweetheart' at the door or the gate. When she said, 'You do love me, little sweetheart, don't you?' I provided the 'Yes' she wanted, and when she acknowledged this assurance with a long hug and kiss, I responded with as able a kiss as I could manage. But it all came from the head rather than the heart; it was a child's willing performance in a play-script written by her.

I recall one summer afternoon when she was expected to tea, and I stood by the french windows in our small drawing-room gazing at our back garden where grew a single tree and wondering whether I would say something that would really please her. Something really strong. I detect here a first effort to be a creator of verbal drama—a dominant ambition which did not flower into consciousness till many years afterwards. When she said, 'You do love me, don't you?' would not I, in my desire to please, reply, 'Yes. I love you better than God'?

She came, and I didn't say it, partly because she didn't give me the exact opportunity, and partly because I was beginning to wonder whether God, who, we were taught, saw every naughty thing we did and heard every idle word we spoke, would take some serious steps about so great an irreverence. And so wilful a deception.

So there we all were in our little 5 Dunsany Road: myself, Ernest Raymond, the centre of the known world; Dorothy Makepeace, my playmate and fellow-ward of Aunt's; that formidable lady herself, Miss Emily Calder; the major-general, George Frederic Blake; and this visiting aunt, Mrs Ida Broenner, bringing perhaps her very tall son, Percy Wilkinson. To Dorothy and me nothing in this multi-surnamed *ménage* was touched with wonder; nothing to prompt curiosity and queries. To children of five and six whatever was, was right. We asked no questions. And no one spoke.

2

THE SECOND HOUSE

One autumn day Dum came home from town and told Aunt—did I hear him or did she tell us of this long afterwards?—that he was being made a director of the Army and Navy Stores, and was soon to be a director of other companies—Hovis Bread and Ilford Camera were two of them—so now he would be able to 'make a home more worthy of her'. He was to go at once to India to open there a branch of the Army and Navy Stores, and while he was gone she was to find a better home for us all. Though excited by this prospect of a 'move', I was surprised because I had imagined that 5 Dunsany Road would be our home for ever. Aunt was excited too and, always relishing a sentimental exaggeration, declared, 'He's another Cecil Rhodes. Everything he touches turns to gold.' Rhodes just then was making an enormous fortune out of his South African diamond mines.

Dum disappeared for India in a fine ship-board ulster which greatly impressed us, and some time in my sixth year Aunt must have decided on the new home.

It was 22 Gledstanes Road, West Kensington, a tall red house of five storeys. Steps led up to a pompous portico whose pillars had leafy and voluted capitals; and, all told, it was a house where a six-foot-four major-general would not look out of scale.

It stood within walking distance of Dunsany Road. You walked beside Brook Green, crossed the dangerous Hammersmith Road, walked the length of Gliddon Road, crossed the railway bridge (Barons Court Station was not yet built) and went onward by the daisy-studded waste grounds of Palliser Road (where now all the quaint little houses stand in their pit) till you were among the tall houses. Best of the tall houses were those in Gledstanes Road because their back windows overlooked the green arena of Queen's Club where in those days the Oxford and Cambridge sports were held, and the inter-varsity matches played—and even a sports contest between Harvard-and-Yale and Oxford-and-Cambridge.

You will not find 22 Gledstanes Road now. I couldn't go and look at it the other day so as to resurrect old memories as I had done on the pavement of Dunsany Road. When it received us and all our expensive new furniture it did not know the fate that was written for it. But in the Second German War a bomb fell straight as a plummet through the midst of it, and for months there was a gap in that terrace of tall houses like the gap left by an extracted tooth in a fine front row. Where our rooms had been and our lives were spent, and where happened all that you may consent to read about now, you could see blue sky and drifting clouds and trees that fringed the Queen's Club Ground.

It was—or seems now—the real house of my childhood. Which is strange because we were there only for five years, and yet, because of the long straying days of childhood between six years old and eleven, it holds one of the fullest chapters of my life.

Dum came home from India, and the axle-tree on which my child-hood turned was in place again. Apprehensions of wrath and slaps had lived close beside me during his absence, but did not, of course, catch hold of me every hour of the day. There were long times when I played happily and Aunt was kind enough and pleasant and amusing. Dum brought home wonderful Indian brasses and silvers to adorn our new bureaux, and an arsenal of Eastern weapons to hang along our entrance hall. 'We missed D—— very much this Christmas,' says Aunt's diary for Dots, 'but had nice letters full of news of travel from him. One day in February he came back from his travels and brought such lots of beautiful things. It was like a fairy story to see them all.'

He now had the best bedroom, the third-floor front, where now the old brass bed and a new walnut suite with a vast gabled wardrobe like the porch of a cathedral, occupied most of the floor. Beneath this room was a 'spare bedroom' which, seldom occupied, served usually as our play-room. Below this again was the 'breakfast-room' and below that the spacious kitchen premises. Of these rooms (except the kitchen which saw only a grey area) the windows commanded the terraces of tall houses: Gledstanes Road to left and right, and Charleville Road ahead of us, leading through porticoed mansions of stucco'd London to the noisy and rather notorious highway, North End Road.

A ruminative child, often self-absorbed and something of a solitary, I would spend dreamy hours with elbows on the window-sill, watching the sequence of events in our long quiet streets. If it was early, here came the milkman pushing his milk-float with its churn and stopping to ladle out a pint or two for a capped and aproned maid who had surfaced from a grey area. In our first days I might still see a man mounted on one of the old 'penny-farthing' bicycles, he dangerously astride one huge wheel while a little wheel trailed behind. My eyes followed him till he had turned a corner because there always seemed a chance that he would become unbalanced and crash to the ground. Which would be interesting. More interesting, and almost as infrequent, was the passing of a motor-car, a new sort of open vehicle that was able to speed at fifteen or twenty miles an hour. Sometimes there was a daring lady in the car with a dust-veil tied tautly from the rim of her large hat to a point under her chin. Her male escort at the wheel would probably be in a peaked cap and goggles. But far more likely than a motor-car would be a one-horse victoria to take a lady for a drive in the park, or a four-wheeler bringing a family home from a holiday, with, on occasions, a man padding along beside it in the hope of a sixpence for helping with the trunks. Interesting too was Dr Owen's brougham going slowly round and round that the driver might save his horse from being bored; this was interesting partly because it meant someone was ill—dying, perhaps—and partly because the horse, after a wearisome circumnavigation, might halt and loose a stream of yellow stale, or lumps of warm dung, on to the roadway. Even in our residential roads there was often a smell, not unpleasant, of horse dung.

Before I leave this window of long ago I must not omit the street entertainers to whom we were allowed to throw pennies. There was the one-man-band with a drum on his back worked from an elbow, pan-pipes tied beneath his lips, and cymbals and other instruments worked by his hands or his feet. There were the Italian organ-grinder turning the handle of his piano-organ while his monkey sat on the instrument or pranced about the pavement on a leash; and the man with a led bear—I can't remember what the bear did, except to be a brown bear, short-legged and upright and lovable, in a London street.

In the fall of the evening the lamplighter came with his long pole and crossed from lamp-post to lamp-post, igniting their gas burners. On Sunday afternoons the muffin man appeared with his tray of muffins and crumpets balanced on his head and his bell sounding in his hand—always it seems now that he appeared on darkening Sunday afternoons to supply us for a winter tea-time.

So much for our play-room first-floor window. Most of our life with the adults was passed in the larger back-rooms of the house. On the ground floor was the long dining-room, all mahogany: sideboard as big as an altar with its reredos, dining table long enough for a city board-room, and a corpulent leather arm-chair by the fireplace for Dum. Here we had dinner when Dum was home from town, and often our two adults at the table were in the desolate aftermath of a quarrel and not, for the present, on speaking terms. Each sat eating and drink-ing in a melancholy silence. We children, conscious of our elders' disunion and loneliness, sat silent too. Often Aunt and Dum had these uproarious rows which might, towards their end, draw tears from both, since Dum wept easily—especially after a bitter quarrel which, I am persuaded, one half of him enjoyed.

Let us have a scene that will be true to these old sorrows but a com-posite picture, blending many similar scenes. It will be a picture of four persons in an old-fashioned dining-room—I was about to describe it as a 'Conversation Piece', but that wouldn't do because conversation was the one thing missing. It is an evening in the later nineties, and we children must be eight or nine, since we are able to sit up for dinner.

At the head of the table sits Aunt Emily, the lady of the house. In the midst of the table's left side sits Dum, and since the table is so long there is an adequate desert between him and his late opponent. We children sit in the midst of the opposite side and swing our eyes from one seated Statue of Speechless Heartache to the other.

Though their relations are temporarily 'broken off' and communi-cation is not desirable, Dum sometimes, without looking at her, addresses us in her interest. 'Koko! Koko!' he says in surprise; even in shock. 'Is it possible that you are not being a gentleman and passing the potatoes to your kind auntie who is so good to you?' Or later, 'Queenie! Really! You are not looking after your kind auntie. Don't you see that her glass is empty? Fill it. What is that decanter for?' Nevertheless words are unsuitable tonight, so next time he just catches my eye, swings his own eye from bread-board to Aunt's empty side-plate, and back to me and the bread-board; I catch the message and offer my kind auntie another slice of bread.

This shadowed meal over, he goes sighing to his big leather chair by the fireplace and to his box of cigars. We hastily set up beside him a folding card-table, and there in his chair, smoking the cigar, he is content to play Bezique or Halma with Mr Koko and Queenie. This always amazes me: I am now older than he was then but I can never catch the pleasing, pungent scent of a cigar box's cedarwood without seeing that card-table and knowing that I could never, at any time, have devoted whole evenings to playing games with two happy and yelling children. But Dum sits there behind his long cigar dealing cards or moving Halma men; finishing one contest, starting another, and if by chance I win, declaring, 'Mr Koko has great gifts. He is surely one of the most gifted players in the country.' If Dorothy wins, it is 'Ah! You see. There! Brilliant youth against poor tired old age.'

'But you win sometimes,' she points out, an intelligent child.

'Luck. Pure luck, my dear. Remember my great age.' He was then sixty-two.

Meanwhile Aunt sits at the dining-table darning his socks or crocheting a present (quite likely for him when the sun shines again) but tonight there is no communication between dining-table and card-table; only these pleasantries across a Halma board between sixty-two and eight or nine.

Eventually Aunt closes the scene by saying sadly (to us only), 'Children, you must go to bed now'; and Dum agrees, though not looking at her, or speaking to her, 'Yes. You must run along now. Always do what your kind auntie tells you.'

§

Above the dining-room was the drawing-room, its velvet-curtained windows overlooking Queen's Club. Here were the Indian silvers and brasses on bureaux or in cabinets, and the Sèvres china on the mantelpiece. It was a room used only for Aunt's At Homes, for her parties to watch the Universities' Sports, for our daily piano practice, and for the evening visits (when such were safe) of Mr Reay. We were instructed never to mention Mr Reay in the hearing of Dum. Diagonally across the top left-hand corner of Aunt's visiting cards were the words 'Last Thursday'. They meant that her At Home day was on the last Thursday of each month, but I, trying as usual to be funny, would point out that this might preclude visitors from ever coming, since the words implied that the At Home was last Thursday and thus, thank God, over and done with.

The daily piano practice I loathed and evaded if possible. Aunt might come home from some neighbour's At Home and ask at once, 'Ernest, *have* you done your piano practice?' And if I had to answer, 'N-no . . .' she stamped her foot at me and said, '*Will* you go and do your practising properly, wuncenfraw!'

Oh, if only I could have done it once and for all, and there left it.

One evening she came home and asked this question, and I, fearing that stamped foot, lied: I said 'Yes' and then like all insecure liars elaborated the lie. 'I did it about an hour ago. For quite a long time. An hour, I should think.'

'You did *not*! You're a little liar.' I perceived her pleasure in catching me lying. 'The room's been locked all day, and the key's not in the door. Come into the dining-room.'

This meant she was going to 'take the stick to me', and I followed her, sobbing. In the dining-room she laid me breast-down on the table so that my legs hung over the edge, and applied the stick. Six times, and not gently.

My memories will not let me doubt that she was glad of the excuse to do this because she got some pleasure from it, though I am certain she turned her thoughts away from this strange fact and told herself that she was doing it for my good. I remember her saying once, the caning over, 'There! You'll be grateful to me for that one day.' Was she burying a doubt within herself as she spoke? She did not wish to be cruel. But, just as Sigmund Freud had not yet come along Dunsany Road, so the Marquis de Sade had yet to be familiar in Gledstanes Road; the unlovely word derived from his name had only just been coined.

But how is it that people forget that children will remember?

I asked for angry words and punishment, of course, scamping the practice, dawdling over it, and lying; I showed no desire to learn, and in the end my music master gave me up as a hopeless starter. Since when a recurring dream throughout my life has been of myself playing at a grand piano with hands running marvellously over the whole gamut of keys, and sometimes overleaping each other, while I express all the sorrows, fantasies, dreams, and soaring hopes of man—all the things that any artist longs to express. One day perhaps someone will unriddle this for me.

Above the drawing-room was Aunt's bedroom, only a passage at the stair-head separating her room from Dum's. Whether she ever crossed that passage after we children and the servants were asleep I cannot know. Nor shall I ever know the limits of her relationship with Mr Reay, who was a good Catholic and went regularly to his duties. He came two or three evenings a week, if Dum was away, and sometimes it was very quiet, wholly silent, in the drawing-room where they sat, not a voice speaking. I lay in my bedroom next to the drawing-room with the door open and if I was still not asleep because daylight was still in the room, I would wonder at these silences. Aunt was usually a voluminous talker.

One thing only I can reveal about Aunt Emily and Dum. On a day

during a prolonged period of injured silence between them I went alone
into Dum's room and saw on the commode by his bed an open letter
which he'd forgotten to pocket or hide. I read it. It begged for a
reconciliation, saying, 'I cannot bear these awful silences. If I have done
something that has bitterly hurt you forgive me and let us be happy
again. Emily.' And many, many years later, after all her loves and
sorrows and secrets had gone into the last great silence we discovered
the old broken diary of hers, written before we were born, and loose
among its torn and time-stained pages was a folded sheet containing a
poem. Often she tried her hand at sentimental poems, but to her
'poetry' meant little more than lines which beat level and rhymed.

> Parody on 'Good Night' (Shelley)
> by E.C.

> Good day! Ah yes! the day is good
> Which brings thee back to me,
> And wasted all the lonely hours
> When spent away from thee.

> How long the night without thee seemed,
> The daylight coming never.
> Ah! Cruel night, so lone, so dark,
> Such faithful friends to sever.

But just as Aunt rarely put a date on any letter but merely 'Tuesday'
or 'Friday', leaving it for ever impossible to say now in what month,
year, or circumstances it was written, so there is no date on these
verses; they may have been written when she was one of Colonel
Calder's five beautiful daughters, young and slim, instead of 'fat and
forty', as she would sometimes describe herself now, but it seems more
likely that it belongs to the years of the diary in which it lay thrust.

Recalling that passage between her room and Dum's, I remember
another problem that will never now be solved. Many times he would
leave his door ajar, and Aunt, when she was joking about him to us,
would remark that, though he never went to church, he always said
his prayers at his bedside. 'I could glance along the passage,' she would
say, 'and see by his heels sticking out that he was down on his marrow
bones praying.' So she said, but I do not think now that these bedside
prayers were regular. I think it was only in his times of agonized despair that he did this violence to Heaven.

When I was about seven or eight, after a long meditation at my window during a summer afternoon, I for the first time questioned Aunt about my unknown parents. This was prompted by no sudden sense that I had a right to know, no sudden uprush of courage; it was only the fruit of a fairy-tale dream at the window. For the first time an enchanting idea had come to me.

'It's rather wonderful not knowing who your father and mother were,' I said to Aunt. 'It might turn out that I'm the son of a prince or a duke or someone.'

Did she pale? Maybe not, but she certainly answered sharply, 'Never that. You'll never hear that. So don't imagine so. Don't get any ideas like that in your head.'

'Well, who were they?' My first question and my last for many a year.

She angered and stuttered. 'I don't know. . . . At least you must ask Dum. They . . . they died . . . when you were two.'

'Did you ever see them?'

'Did I . . . ? No. . . .'

'Did they both die together?'

Surprisingly her foot stamped. 'Don't worry me about it. Ask Dum if you want to know. He is your real guardian. I'm not really.'

'Yes, but—'

'Now *will* you leave me alone?'

Frightened by her manner, I did not go on to ask who Dorothy's parents were. I walked slowly away.

And I didn't ask Dum. Never in his lifetime did I ask him, and never did answer come from his lips. In these early years my silence with him persisted because Aunt's voice had frightened me; in the later years because I suspected many things and dreaded even a single moment that might embarrass both him and me. I did not want this discomfort for myself, but, more than this, loving him as I loved no one else, I did not want, even as a child, to let any displeasing moment spoil my memories of exultant happiness in his company.

§

That other diary of Aunt's, begun before we were born and surprisingly found but a few years ago, is written in slap-dash style within the black covers of a cheap exercise book. It begins with the Golden Jubilee of 1887, and it was probably this glorious affair, an excitement in the streets after her own heart, which inspired the thought, 'I really ought to keep a diary.' Only a few of her years lie within the tattered pages of that old broken-backed book, and these years, because of the casual and intermittent writing, are in fragments small or large. They tell scrappily, though delightedly, of her visits to Brittany, Paris, and Switzerland. These were years when she was young-hearted and avid for life in any and every form—as indeed she remained till her death in her eighties.

But there is a mystery in the last sixty pages of the book. Apart from her friends and her old mother in London and her elder sister Ida, later my 'sweetheart' (officially), who accompanied her to Brittany with her huge and lusty infant, Percy, then three years old, no names are mentioned. We are never told, either by an initial or hint who are the 'we' who visited all the obligatory sights in Paris, went to the Great Exhibition of 1888 over and over again, and in Switzerland 'made a lovely expedition by steamer to Tellsplatte where William Tell jumped from the boat in the storm'. But clearly the 'we' are not two sisters alone; there is another adult with them. 'We lunched at the Hotel de la Tellsplatte from where there is a lovely view and then Ida, I, and —— walked by the Axenstrasse to Flüelen and back two and a half miles either way a lovely walk hewn in the rock on the mountain's side.' Sometimes she seems carefully to avoid even the 'we'. The verb may describe a 'lovely' occasion but it is denied any subject. 'Walked one day to Weggis and saw the Pension Gottliber opposite the Rigi. They asked six francs a day. Grounds very lovely. Went today to the Rigi—boat to Weggis. Walked up the mountain for some hours it was pleasant and not too steep.'

Like the diary, addressed to Dots, this old crumbling volume, late in my life, shewed me that, because of the temper, the slaps and the beatings, I had never been fair to Aunt Emily. Fifty years too late I discerned many pleasing facets of her character. My heart struggled out at last to this young Miss Emily Calder chasing after life and experience where they were to be found, warming with appreciation for whatever, sparsely educated, she supposed to be high art or poetry, full of affection for her lonely old mother in London and for her chosen friends—and palpably, if silently, loving the hidden member of the 'we'. I could not, now or ever, feel love for her but there came an amused admiration, and a large measure of compassion. She could suffer. The writing of the diary stops while there are still many pages of the exercise book unused. Obviously she had laid it aside carelessly and never touched it again. Nowhere in it are there any attempts at fine writing or dramatic effects; it is just a woman's prattle hastily scrawled. None the less, when at last the curtain falls on the careless but vivacious record, the closing lines by a happy accident are sufficiently poignant and winning to bring a curtain down. 'We had a most lovely sermon today on the furnace of pain. The vicar is a wonderfully sympathetic preacher and his congregation all seem to be so responsive. I think I have gone through my furnace of pain, mental pain, but oh, how acute sometimes.'

§

Since Dum had been made a director of the Army and Navy Co-operative Society he would allow us to buy hardly anything except at the Army and Navy Stores. It was a joke of Aunt's that if he wanted a twopenny pencil he spent twice as much travelling on the District Railway to Victoria so as to buy it at the Army and Navy Stores. A faithful director, Dum. He was equally faithful to Hovis Bread. There would be an inflammatory, if stately, row at any restaurant to which he took us if they could not serve Hovis bread. Generally, shocked, we walked out.

Accordingly one late December afternoon he took us to Victoria and the Army and Navy Stores so that we could consider the Toys Department and choose our Christmas presents. On our way to the Toys through the China and Glass he recognized a small grey old gentleman and stopped to talk with him. He introduced us. 'These are two little wards of mine. Mr Ernest here is the son of my old friend, William Raymond. William *Bell* Raymond,' he emphasized. 'Who died. . . . In Switzerland a few years ago. One of my lifelong friends.'

I am sure I was not meant to overhear this name, William Bell Raymond, and at the time I was not certain what I had heard. It was only later that I learned exactly what Dum had said.

The old gentleman smiled down at us. Leaving him in the China and Glass, Dum told us proudly, 'That was Colonel "Choky" Morrison, a very famous officer. Distinguished himself in the Crimean War, and afterwards at Kandahar and Jalalabad in the Second Afghan War—which of course you know all about. I wish I had half his medals. My only active service was in the Baltic. An undistinguished career.'

That you may not accept this slander on his career let me recount here that when he was nineteen he had his part as a first lieutenant in the blockade of the Russian ports in the Gulf of Finland, before Sebastopol fell and the Crimean War ended; that he served three years in H.M.S. *Cadmus* in the Mediterranean, North American, and West Indies stations; and that when he was thirty-one he became a barrister of the Middle Temple and was duly appointed a Deputy Judge Advocate, relinquishing this appointment on attaining the rank of full colonel when he was forty-nine; and, finally, that he was retired the following year with the rank of Honorary Major-General, his retired pay being £450 a year.

In the Toys Department he said, 'Now choose. Choose what you want. Queenie and Mr Koko must have exactly what they want. Naturally. And nothing but the best is good enough for two such admirable children. Besides, the best is always cheapest in the end. Remember that. All the same, may I timidly suggest that you limit the cost of your purchases to about a pound each. One-pound-ten perhaps. But remember that I am but a poor man.'

With that strange consideration which sometimes the least attractive children show for an adult's purse, and even though we had no belief in that 'but a poor man', we were careful not to exceed too far the limits he had suggested and were apologetic about the slight excess. Besides, did we not know that on Christmas morning at the breakfast table he would unpocket his little soverign case, open it, and slide out a golden sovereign, probably newly polished, for each of us. 'That, I think, should meet the occasion. It might well be more, of course, but I am but a poor man. . . . No, please, *please*! It is nothing, nothing—' this as we flung our arms around him.

That Christmas occasion in the China and Glass was the first time I heard of William Bell Raymond, Dum's lifelong friend. Who had died. I don't think he mentioned Dorothy's parents; if he had, we must have discussed them later and so planted a name in our memories.

Once again I must set down that after my romantic suggestion to Aunt that I might be a prince's son, the years drifted on and neither Dorothy nor I troubled Dum or Aunt with questions. And why? In part because children avoid angry tones, but in the main because as yet we were not really troubled. Our home was our home, and whatever was happening in it was reasonable and right. A calm sea of silence lay all around us with never an underswell to disturb its surface. Years were to pass before we disturbed it.

3

MR HILLIARD AND OTHERS

Sometimes it seems to me as if there were no natural seasons in the roads of tall houses I commanded from my window. Or as if the seasons were but faintly apprehended as they went by. Evenings would darken earlier, of course; the incandescent gas lamps in our rooms be turned up as soon as four o'clock; and the lamplighter in the street might pass with his pole before it was five; but what else? There were no trees in these streets to drop rusty leaves; only stone pavements, cambered carriage-way, and lamp-posts alternating with one another along the kerbs; no birds except the sparrows which changed not at all throughout the year; no flowers except those in the window-boxes—scarlet geraniums, white marguerites and blue lobelia—but these boxes were so few and separate that we hardly noticed when they emptied. There was no stream to freeze; all one could say was that everything in the winter months—pavements, metalled roads and brick walls—*looked* harder. If we walked along Palliser Road towards Hammersmith we did not notice that the long waste grounds, daisy-sprinkled in the pride of summer, were empty now of all but their tired grass, dandelions and chickweed.

Chilblains might redden my toes and heels, and so tease them that in church I kicked them against pews or floor to stop the maddening itch, but I never associated this with the months of the year. Memory suggests that, apart from the rare falls of snow or the glitter of ice in the gutters, it was only the November fogs, and the brown darkness before and after them, which reminded us that it was winter. Even so, the thick, acid, soot-smelling fogs of those old Novembers served in part to conceal the season in the streets.

Or am I right in thinking that the muffin man with his bell signalled winter by coming more often along the streets in the gathering dusk before tea-time?

Chilblains in church? Yes indeed. If the natural seasons were but dimly remarked the ecclesiastical seasons had suddenly impinged upon our household in full power—if by household you understand only Aunt and Dots and me; the steeple of St Andrew's Church, Fulham, which we could just see over our roofs, had inspired Dum not at all, he who prayed only by his bedside—occasionally.

St Andrew's was a large parish and, curiously enough, its large and ugly Victorian church stood with geometrical accuracy between its residential streets of 'ladies and gentlemen' and the streets of the poor. The pretty little St Andrew's Road, holding the church and named after it, separated, like a straight chasm, gentles from plebs. 'Ladies' children', as we were called, were allowed to play together in our roads —cricket perhaps against a lamp-post—but forbidden to associate with the 'Board-School children' on the other side of St Andrew's. The church might be 'St Andrew's, *Fulham*' on that farther side, but we on our side called ourselves 'West Kensington', clinging to the hems of a fashionable borough.

As far as I can remember, no church threw its influence over us in Dunsany Road, but now! Well, now Church life, like June in the song, was busting out all over. Now Mr Hilliard appeared in our streets, and here he was in our house. Vicar of St Andrew's, he had a magnificent sculptured face beneath silver hair parted down the middle, and his appearance would have been majestic if his figure had been less broad and squat. No saint, as my older eyes perceived, he was yet the most successful parish priest I have ever encountered, if numbers are to serve as the measuring rod. Not only did he draw into his church most of the 'ladies and gentlemen' in their fine Sunday clothes, but he had in his Sunday schools fully two thousand children from the poor and noisy streets. In my day he had to enlarge an already large church to hold a queuing congregation and to hire huge board-schools to hold these children. The 'ladies' children', separated from the vulgar, had a crowded morning service to themselves in the parish hall.

Mr Hilliard was an actor born, and might have earned fame on the stage; his three children, our friends and schoolfellows, Stafford, Harry, and Evangeline Hilliard, all went on the stage and won some distinction there. He looked like an actor: many noticed his resemblance to the silvery Wilson Barrett who, round about this time, was drawing all London to his own play, *The Sign of the Cross*. Hilliard's reading from lectern or sanctuary of great Bible passages could not be surpassed by any of our actor knights today: it echoes in my mind after seventy years. He had three curates, but if the lesson for the day was a gift to any actor who loved to hear himself speaking great words, no curate went to the lectern; it was Mr Hilliard who stood there; there would be a silence of nigh on a thousand people waiting to hear him; he let the silence serve as an introduction to the splendour that was to come— and then began to read. 'Comfort ye, comfort ye my people, saith your

God. Speak ye comfortably to Jerusalem and cry unto her that her warfare is accomplished, that her iniquity is pardoned. . . .' Or Ecclesiastes: 'Remember now thy Creator in the days of thy youth, while the evil days come not, nor the years draw nigh when thou shalt say, I have no pleasure in them; while the sun, or the light, or the moon, or the stars be not darkened, nor the clouds return after the rain . . . when the grasshopper shall be a burden, and desire shall fail; because man goeth to his long home, and the mourners go about the streets.' Or Mary is at the sepulchre weeping . . . 'and Jesus saith unto her, Mary.'

I can hear that 'Mary' now.

Throughout Holy Week it was not the Vicar who celebrated at the altar; he stood on the gospel step that he might read the long heart-wrenching Passion stories.

One who often sat enthralled, with mouth open and eyes staring, was a boy of nine or ten in his Eton suit and starched white collar: myself. And so it was Mr Hilliard who cast into a soil, unbroken till now and virgin, the first seed of a love for words that could shiver and shake one's being. I may still feel an inadequate gratitude to Aunt Emily for her beatings, but I do feel a full gratitude to her because with her love for all sentiment and poignance she too sat enraptured by Hilliard's performances and raved about them to us afterwards so that at an early age we were infected with a delight akin to hers.

Aunt read none of her country's historic literature but only the popular novels of the day, the halfpenny *Daily Express*, and the gossiping weeklies like *M.A.P.* (Mainly About People). Thus, except for Hilliard's superb rendering of the Bible and of the Elizabethan and Jacobean language in Collects and Prayers at Matins and Evensong, so noble in diction, balance, and rhythm, little of true literature would have come my way in childhood. I loathed the Sundays when the Litany extended Matins almost beyond bearing, but I began to hear, dimly and as it were distantly, the beauty of its suffrages. 'That it may please thee to strengthen such as do stand, and to comfort and help the weak-hearted; and to raise up them that fall, and finally to beat down Satan under our feet. . . . That it may please thee to preserve all that travel by land or by water, all women labouring of child, all sick persons and young children; and to show thy pity on all prisoners and captives.'

Oh, yes, if I was listening and not day-dreaming on my knees, a little of the magic broke through.

We had not been long in Gledstanes Road before Hilliard had Aunt in his pocket together with most of the other ladies in our genteel streets. On one page of her 'diary for Dots' she writes, 'Yesterday was an important day and marked a new era of my life. The Vicar Mr Hilliard came to see us. We found him awfully nice so humorous and mischievous and he came several times and somehow or other has commandeered me and by now I am a fully fledged district visitor. I do hope I shall be able to be useful for however humble the instrument it may be of some use. In the meantime it fills my lonely hours.'

And so from now we children were safe in the Church's laager, and thanks to the voice of Hilliard, that fine instrument so skilfully played, my education in the wonder of words was begun.

But, as I think now, it was a lesson in word-music only; it rejected the one thing which, more than all else, anyone who seeks a full culture should get from his schooling: the gradual liberation of his thought so that at the last it is totally and fearlessly independent: his own private and personal vision.

Here was Aunt Emily, a woman of restless vitality, and the Church of her time with its ingrained puritanism, its excessive niceties, its credal insistencies, and its Biblical infallibilities, shrivelled much that might have been richly creative thought in her. It inhibited and drove underground to their detriment the true realities of her private self, and of ours. Our churchmanship at St Andrew's was neither High nor Low; it was of a precisely middle stature; and yet Mr Hilliard could have largely underscored Cardinal Newman's typically fearless and ruthless statement in his *Apologia*: 'The Church claims, not only to judge infallibly on religious questions, but to animadvert on opinions in secular matters which bear upon religion—on matters of philosophy, of science, of literature, of history, and it demands our submission to her claim. It claims to censure books, to silence authors, and to forbid discussions.'

Seldom has there been a richer period of liberating and provocative books than at the nineteenth-century's turn, but no Shaw, no Ibsen, no Morris, no Samuel Butler, no Wells, no Hardy (except furtively), no *Yellow Book* (just founded), nothing of the Naughty Nineties, came through our doors to startle and shock us but also to quicken us into life. The powerful Church had erected an invisible but substantial barricade around its subjects, and tied golden bands around the brows of its children lest their thoughts ran too free. In my own case I know, as the close of this story will show, that I never wrote a book which can satisfy me now as the work of a free individual mind until I had laid aside, while still loving the Church which I had been serving as a priest, some of the impossible loyalties she had laid upon me.

But at nine or ten years old my ambition to be a writer had not yet come. At this stage my daily dream was to be a hero of some sort, unknown and unsung perhaps, but preferably one of a resounding fame. For a little while my desire was to be a Christian martyr. Aunt, missing no excitement that was the talk of the day, had hastened to see Wilson Barrett and Maud Goodman in *The Sign of the Cross* and had wept so generously when Wilson Barrett as the Roman officer approached the Christian girl to seize and rape her and she whipped a cross from her breast, held it on high (while Heaven's lightning flashed around it) and cried out (the lovely girl) 'Thou cans't not harm me now'—then, I say, Aunt was so damp with tears, and exalted, that she decided, 'The children must see this.'

I may make fun of Aunt's trembling lip and smothered tears at anything that sounded beautiful, but I wept quite as gulpingly, and more openly, when at last the Roman officer, giving himself to Maud Goodman's beauty, walked with her, hand-in-hand, to the lions.

For weeks afterwards, as I walked homeward from school, I was a Christian martyr walking, head erect, not to Gledstanes Road, but to the Colosseum gates and the waiting lions. Sometimes I walked hand-in-hand with a Christian girl giving to her, a weaker vessel, something of my strength.

At other times I was in some other heroic condition. I was driving Nansen's ship, the *Fram*, through the ice-packs towards the Pole and discovering it before anyone else. Or I was winning the three-mile race in the Queen's Club ground, while Aunt and all her sports-party guests watched from our back windows. I won it for Oxford, my fancy just then. I was especially good and graceful over the hurdles, winning with ease—and with modesty. I walked back to the pavilion, as if unaware of, or indifferent to, the cheering crowds.

It was Aunt's raptures over Hilliard's reading which awoke me to the fact that we had another stirring elocutionist near at hand. In the house, in fact. Dum was another who had a rich musical voice and liked to hear it reading poetry to an audience—especially if the poem was tragic and Aunt was one of the audience brushing wet eyes and blowing a troubled nose. I now had the ears to hear a real, if self-conscious, beauty in Dum's reading, and since it was the poetry of the masters that he liked to read, I learned a little more about literature from him. Perhaps one may say that Mr Hilliard was the Paul who planted the seeds, and Dum was an Apollos who watered them.

It is after dinner again, and we are in the dining-room, Dum in his easy chair with the oil lamp on a table beside him because he is about to read; Aunt is at the newly cleared table with her work-basket; and we children are on the saddle-bag chairs or on the floor.

And Dum begins. At Aunt's request he reads a pathetic poem that she loves and that we children love too, though not understanding it fully, and that Dum probably loves most of all. When he comes to really moving lines he lets the book drop to his knees so that he can speak them with eyes gazing ahead at all the sorrows and tragedies of mankind. At first his eyes are down upon the book. Then it is plain, from the deep feeling and slowed measure with which he begins to read, that if there is one poem in the language which has the whole of his heart it is this.

> Take her up tenderly,
>   Lift her with care;
> Fashioned so slenderly,
>   Young and so fair. . . .
>
> Touch her not scornfully;
> Think of her mournfully,
>   Gently and humanly;
> Not of the stains of her,
> All that remains of her
>   Now is pure womanly.

The book drops for the next verse, and his eyes lift.

> Make no deep scrutiny
> Into her mutiny
>   Rash and undutiful:
> Past all dishonour,
> Death has left on her
>   Only the beautiful.

Aunt is broken here, weeping over her work, greatly to his satisfaction, I am sure. He doesn't spare her from more of the same treatment, and why should he, if both are so enjoying it? The eyes lift again and the book drops for:

> Alas for the rarity
> Of Christian Charity
>   Under the sun!
> Oh, it was pitiful
> Near a whole city full,
>   Home she had none. . . .
>
> Where the lamps quiver
> So far in the river,
>   With many a light
> From window and casement,
> From garret to basement,
> She stood with amazement
>   Houseless by night. . . .
>
> In she plunged boldly—
> No matter how coldly
>   The rough river ran—
> Over the brink of it,
> Picture it—think of it,
>   Dissolute Man!
> Lave in it, drink of it,
>   Then, if you can!
>
> Take her up tenderly,
>   Lift her with care;
> Fashioned so slenderly,
>   Young and so fair. . . .

The book is closed—dramatically—for the last lines, which none could know better than he.

> Cross her hands humbly
> As if praying dumbly,
>   Over her breast.
>
> Owning her weakness,
>   Her evil behaviour,
> And leaving with meekness
>   Her sins to her Saviour.

But it is not emotional incidents only that he loves to declaim, but words also that are great and lines that are mighty, though empty of drama. There is silence in the dining-room, so absorbed are we all; Dots and I sit spellbound with lips parting; Aunt is listening rather than sewing; as he reads—no, 'delivers' is the only word—the grand crescendo organ close of Matthew Arnold's *Sohrab and Rustum.*

> But the majestic river floated on,
> Out of the mist and hum of that low land,
> Into the frosty starlight, and there moved,
> Rejoicing, through the hush'd Chorasmian waste,
> Under the solitary moon; he flowed
> Right for the Polar Star, past Orgunjè
> Brimming, and bright and large; then sands begin
> To hem his watery march, and dam his streams,
> And split his currents; that for many a league
> The shorn and parcell'd Oxus strains along
> Through beds of sand and matted rushy isles—
> Oxus, forgetting the bright speed he had
> In his high mountain cradle in Pamere,
> A foil'd circuitous wanderer—till at last
> The longed-for dash of waves is heard, and wide
> His luminous home of waters opens, bright
> And tranquil, from whose floor the new-bathed stars
> Emerge, and shine upon the Aral Sea.

The book shuts, and that is the only sound in our silence.

I will only add that Dum, when enacting for us a show of being lonely, unwanted, and a failure, liked to call himself 'a foil'd circuitous wanderer'.

§

If Mr Hilliard was a sovereign reigning over our West Kensington streets, he was but a small figure compared with the little old capped lady who from Balmoral or Buckingham Palace not only reigned over all the red on the map of the world but was mother to half the royalties in the West. As I think again of our play-room window, it seems to me —though this is but fantasy—that I could *see* in that last decade of the century an extraordinary peace brooding over our streets. It was as if I saw a Pax Victoriana in quiet possession of the world. But, whether or not I saw it, this Pax was there. It lay over the whole civilized West, and as yet there was no foreboding anywhere.

We believed that this peace, of which she was the crown and symbol, ensured that there would never be war in Europe again. There might be picturesque skirmishes on the fringes of her empire, with our soldiers in their red coats punishing the dark skins of Zulus or Mahdists or Afghans, but it was not to be conceived that any of the European powers would touch us. Had not the French dared to occupy Fashoda on the Upper Nile, so clearly our rightful terrain, and did they not discreetly withdraw after Lord Kitchener had marched from Khartoum to take care of them?

That was in '98. In '96 and '97 all of us children were as excited as at a long cricket match to see if the Queen would beat George III's record of sixty years on the throne. An exciting question because she was already touching eighty, but in 1897 she did it, and then scored, as you might say, three runs to spare.

On 12 September 1898 I began to write a diary. It is before me now in a feint-ruled exercise book far more stained and tattered than Aunt's. It extends over fully thirty pages; and these cover three years of my life, so often did I abandon the wearisome writing and then start it again. Again and again; some pages being written with a laboured neatness, only to slither into hasty scribbling. It is headed:

MY DIARY
Introduction

which suggests that at nine years old, like an early spring crocus, my desire to be a writer had broken surface and was peeping above ground, but the opening paragraph shows that I was far from sight of the truth that good writing is not a matter of words alone, and cannot exist apart from an unflinching truth to one's own obstinate vision. It runs: 'My dear Auntie with whom I live wishes me to write a diary as she thinks it will teach me to comp Ose and also be interisting when I am grown up to read what I did when I was a little boy', but, alas, there is no sincerity in that 'My dear Auntie' because I disliked the woman. Either she dictated that paragraph to give me a flying start, or it is a piece of sycophancy, of which I was quite capable: remember 'I love you better than God'.

Five and a half pages, and we are in a December of two years later.

Five more pages of jottings, and we come to really exciting stuff on 22 January 1901.

'Lately there has been much anxiety throughout the British Empire Because of the Ilness of Queen Victoria and this evening we heard a boy going about calling *"Death of Queen Victoria"*—[this is in larger letters, heavily underscored]—What a rush there was for papers! All the servants coming to the doors! and people looking out of their windows! the boy sold all his papers out so when he came to us he had none to sell so we did not believe but afterwards many other men came round and the next morning when we found the papers thick with black we knew it must be true.

'January 23rd 1901. I did not say yesterday that we went back to school because I was so taken up with writing about the Queen.'

No more till 15 September 1901, so let Aunt take over from 23 January. Her thrilled descriptions are written in my diary since she had despaired of my dealing justly with these tremendous days.

'The next day, Jan. 23rd. I went to town and heard the eighty-one guns fired in memory of her age on the Horse Guards Parade. It was very solemn. The next day I went to hear the King proclaimed by the heralds but as it was done earlier than anyone expected I missed it altogether. I was at Temple Bar at ten where a silk cord had been drawn across the street. I waited and saw the return procession but not the heralds. I went to St Paul's Cathedral and heard Evensong. The pulpit and reredos were draped in black and they sang God Save the King the first time after the accession. The Cathedral is very beautiful now and the singing of the choir pleased me muchly.

'*Saturday the 26th.* We had a good many at our At Home and some nice music.

'*Sunday, Jan. 27th 1901.* Mr Hilliard preached this morning the funeral sermon for our late Queen. He read the chapter as lesson, Remember thy Creator in the days of thy Youth and his exquisite voice made the strange sad words of that chapter sound like a beautiful poem as he said, "Man goeth to his long home and the mourners go about the streets." There must have been few who were not touched. He certainly is a great reader.

'His sermon was beautiful, the text being, "And I saw a great white throne." Rev. 20.11. He alluded first to the *greatness* of Queen Victoria and her reign and said it seemed as if God had forced on her endless possessions and countries and people till her dominion was spread in all parts of the world for God knew that she was good and could be trusted to govern all these peoples and lands. He alluded to her great grief for her husband which was the only fault anyone ever could find with her, and he added that she never let her grief cause her to neglect her duties but only to give up pleasures—and her heart was more sympathetic because of her own sufferings. He said much that was beautiful in praise of the Queen, and then he alluded to the whiteness of her throne and the purity of her character and how all nations respected her, and those who hated England honoured and loved England's Queen—how she had endeared herself to all the monarchs of the world—and he ended by a most touching reference to the King as chief mourner and King at the funeral on Saturday—implored us to give him all our prayers and make intercession for him, to remember he was our Queen's son, bone of her bone and flesh of her flesh, trained by her and called to fill the greatest position and rule over a great empire and to ascend the purest and greatest throne monarch ever inherited. He then asked us to remain kneeling while the Dead March was played and to give silent thanks to God for his mercies to England during her Majesty's long reign—after which we were all to sing God Save the King.

'The church was quite crammed, chairs everywhere, and many standing. Everyone wore black.

'The wind was so high and rattled so in the roof of the church I sometimes could not hear every word. When we came out of the church we were literally blown round the corner home.'

4

SCHOOLDAYS AND HOLIDAYS

'I did not say yesterday that we went back to school because I was so taken up in writing about the Queen.'

This I have quoted from my insincere diary under a date in 1901. I have called it insincere because so often it tells, not my real thoughts, but those that Aunt would like to see written down. After that grossly insincere opening, 'My dear Auntie with whom I live . . .' there come the words, 'I was very much excited this morning because I had to be introduced to Mr Bewsher headmaster of Colet Court Preparatory School for St Paul's.' As far as I remember, I was not at all excited, but heavy with premonition, and this the diary conceals behind a proper show of liveliness. 'We called on him soon after ten and I found him very nice and kind.' One of Aunt's nieces, Edythe Blaine, being of an age with myself, was much with us at Gledstanes Road, and she too was going to school for the first time as I was, and writing a diary about it—Aunt persuading everyone to keep a diary. She has shown me this diary, which was as scribbled and fragmentary as mine, and in it I read that both Ernest Raymond and she 'had been dying to go to school ever since we read *Tom Brown's Schooldays*.' I have no doubt this was true of herself, but it suggests to me a yawning difference between small girls and small boys, or between girls' schools and boys' schools. I was *not* 'dying to go' and Aunt had perceived this. In *her* diary occur the words, 'Dots, Edythe and Ernest are all at school now. Edythe was so excited about it she could hardly walk across the street. Poor old Ernest was much more sober, he not liking the idea overmuch.'

Very true.

Nevertheless Tom Brown and his schooldays were obviously in my mind because the next words of my diary run, 'Now I will end this brief preface and start tomorrow to write

Ernest Raymond's Schooldays

CHAPTER I

'Very early this morning Aunt woke me up. It is the first day of my school life so Dum took me—'

These three small words, 'Dum took me', cannot contain the story.

I tried to tell it long afterwards in an early and, on the whole, weak novel.

What happened was this.

As Dum and I left the house in Gledstanes Road to walk to Colet Court in the Hammersmith Road, I in knickerbocker suit and Eton collar, hanging nervously on his arm, but hiding my fears, he said, taking his tall hat from the hat-stand, 'This is undoubtedly a historic occasion, but I do hope Koko's arrival at this school will be treated as quietly as possible. I trust there will be no flags or bunting to welcome him. Obviously it is my duty to accompany him on his entry into the world of scholarship, but my nerves at my great age'—he was then still only sixty-two—'will not stand any uproarious ovation.'

Our entry into the school's forecourt converged upon that of another small boy with school cap on head and satchel slung. He was about my age, nine years old, but seemed as comfortably at ease as I was tremulous with nerves. Dum greeted him with the words, 'Good morning, sir. I thought that you would like to know that this is Mr Ernest Raymond who is about to become one of the most distinguished members of your excellent school.'

The small boy, alarmed, ran to a place of sanctuary in the school.

'*Il ne comprend pas,*' Dum said, as he usually did, sadly, when his humour had not been grasped and appreciated.

The school was acting as he had hoped, and making no noise about my arrival, but he was not wholly happy about an indifference so complete. We were left standing together in the entrance hall, alone and unnoticed, I still hanging on his arm and nervously watching the rush of other boys, some of whom, though none could have been over twelve, seemed tall and towering.

Not pleased to be left on the mat like a can of milk, Dum waited, tut-tutting, till a porter in a brown uniform and with a bristling ginger moustache issued from his office in this vestibule. Immediately Dum addressed him, 'Pardon me, sir, but are there any arrangements in this establishment whereby people awaiting attention can sit down?'

The porter gaped, and Dum sighed, '*Il ne comprend pas.* Has the place a chair, sir, or perhaps a wooden box, on which one could sit?'

'Oh, a chair. Certainly, sir,' said the porter, bright now with understanding.

'Exactly. A chair,' Dum encouraged him. But at that moment the headmaster, Mr Bewsher, in gown and mortarboard, emerged from a door opposite, and Dum, after saying, 'Come, Koko,' which made me blush, turned to him and explained, 'This, sir, is Ernest Raymond, my young ward. He commences with you today.'

Mr Bewsher smiled his welcome. 'Oh, yes. It is very good of you to bring him. He'd better come into Prayers.'

'Quite so,' said Dum, now eager to escape. 'Koko, go into Prayers. Always say your prayers. Now follow that excellent headmaster. Good-bye.'

I withdrew my hand from his arm, and it was like loosing the painter of my boat from a strong bollard on the wharf of life, and drifting away, rudderless. Apparently Dum saw the moisture glistening in my eyes, for his large hand gripped my shoulder, pressed it strongly, while he said almost exactly what he had said to our poor lost Annie Olden years before. 'Keep a stout heart. We're a schoolboy now. Keep a big heart.'

§

I did well in my first term at Colet Court, getting top marks week after week, and coming out second in the exams. But this was in the lowest class, and I did less well in subsequent terms and in higher classes, as I got older and lost myself more and more to dreaming.

This very first term I got a prize and have it still, a handsome book bound in full calf and gay with gilt, its title *Country Pastimes for Boys*. What those pastimes are I do not know to this day.

Dum professed an immense appreciation of this scholarly achievement, and declared to Aunt that he must certainly come to the prize-giving and see Mr Koko publicly honoured. But the day of the prize-giving unfortunately followed a day when there had been one of those heart-searing quarrels between him and Aunt, so that they were not, just now, on speaking terms. They were moving past each other, or sitting at the same table for lunch, in one of their Greater Silences—except when, possibly, he enjoined me, 'Koko! Koko! you're not looking after your kind auntie who's so good to you. Pass her the red-currant jelly.'

This schism between them meant that he came alone and sadly to the school's Great Hall and sat humbly at the back behind a full congregation of parents. It was an established custom at the school that all applause for prizewinners should be withheld till the last prize had been given, and silence accordingly prevailed for perhaps thirty minutes till the name of 'Raymond, E.' was called, whereupon Dum, with that strange and lonely indifference to what people around him might think, clapped slowly but steadily—clap . . . clap . . . clap— while Raymond, E. mounted the platform from one side, passed across it, and descended with his prize down the steps on the farther side.

Let the silence of others be what they fancied, he was not going to have Mr Koko-man denied his meed of applause.

§

Parts of a birthday letter from Dum at this date, I then nine years old.

'Hôtel de la Plage, Cannes, 31. Dec. 98.

'My dear Koko,

'I have thought of you today, and kind Dame Nature has celebrated it with the brightest sunshine all through the day, ending with a magnificent sunset. I left Genoa at $\frac{1}{4}$ to 9 and almost the whole way we were coasting the blue Mediterranean which sparkled in the sunshine. Arrived here had a cup of tea, and am now writing to you by way of keeping your birthday. . . .

'I mean to go to bed very soon and hope sleep will soon come and stay till the morning when, if the sunset keeps its promise, I shall see the blue sea sparkling in sunshine. I wish you, dear little man, a happy year and many more to follow. Try each year to get better in every way—health, learning, temper, manliness, and gratitude to your most kind Auntie who is so good to you. Get more honest and good each year. My address in Paris will be Army and Navy Co-operative Society Office, 253 Rue St. Honoré. I congratulate your new school on having you to ensure its success. Now goodnight. Lay my homage at Queenie's feet.

Always your old friend,
Old Dum.'

§

It happened that after the Easter term of 1900 Dum in his capacity as a director of the Army and Navy Stores had to go to Brighton to complete an arrangement with the Palmeira Stores in Hove, which was at that time affiliated in some way with the original Co-operative Society in Westminster. And he suggested to Aunt that after two terms of unremitting scholastic labours Koko deserved a second holiday and he would take him with him to Brighton. He would be a pleasant companion, he said, and the sea air would be exactly the thing for him after all these weeks of scholarly work. Just as it amazes me that he was usually ready to play Bezique or Halma with noisy children of eight and nine, so it amazes me that, at sixty-three, he was ready to take with him to the seaside as his sole companion a boy of eleven.

But he seemed almost as pleased and excited about our excursion together as I was. 'Koko must certainly have a new suit if he is to stay at a fashionable hotel.' And off to the Army and Navy Stores I was taken by Aunt to be fitted at Dum's expense with a dark suit for important occasions. Had Mr Koko a suitcase, or a Gladstone bag, for his travels? 'What? No Gladsone bag? Good gracious! This is ridiculous. You will kindly take him to the Army and Navy Stores and choose a suitcase for him. One of the best. He likes nothing but the best.'

The morning came when a four-wheeler arrived to take us to Victoria, I, wearing my expensive new suit and insisting on carrying my new suitcase. In the Brighton train we had a first-class carriage to ourselves—the first time I'd travelled first class. 'What? Don't you always travel first class, a gentleman of your distinction? I must speak to your kind auntie about this.' In the carriage sitting opposite me he surveyed my new suit and said, 'Mr Raymond is certainly one of the best dressed men in town.' In Brighton we took a 'fly' to the Grand Hotel and there at the Reception bureau he asked for a large bedroom and 'Perhaps you will be so kind as to put a small extra bed in it for this young gentleman.'

He, sixty-three, was prepared to have me sleeping in a second bed at his side.

In the morning we came down to breakfast in the fine restaurant, and sat together at a table that overlooked the esplanade and the sea. A waiter came towards us to ask us what we wished. Now, just as Dum could sometimes be observed kneeling in prayer by his bedside, so he would occasionally—and quite unexpectedly—say with bowed head a grace before beginning to eat. It was always the same grace, 'For these and all his mercies may God's holy name be praised.' This morning, seated and with bent head, he was half-way through this grace—probably offered to Heaven as a good example to me—when the waiter interrupted it with a question about porridge. Dum raised his head at this profane interruption and indignantly fired the grace's final clause straight into the waiter's face: '*May God's holy name be praised!*' The waiter started aback as if shot, but Dum immediately recovered from this moment of indignation and said, 'Koko, listen to what this kind gentleman is offering you. Tell him if you would desire porridge or not.'

After a notable meal (so far as I was concerned) we walked out into the great vestibule and there saw a uniformed commissionaire staring vacantly out to sea. Dum, greeting him in jocular vein, asked, 'Good morning. Is the sea still there?' at which question the man looked a trifle soured—justly I now think—and walked away, answering Yes, it was. Dum, accepting that his jest had gone astray, murmured only, '*Il ne comprend pas.*'

On the Sunday of this week-end we went to church—'Of course you must go to church. All children should go to church. I will take you'—and like a dutiful guardian he walked me towards the nearest church he could find, which chanced to be St Paul's in West Street. Here the service was extremely High—as High as you could get in the Church of England without going through the roof and out of all touch with Canterbury—with the result that Dum tut-tutted frequently as we seemed to jack-in-the-box up and down, now genuflecting, now standing, now bowing, and anon and inexplicably sitting down again. At a point in the first ten minutes of the sermon the preacher referred to Martin Luther as a 'contemptible heretic', and straightway Dum rose to his six-foot-four-and-a-half, and said 'Come, Koko.'

And he began to slip past people's knees and over hassocks into the centre of the nave. Down the nave he walked at no hurried pace, with his usual lonely indifference to what surrounding people might think, while I clopped along behind him, both of us seeking the West Door and the daylight. He never once looked round to see if Koko was duly coming, or the preacher was watching and waiting, or the congregation was astir. But Koko was there, following.

Having no knowledge of theology in those days I did not ask, when we were out in the sunlight, why he found it intolerable that Martin Luther should be called a heretic, so I cannot answer that question now. My only submission would be that in the nineteenth century—and this was only 1900—upper-class and middle-class gentlemen who never went to church at all were warmly opposed to 'Ritualism' and 'Pusey-ism' for those who did.

Our protest made, we walked together up and down the fine Hove Lawns, in the fashionable Church Parade, he in his top-hat and frock-coat, I in my Eton collar and still immaculate new suit. Among the other well-dressed people parading up and down he noted and pointed out to me a curly-haired old gentleman being pushed along in a bath-chair. 'Toole,' he said. 'John Laurence Toole, one of the greatest comedians our stage has ever known. You must surely have heard of Toole's Theatre in London.' A few minutes after this he met an old military friend, as he had done in the China and Glass at the Army and Navy Stores, and again he introduced me as his little ward 'who is very kindly taking care of me during this important business com-mission'. This was the time I really caught the name, 'William Bell Raymond. Who died.' Whether on this occasion he described him as 'one of my dearest friends; a lifelong friend' I do not recall.

§

Two of my letters survive, describing this holiday to Aunt Emily, and they are of some interest as showing a child's-eye view of a famous adventure.

I give them exactly as punctuated and spelt.

Grand Hotel Brighton. May 13th 1900
Dear Aunt Emily
We arrived safely here; at about half-past one. We had a first class carriage down and a carriage from the station to the hotel. The hotel is such a big one that I felt quite bewildered when I first went in however I got used to it soon. Dummie showed me the new solicitor-General as we were in the carriage, he has a house in Rottingdean. Dummie was so funny in the way he talked to the secretary he asked him whether I could not go cheaper, he said 'surely you will let such a nice little fellow as this go cheaper, he has got a very good appetite'— (I don't know what my appetite has got to do with it I think it would only make it dearer) and he let us go for a guinea a day, 12.6 Dummie, 8.6 me. After we had had some lunch we went out and Dummie ordered a little carriage and we drove part of the way to Rottingdean. Then we got out, had some tea at a little shop in which Dummie got

so cross because there was no Hovis bread then we walked a little way up the pier and then came back, Dressed, and had Dinner which was such a large one we could not eat nearly all, and there was such a nice old chap who sit's next to me, and he said that he had one son at Uppingham and the other one in the army and two daughters. There is a band every evening except tonight when we have a concert. This morning Dummie ordered a hot bath for each of us. Bye the bye, we have got such a lovely room, viz, two beds, two dressing tables, two washing basins, a chest of drawers and a wardrobe. When we came Down to breakfast Dummie was so funny he saw an attendant and he said to him, 'Is the sea still there' I felt inclined to say, 'The tide's gone out and people say it is never coming back.' It is five and twenty minutes to seven I must go and dress for dinner I will write again tomorrow

Your loving little

ERNEST

Dear Auntie

I continue my letter now because as you know I had to stop to dress for dinner which was such an enormous one that I enclose the Menu—Notice that the soup was Real turtle and was so nice. I wanted to tell you that we went to church yesterday and the sermon was about only to speak of others behind their backs as you would before their faces then he went and called Martin luther a contemptious heretic so dummie came out because he did not like it and he said that he was sure he would not say that before Martin Luther. Yesterday we were walking up and down with Mr. Carrington and Dummie said that I was taking care of him and then Mr. Carrington said that I was to keep him out of Mischief. Yesterday we had such a beautiful concert, one lady and Gentleman sang 'where are you going to my pretty maid' and they did it very well.

This morning I have had a donkey ride

With love to all

I remain

Your loving

Ernest.

§

Poor Dum. I wish I had a full understanding of the distressful relationship between him and Aunt Emily. I cannot hope to know the
truth of it now. But this brief holiday with him at Brighton reminds me
of a long summer holiday in Boulogne with Aunt Emily and Dorothy,
perhaps two years before, when I was nine. Aunt loved to go to
Boulogne because she had lived there for all her childhood and youth.
And one bright summer morning we were at play on the sands with
our spades and pails while she sat under a parasol in a deck-chair. Not
on the sands of the Boulogne Plage des Bains which we avoided
because of the many holiday-makers there, but on the broad Capécure
sands west of the Old Town which were unfashionable and quiet. We
would go towards them by the Rue de la Lampe and the Boulevard de
Chatillon and so down to those stretches of largely unvisited sand.
Here there were only a few bathing machines, or *cabines roulantes*,
wheeled and sandy wooden huts which, when we were undressed and
ready, a horse would draw right into the waves of the sea. From one
of these gabled huts, which in the interest of propriety had two com-
partments, Aunt and Dorothy would emerge in voluminous bathing
frocks, waisted, sashed, bloused and bloomered, to be received in the
water by a bathing woman, who there encouraged, supported and
fortified them among impudent and unseemly waves. I followed them
in a bathing costume that covered me with decency from neck to
thighs. Often when we had finished our bathe we came out of the water
to discover that the horse had taken our machine back to its original
stance under a sea-wall. Then in wet clinging garments we had to
search for our sandy-floored machine, together with other bathers,
who, soaked and dripping, were looking for theirs. It was rather
embarrassing, Aunt said, this long walk over the sands in sodden
garments that clung to one's figure.

On one such morning, after a bathe, Dorothy and I dug moated
castles, aqueducts and dikes in the sand for a long hour till Aunt called
from her chair that it was time to go home for *déjeuner*. We picked up
buckets and spades, and I was returning towards her chair when in the
distance I saw Dum coming towards her too from the direction of the
Rue Henriville. *But*—he was brandishing distractedly his handsome
Malacca cane towards us and—unbelievably—*crying*. I had never
known a moment like this: Dum splendidly tall, grey-bearded, long-
moustached, a major-general—crying. Never before had I expected to
see a grown-up man in tears, and least of all a man fifty years away

from his childhood. I know that at sight of his tears my heart raced out to him; I could have cried bitterly with him; I begged, though he could not hear me, 'Oh no . . . don't cry. Don't cry. Please'; sobbing within myself, I walked onward to Aunt's side where I pretended to have seen nothing. He was now standing at Aunt's side too. We children did not know what part to play in a scene so unexplained and so shaking. We knew he had come separately from London, following us, but had gone to his own hotel, and we could only guess that last night, probably, when we were in bed, there had occurred one of their unhappy quarrels, and that now, after a night and morning of sadness, he was aching for a reconciliation. We just stood near them while they spoke together. What they said we did not understand, and I don't remember, but at last, and plainly, there came the reconciliation which they both craved, and they were now at the top of happiness, and full of love again, as we all are once a quarrel is analysed, forgiven and ended. Dum turned joyously to us, saying, 'Come along, children. Peaches, perhaps? Ices? Surely it is time for one or the other.'

Here was a dilemma that paralysed speech. If we chose peaches from the fruit and flower market we would lose the incomparable ices at Caveng's famous *pâtisserie*. But those peaches on the market stalls! Dum perceived this Gordian yoke and cut it in two for us. 'Perhaps with a little skill we could manage both. Peaches *and* ices. But only if you swear an oath that you will not eat the peaches till after *déjeuner*, and when your kind auntie says you may.'

Willingly we swore anything demanded, and all four of us walked back together by the Quai de la Crique and the Arrière Port to the Basse Ville and the Market. The market all around the steps and walls of St Nicholas Church was a splendidly coloured spectacle to close with happiness a morning which had touched despair—the old market women, in their clean white caps and kerchiefs sitting under their large umbrellas by their baskets or stalls of fruit and vegetables. Dum bought six peaches for three sous each. Then on to Caveng's in the Rue Victor-Hugo for ices.

5

THE CALDER GIRLS

Five Calder 'aunts' I had, as I have told you. Whether they were truly aunts had yet—and waited years—to be disclosed. In order of age they were Aunt Sophie, the eldest, Aunt Clara, Aunt Ida (my self-appointed 'sweetheart'), Aunt Emily (my effective guardian) and Aunt Mary. In my schoolboy humour I liked to call these handsome, well-rounded and redoubtable women the 'Calder Girls'. There were two Calder uncles, Uncle Gus who died early, and best, kindest, jolliest of all, Uncle Edwin.

Let me go back to a hazed and now ghostly past to open the story of the 'Calder Girls'. Back to no less a place than a gun-deck of the *Royal Sovereign* as it sailed beside Nelson's *Victory* to cut in two the battle array of the French and Spanish before Cape Trafalgar. In the early forenoon the *Royal Sovereign* with its hundred guns, flying the flag of Lord Collingwood, Nelson's second-in-command (who stood on the quarter-deck with Captain Rotherham) went slowly forward under a press of sail towards this encounter. The *Victory*'s order had been to make all sail and form the sailing ships into two parallel divisions, *Victory* leading one, and *Royal Sovereign* the other. A light breeze blew from the north-west, as the ships moved eastward towards the centre of the enemy's array, *Victory* leading the weather column, *Royal Sovereign* the lee. At half-past ten, as the two columns neared the Franco-Spanish line, the *Victory* telegraphed 'England expects every man will do his duty', and a great cheer went up from the crew of the *Royal Sovereign*.

Among those who cheered this signal was a midshipman of fifteen, acting as powder-monkey. Probably, like most of the men, he stood at his action station, naked to the waist. It was exactly twelve o'clock as the *Royal Sovereign* with enormous cheering first broke the enemy line, firing a broadside at the Spanish *Santa Anna*, and then laying herself alongside the French *Fougeux* to give it battle. Collingwood said to Rotherham, 'What wouldn't Nelson give to be here,' and the powder-boy rushed from magazine to gun with his powder. Twelve-twenty, and the *Victory* flew the signal 'Engage the enemy more closely', whereupon Collingwood flung his *Royal Sovereign* and all the ships astern of him against the enemy line at point-blank range. By fifteen minutes past four the *Royal Sovereign* with only one mast left standing, and all its proud canvas no more than ripped and pendent rags, was rolling like an old hulk in the smoke and the sea-swell, but on one side of her was the *Santa Anna*, wholly dismasted and a capture, and on the other side the *Victory* with surrendered French ships, half shrouded in their own tumbled sails, lying helpless around. By five the battle was done, two-thirds of the enemy's ships having been destroyed or captured.

And the powder-boy lay near a gun with forty wounds in his body (grape-shot?) one eye gone, and seemingly dead. 'Throw this stiff overboard,' said someone from among the survivors who were scavenging blood and bodies from the decks. But at that moment an officer, passing by, ordered, 'Wait. I don't think that boy's dead,' and they desisted from their immediate purpose.

He was not dead. Good; but why, you may wonder, in a picture of my childhood, all this eager and affectionate detail about a battle that belonged to a hundred years before? The answer is simple and perhaps pardonable. Had that officer not passed by and saved the powder-boy from being cast overboard, there would have been no Calder Girls, and no author to write this story.

The middy lying there was a parson's younger son, Gilbert Kennicott—more, he was a grandson of the 'great' Dr Kennicott, the eighteenth century's most famous Hebraic scholar—and he lived to enjoy a long and adventurous career, dying as an admiral in his eighty-sixth year. Trustees of Lloyd's Patriotic Fund, founded only two years before Trafalgar, held a meeting after the battle and voted grants to Officers and Men who had been wounded on that 'glorious day'. Among the grants was '£60 to Mr. Kennicott'—that is £1 10s. od. for each of his forty wounds.

An article in the Fund's annual report of 1934, a hundred and nineteen years later, speaks of the middy at Trafalgar and contains this paragraph. 'Mr. Kennicott had an adventurous career afterwards, as he was wrecked in the *Hind* off Cyprus in 1807 and kept prisoner by the Turks until 1809. As a lieutenant in H.M.S. *Minorca* he was taken prisoner in an American prize and detained until 1814. He finally retired in 1867 and died in 1874. His grand-daughter is now 78 years of age and has received regular help from the Trustees for the last eleven years.'

This old lady, helped in her age by those who still honoured the men who fought at Trafalgar, a hundred and thirty years before, was my Aunt Emily.

What is of major interest here is Lieutenant Kennicott's second imprisonment after the capture by the French of the American prize. O'Byrne's *Dictionary of Naval Biography*, 1849, records, 'Mr. Kennicott was nominated by Lord Collingwood to a lieutenancy in his own ship, the *Ville de Paris*. Removing not long after to the *Minorca*, 18 guns, Lieutenant Kennicott, in November 1810, was again placed in command of a detained American vessel, whose crew, of themselves equal in number with the British, conjoined with one-half of the latter and succeeded in recapturing her and carrying her into Marseilles. A second time thus a prisoner of war, the Lieutenant, after he had been for some time confined in a common gaol, was conducted to Verdun and there kept *en parole* until the conclusion of the war.'

Now, among the *détenus* at Verdun was 'a very beautiful Spanish girl of high degree'—so the family records phrase it. She was the widow of a Captain Collins whom she had seen shot before her eyes. Lieutenant Kennicott comforted her, we are told, and I can well believe he did. She was liberated before him and came to England. When, in turn, he was liberated, he hurried to England, woo'd, and married her. They had two daughters, and one of these, Sophia Kennicott—but no: here let us turn to Colonel Calder, father of the Calder Girls.

Born in 1797, only eight years after Gilbert Kennicott, Colonel William Calder was gazetted Ensign in the 8th Foot when he was seventeen, Lieutenant ten years later, and Captain in 1835. He served at various stations—Malta, Ionian Islands, Ireland, Sunderland—but I know of no active service on which he was engaged. On a day in 1841 he was at Windsor Castle with the young Sophia Kennicott, probably because one of her uncles was a Military Knight of Windsor, having served with distinction in the Peninsular War. At this time Captain Calder was forty-four, Sophia Kennicott twenty-two, and together they climbed to the top of Windsor's Round Tower. Up in that exalted solitude, she, no doubt gazing shyly across the timbered lawns and the silver, winding Thames towards the turrets of Eton, listened as he asked her to marry him.

Captain William Calder and Sophia Kennicott were married a few weeks later. So the houses of Kennicott and of Calder were united, and from this union sprang ten children, five of whom were the Calder Girls.

Responsible for a large family of eight surviving children, William

Calder, then Major, retired with the brevet rank of Lieutenant-Colonel, and in 1857 exiled himself to kindly, welcoming Boulogne-sur-mer, where a colony of British officers had preceded him, because their pay was small, their families large, and the living cheap.

One of them, by the way, was Thackeray's Colonel Newcome. Ruined, you may remember, by the failure of his Bundelcund Bank, he had sought 'an abiding place in Boulogne, refuge of how many other unfortunate Britons'. And there, like Colonel Newcome, Colonel Calder would sit upon the Boulogne Ramparts with his newspaper and some of his children playing around him. Impossible not to think of him, when I read in *The Newcomes* how Arthur Pendennis went to find Colonel Newcome in Boulogne. Word for word, it might be the picture of Colonel Calder, as painted on my memories by Aunt Emily's or Aunt Ida's tales of him.

'To this friendly port I betook myself speedily, having the address of Colonel Newcome. His quarters were in a quiet, grass-grown old street of the Old Town. None of the family was at home when I called. There was indeed no servant to answer the bell, but the good-natured French domestic of a neighbouring lodger told me that I should probably find the old gentleman upon the Ramparts where he was in the custom of going every day. I strolled along those pretty old walks and bastions under the pleasant trees which shadow them and the grey old gabled houses from which you look down upon the gay new city and the busy port, and the piers stretching into the shining sea, dotted with a hundred white sails or black-smoking steamers, and bounded by the friendly lines of the bright English shore. There are few prospects more charming than the familiar view from these old French walls—few places where young children may play and ruminating old age repose more pleasantly than on those peaceful rampart gardens.

'I found our dear old friend seated on one of the benches, a newspaper on his knees. . . .'

§

Because of my childhood love for Dum, and my boyish delight in him as a man of infinite odd jests, he, or rather, a fictitious character flowering from my memories of him, persists in novel after novel of mine, though, inevitably, he is given imaginary actions, words, and behaviour to meet the requirements of each plot. The portraits that are truest to him are in a novel called *Newtimber Lane* where, as the central character, Sir Edmund Earlwin, he holds the stage for all of its five hundred pages, and in *Gentle Greaves*, where in the figure of General Allan Mourne, he is apt, like a good general, to take command of all the battlefield around him. These two fictitious characters I like best because they are so nearly true portraits of him.

In *Newtimber Lane* the Boulogne of 1857 to which Colonel Calder took himself and his large family is lovingly painted, because we children and Aunt and Dum all so loved the place, and the stories of it.

'Ah, Boulogne, city of refuge, just under the walls of England. Dear sanctuary (what a word for Boulogne) creeping up close to the Folkestone Gate, so that we had only to cross the moat and we were in the safety of your generous welcome. The walls of England were white as we saw them from Boulogne on a clear day; and the streets of Boulogne were somewhat soiled; and this was a parable, because England (or the face of her) was very virtuous at the time of which we write; as virtuous as she had ever been, and much more virtuous than she can stand for any length of days. . . . Not that the English colony in Boulogne were scapegraces all. We shall be close to the truth if we see three "sets" in that society. First and dominant, the outlaws: those who for one reason or another had made England too hot for them and decamped—pull devil, pull baker—*à Boulogne*. Then the wealthy tourists who were come to patronise this gay continental town. And thirdly the old half-pay officers, so different from the others, so admirable in their probity. These were there because living was cheap and their families were large, and they were mostly good men, loving duty. They read their Bible and Dickens and kept themselves apart from the outlaws in the security of their narrow homes. But they did not always keep their daughters. The eyes of these pretty creatures strayed sometimes towards the sparkling life of the Etablissement des Bains (later the Casino), the Théâtre Municipal, and the tall hotels. And quite often a drama sprang up and waxed warm between an ambassador from these brightly lit booths of gaiety and a daughter from the tents of righteousness. Is much of what follows some such tale?

'Three sets then: for the sake of brevity shall we describe them as those with money, those without money, and those without morals?'

Is much of what follows some such tale?

Two long white jetties with lighthouses on their prows enclosed the channel of entry to the Avant Port of Boulogne, and it was a fashion for many of the citizens, especially the English, to line the rails of the southern jetty so as to see the Folkestone steam-packet come slowly towards the Quai des Paquebots, and to wave a welcome to all aboard.

On a day in 1866, if my estimate is right, three of the Calder sisters left their small *appartement* in the Rue Royale to take their part in this merry custom. Sophie was then twenty-four, Ida twenty, and Emily only ten. They walked from the Rue Royale along the Rue de l'Ecu (Heaven knows what these streets are called now) and so came to the quays. Here, round and about the quays, beat the real heart of Boulogne, with its fishermen in their brown blouses and peaked caps, its porters in their blue smocks and, most famous of all its fishwives, *les Boulnoises*, with their white frilled caps spreading like an aureole behind their faces, their long gold ear-rings, their gaily coloured shawls, their baskets on their arms, and their short striped skirts revealing ankles and feet in high-heeled *patins*. We can say with some certainty that the three Calder girls passed through a well-loved smell, blent of seaweed and fish, and that one of them (not Ida, who till death considered every detail of her dress from hat to shoes) probably trod on the cold head of a fish lying crushed on the cobbles.

On the jetty they stood together near the lighthouse at its end; and the Folkestone boat came in to be greeted by a hundred waving hands. The two younger sisters ran along the jetty abreast of the boat and then stood and watched while it berthed against the Quai de la Douane and the passengers disembarked. One who came ashore caught their eyes and held them, he was so tall and handsome, with black hair curling a little above the ears, black moustaches and neatly pointed black beard: Sophie, the placid sister and one never given to the exaggerated sentimentalities of Emily, was to call him to the end of her life 'the handsomest man she had ever seen'.

§

He was a Captain Blake of the Royal Marines, then thirty and serving at their Woolwich Headquarters while studying to become a barrister as well as an officer of marines. Having a love of Boulogne, where he had friends among the old English officers and their children, he came often there on holiday. It was always a pleasure to him, this sea approach to Boulogne with its Haute Ville on the heights, its dome and roofs rising into the pale sky, its fort and calvary looking out to sea, and its twin white jetties to embrace the Folkestone boat with a welcome of waving hands. He stepped ashore this day—to what? I have no reason to suppose he observed the three Calder girls who had observed him so closely. But thereafter—to what?

How can I know what happened, since no word was spoken of it by Aunt Ida till the eve of her death, and then only a few nervous sentences; and from Aunt Emily came only occasional answers, embarrassed and quickly evaded, since she too had a part in the story to hide. My surmises and guesses as to how it all came about are written at length in *Newtimber Lane*, but much of this is fictional, a guess-work journey into the hidden past, only the characters, as I like to believe, being true to their originals, Ida, Emily, and Captain Blake.

It would seem that the young and handsome Captain Blake was soon brought into touch with the Calder family, perhaps by some of his friends in the English colony. And that he quickly fell in love with Ida. Few and small are the scattered facts on which I build my guesses, but when we were grown up and Aunt spoke a little about Ida and Dum (never about herself and Dum), she would say in her sentimental way, 'He couldn't keep away from beautiful women, but she was the real love of his life. That was his real love story—' and her lips would begin to quiver.

Once when, as usual, we were in Boulogne for the August holiday Aunt took us to the Rue Royale to see the *appartement* where she and her sisters had lived for all their childhood and youth. It occupied the straggling first floor and the attics above of No. 11 Rue Royale, a tailor's house, whose shop and living-rooms were below. Like many old French houses it was built around three sides of a flagged courtyard, the high wall of the next house forming the fourth side of the quadrangle. Many of the Calders' windows overlooked the *cour*, and Aunt, pointing up to her window, told us how, on a market day, she would throw open her green shutters to see the stone flags below piled with vegetables and flowers, for the tailor allowed the market-sellers to dispose their stocks there at call. Almost overpowering, she said, would be the fragrance of massed flowers and damp earth coming up to her window in the fresh clean morning air.

There were no flowers on this day of our visit, all was bare in the *cour*, but, ever a dreaming and imaginative child, I waited there till I saw the Aunts as girls, and even the old Colonel himself, looking down from windows at the rich market flora below. As yet I did not know enough to imagine a Captain Blake seated in one of those rooms and coming perhaps to a window.

I have said that he fell 'soon' and 'quickly' in love with Ida because I have a fat old Paris guide-book, published in 1867 as a special edition for the great 'Universal Exhibition' of that year. It has 'G.F.B.' (George Frederic Blake) on its flyleaf, but it was in Ida's possession till the day of her death, and—because of what she did with it on the eve of her death—I can but wonder whether, she being twenty-one, Captain Blake took her to Paris. Difficult to conceive of a strict old Colonel, in a mid-Victorian year, allowing a handsome captain to take the most beautiful of his daughters to Paris—Paris of all sinful places— but it may be that others of the English colonists were of the party, and all seemed safe. The Colonel and his wife did not know, I am sure, that this young Captain Blake was a married man finally estranged from a wife who would not divorce him. Dum would not have told them this. All his life Dum's devotion to Truth, if it was the least embarrassing, stayed well this side idolatry. He rejoiced in the creation, whenever necessary, of impressive fictions, and, did any standers-by know the real truth, he decided that a few outrageous lies, devised for their entertainment, would amuse them. But, whatever may be the truth, now lost, of the old fat Paris guide, fifty years in Ida's keeping, here it is before me; and of the significance in its destiny after her death you shall be told when the time comes.

Certainly, if I am right, that this 'real love story' began in 1866, it lasted—not without infidelities—for twenty-five years. He was with her alone in Argentières, near Chamonix, in 1889, as a strange ecclesiastical document attests, and with her again in Switzerland in 1891, Aunt Emily being now in attendance upon them.

Then I have on my bookshelves a parade of elegant volumes, leatherbound and gold-tooled, but looking their age now; they are all the English poets, from Shakespeare and Milton to Moore and Mrs Hemans, and include, no less elaborately bound, such a lost poet as Henry

Kirke White. Each volume has an inscription on its flyleaf, in Indian ink and black-letter script, 'Ida Calder, 1874'. These inscriptions, all similar, were ornately contrived by Dum; all, one would imagine, on the same happy day. They were his gift to her. As we have seen, he loved poetry and loved to hear himself reading it aloud, in good voice and with abundant expression. Whether Ida ever read much, or at all, in these volumes I doubt, but she loved their beautiful outsides and would polish them with beeswax so that they shone prettily on her shelves, much as she would spend long hours polishing and garnishing her own pretty outside. She loved them in her fashion, and on her death, they went the same way as the old Paris guide.

I turn again to Aunt Emily's private diary in its battered black exercise book. It covers only a little over two years to August 1890, with two scraps added in 1894 and 1900, breaking off, never to be continued, with the words about the furnace of pain, mental pain—'oh, how acute sometimes'. I have told you how she omits names when it seems wise to do so. She is now in St Lunaire on the Brittany coast with Ida and Percy, Ida's enormous three-year-old baby. Mary, the youngest Calder sister, and Tom, her husband, have joined them.

'*Sunday August 14th 1887* Mary and Tom arrived yesterday. We took them for a stroll in the afternoon and showed them the views. This morning Ida and Mary went to mass and I went to bathe with Tom and D—— and tried to swim for the first time but never succeeded in keeping above water. . . . [Aunt always spoke of General Blake as "Dum".]

'*Friday August 19th* We bathe daily, sometimes from the rocks, sometimes from the cabines. The other day we chose a spot but found as soon as we were in our bathing gowns that we could be seen so we all adjourned bag and baggage to another rock and we looked sufficiently comical in our gowns carrying huge bundles, boots and bustles, stockings, corsets *etc.* all in hopeless confusion surmounted by the hats, Tom bringing up the rear with some of Mary's goods and chattels. We have great fun bathing, Tom and D—— helping us to float. I am sorry to say Mary and Tom leave tomorrow. Mary really looks sweetly pretty in her bathing dress. I tell her it is far more becoming than her general attire.

'*Sunday August 28th* Hotel du Centre, St. Brieuc. We left the Hotel de Paris yesterday and came here. It was pouring rain. Percy and I came in the diligence leaving the others to follow. We amused ourselves watching by the hotel window for them as they were so long in coming but at last baby went to sleep tired out. . . .'

Who were 'the others'? Tom and Mary having gone, Emily and Percy having come ahead, the others can be only Ida and D——. No wonder they delayed their coming. At this time, 1887, Ida was forty-one; Emily, thirty-one; Dum, fifty-one; and already an honorary Major-General, having been gazetted in January 1886 on his retirement with the pension of £450 per annum. I must explain that Ida had married a distinguished civil servant but was now legally separated from him, without hope of a divorce, but enjoying an allowance of £250 a year. If she and Dum, when living together at Argentières and in Switzerland in 1888, the following year, blent their incomes, they were well enough off for those days.

Now the diary passes into the early months of 1888, and a strange white mist lies over so much of it that no one in the world will ever know, henceforward and for ever, what is hidden in the haze. The 'we' is still there but not often; more often, as before, any clear subject is withheld from its verb. Once, when getting older, I again risked with Aunt Emily a question about our parentage, and she, as usual, warmly evaded it, saying, 'You must ask Dum. He is your guardian.' I persisted, 'Well, would Aunt Ida know?' and she snapped forth, 'Perhaps. It's not for me to say. Wuncenfraw will you leave me alone about it?'

I left her alone, and as with Dum, so with Aunt Ida, I never once in her life spoke to her on these veiled mysteries, never once asked her what she knew—till the very end, till my last sight of her, and then she spoke first.

Why did I not ask her? Never in childhood. Never once in twenty-eight years. Because as my perceptions brightened I told myself that 'things' would never be the same between us after that shaking moment. Let old and distant things stay where they were, within their cloud of silence.

Now the diary begins to cover what must have been one of the most momentous years in Emily's life, if not *the* most momentous. Behind the scribbled entries speaking only of superficial things, there must lie a story of pain, even great pain, and of some joy. In these months there were love, pregnancy, a birth, a child to worship, and—I can only imagine—an occasional torment of jealousy.

'*Sunday Jan. 29th 1888* [Aunt Emily is in Paris, but not alone. There is an unnamed presence with her and it is not Ida's.] I went and fetched Mother's letter and read it in the P.O., such a dear letter though she began by blowing me up, which makes me laugh—and then finishes up with loving words and thoughts which makes me cry.

'*Thursday Feby 2nd* Went to a matinée today and saw some of the celebrated actors and actresses. Heard Sarah Bernhardt read a little simple story most touchingly, Coquelin recite and give us an encore "Enragé" which made me laugh. Sarah was swathed in grey silk hitched up into a silver chain round her hips, her throat encircled with skunk which continued half-way down the dress, and a large bunch of pink roses at her waist. I didn't admire her appearance in the least though I should like to see her act something tragic, her voice and manner were sympathetic and most emotional. There was an address by M. Ernest Renan, very witty, only I could not help feeling a little shocked to hear an old man so feeble that he could not stand, his voice so weak that he could be scarcely heard, chuckling and enjoying a good joke of a rather blasphemous nature. His address was on the French language. After speaking at some length about the beauties of French, and the many beautiful sayings that were first given to the world in that language, he went on to say that they should make it last till Doomsday because "only fancy how distressing it would be if *les affaires* were conducted in German". This provoked a roar of laughter which encouraged him to proceed, and he then said that if all the anonymous letters he received informing him of his certain damnation were true, how much easier it would be for him to "arrange himself" with the Bon Dieu if He spoke French. "If He speaks German I shall be lost." People laughed all the more and I could hardly suppress a smile, but there was something very shocking in it all the same. Certainly it did not make his old age appear venerable in my eyes.

'*Monday July 9th* Left Paris. Train passed through pretty country. Took our *déjeuner* with us in a basket and enjoyed it very much. We had a carriage to ourselves. Arrived at hotel safely but find it exceedingly cold. We feel very seedy indeed. Suppose it is the cold. ["Our"? "We"?]

'*Thursday July 15th* Day turned out very fine. I bathed at 4.30. Enjoyed it very much. The sun was shining very brightly and there were big waves over which the "baigneur" lifted me as he was helping me to float. We took a walk through the fields beforehand. [The "We" here is a bold correction from "I"—perhaps in an uprush of truthfulness.]

'*Monday Aug. 20th* Still feeling very seedy and depressed. Not been able to bathe on account of the cold weather. Everything going wrong. Am so tired and worn out and wish I could go home to mother.

A lapse of four more months—and then:

'*Jan. 1st 1889* Day of suffering—sick headache all day long. Begun the year badly. Nothing ever occurs worth recording. *Ida away still.* [I have italicized these last three words because it will be well to remember them and their date. They were written in London, during a stay there of some months before she returned to France and spent a few months in Paris, whether alone, or with whom, I cannot even conjecture.]

'*June 26th Wednesday* Crossed to England via Calais. Crossed the Liane (Boulogne's river) and recalled happy youthful days and picnics and pleasant times, so often did we boat on that river. The sun shone full on the Cathedral surrounded by the Old Town and Ramparts, looking very picturesque and pretty. The town never looked better seen from the tráin. Stopped at the Tintelleries station where we used to see the train go by as children, and from which they used to set off the fireworks at the fêtes.'

In England Aunt lived for nearly a year at Rottingdean on the Sussex cliffs.

'*Rottingdean, July 1889* Have been here some days now. Such a funny quaint little place. Nothing ever occurs here worth recording. It is healthy and bracing but nothing ever occurs. We have got tired of the beach and have been walking inland watching the harvest. It is nice to climb the hills and get a blow but on the whole it is rather dull.

'*Feb. 4th '90, Rottingdean* Copied from "Hawk"

> 'Little white sweetheart gracious and good,
> I wish we were far from the world of men
> We two in our Sussex weald again
> With moonlight and starlight and meadow and wood,
> For then . . . Ah, then!

> Summer nights are like wine to drink,
> My woodland blossom, my wee wild wren,
> When one is far from mortal's ken
> One doesn't reason and one cannot think,
>   And then . . . Ah, then!'

By another unintended dramatic effect in this fragmentary and scribbled diary the words 'Ah then!' are followed by a procession of dots right across the page from left to right. They appear to have been penned there because the next entry is abrupt and, as it were, surprising to the writer: *'Thursday, May 21st, '90* Left for Switzerland. . . .'

After a rapturous description of the train journey through the mountains to Lucerne, the next entry for June 1st is the description of how 'we' went by steamer to Tellsplatte at the other end of the lake and then walked along the Axenstrasse to Flüelen. The day after this they walked up the Rigi but did not reach the summit because after passing Kaltbad the heat became intense and Emily felt very sick and tired. She took the mountain train back to Kaltbad, but 'Ida walked down to there alone and slipped and fell'. So Ida was one of the 'we'.

Now there is drawn right across the diary's page a shaky line dividing this entry from one nearly three months later. This is weakly written in pencil so that, after eighty years, it has faded almost out of sight. *'Interlaken Saturday 23rd August, 1890.* Got up for half an hour for the first time, having had typhoid very severely.' Then a second shaky nervous line stretches right across the page, and thereafter it is four years later, and she is in West Kensington at Gledstanes Road. *'June 10th 1894.* Mrs. Hughes had an At Home today. It was very crowded. and there were many interesting people there. The singing as usual was good. Mrs. Alfred Barker recited "The Creation of Woman".'

§

Well, there is the piecemeal diary with the mist over so much of it. Let us take our stand on a few hard facts now known for certain, and with these for a view-point see what we can deduce, or guess, from shadowy shapes and movements in the mist.

The certain facts are these. General Blake and Aunt Emily were together in Paris in the spring of 1888. We have seen the birth certificate of a child born to them in Paris at that time under the name,

Dorothy Makepeace. Ida must have been there at the same time—or accessible—for the following reason.

There is no doubt that in August of the next year Dum was living with her in Argentières, Haute Savoie. I have the certificate of the private baptism in Argentières of a child born to them seven and a half months before, on the last day of 1888—that is to say a child conceived either just before or just after Aunt Emily's child was born. Could this explain the brief entry in Aunt's diary for January 1st. 1889, the day following the birth of Ida's child—Emily in London, Ida and Dum in Switzerland: 'Day of suffering—sick headache all day long. Nothing ever occurs worth recording. Ida away still.'

(The furnace of pain, mental pain—oh, how acute sometimes.)

This private baptism certificate, written on hotel note-paper is the 'strange ecclesiastical document' I referred to before. Attached to it by a now bent and rusting pin is a note on the same paper: 'To the Officiating English Clergyman at Chamonix. Dear Sir, Please enter in your Register of Baptisms (if you have one at the English Church) the name mentioned within of a child privately baptised by me at the Hotel Couronne, Argentières this day, August 14th 1889.' The names on the certificate will be disclosed in their proper place. When this certificate and letter were first shown to me twenty-three years later, in circumstances which will also be uncovered for you, there was with them a letter from the priest who had performed the baptism, authenticating his certificate:

'Shrewsbury Hospital, Sheffield. March 5th 1912.
'Dear Sir,

'It was curious and interesting to me to see a memento of my first visit to Switzerland more than 20 years ago—[though Savoie had been ceded to France in 1860 people always called parts of it "Switzerland" because of the Alps all around]—Yes, it is perfectly genuine and you may safely act upon it. I think the parents told me they had let their house in Paris and were living quietly in Switzerland. There was then no chaplaincy at Argentières, and they did not know when they would come across a clergyman of their own church. We grew very friendly the few days I was there. So at their particular request I baptised their child as stated.'

With my love for the Dum of my childhood and with my memories of him ever since, it is hard to write down what seem the only possible deductions from all these facts. Once in my adolescence I remember arguing with Aunt Emily whether Dum was a good man or not, and declaring hotly that *of course* he was; and Aunt replying in her best tragico-sentimental manner, 'Keep your dreams. Keep your dreams.' I did keep them, and I do still; I can do no other when I remember Dum. I deny that they were dreams pure and simple because I must always believe that in Dum there was a quality of goodness, deep and lovable, even if he was morally—and if you like, gravely—at fault with these two Calder sisters, and perhaps with other women. He is not the only person in my life whom I have known to be morally amiss (giving 'morality' its limited sense) all too often perhaps, and yet to have beyond question, in my eyes, a basic goodness; he is just the chief of them.

Aunt should take a word of credit here too. In this that, though she went to her death without once admitting that she'd had a child by Dum, she had certainly done so, and yet she would always allow generously that Ida was 'the love of his life', and so put herself into the secondary place.

So much said, let my only possible conclusions be stated faithfully. Dum in early 1888 must—in some manner—have been living with both sisters in Paris, and in the months round about Emily's later pregnancy, she not being available, he must have begotten a child on Ida. The 'we' in Rottingdean on a day in July 1889, who walk over the hills and watch the harvest, cannot be Emily and her one-year-old child, Dorothy or 'Dots'; but the verses 'quoted from "Hawk"' in February 1890 could well refer to herself and the child, who would then have been nearly two years old.

> Little white sweetheart, gracious and good,
> I wish we were far from the world of men,
> We two in our Sussex weald again. . . .
> My woodland blossom, my wee wild wren
> When one is far from mortal's ken
> One doesn't reason and one cannot think. . . .

When, soon after this, she suddenly 'left for Switzerland', Ida's child by Dum would have been a year and a half old, and I have little doubt that he had summoned Emily to be a companion for Ida and to help her with the two children there, Percy, now six, and the infant christened in Argentières. It is certain that the typhoid fever at Interlaken seized her while she was living with Ida and Dum, because she would tell us how they cared for her there and brought her away from the hospital to their home—in Lausanne, I think: a cabinet portrait of the Argentières infant has the name of a photographer in Lausanne. When a happy mood was on her she would tell us amusingly, but affectionately, of Dum's many despairs after steamy quarrels between him and Ida; how he would plunge into one of his 'awful silences' and, wounded to the heart, would climb slowly up the nearest available mountain, the very picture of a tall and lonely Man of Sorrow, while a little boy, Percy, toiled up behind him like a faithful dog. Of Dum, Ida, Percy, and herself she would tell these stories, but she mentioned no other children in that little Swiss company, neither Dorothy nor myself; and we probed no further because these occasional tales were told either when we were too young to have any questions to ask, or too old and considerate to press, or even pose, them.

As far as it was in her to do so, Ida, ever abounding with verbal affection, loved the Argentières infant, calling him her 'little Swiss boy', and there is a pleasant story told us by Emily in our adult years when she hesitated no longer to talk to us about Ida and Dum (though never speaking that word about herself and Dum). On some Swiss occasion Dum and Ida showed the two-year-old child to the *patronne* of a *pâtisserie* by the lake of Lucerne, and the good gushing woman exploded with the suitable admiration. '*Mais il est merveilleux, Madame. Vraiment. Il a dans ses yeux un coin du lac.*' Turning to Dum, she inquired, '*C'est votre petit enfant, Monsieur?*'

But Dum, never slow with a lie for the entertainment of Ida, protested, laughing, '*Mais non, Madame! Non, non!*' And, fifty-four at the time, with silver threads in his dark hair and a grey beard, he pointed to them as if they demonstrated the unlikelihood of paternity. '*Regardez mes neiges.*'

Quick as a tennis ball slammed home across the net, came the good woman's wit. '*Ah, oui! Oui, bien sûr, Monsieur, mais souvent sous la neige il y a des volcans.*'

An apt evaluation, maybe, of Dum.

§

From here onward the mist is in full possession. I cannot break it anywhere. It would seem that some time in 1891 or '92 Dum and Ida returned to England with Percy and the Argentières infant; and that, possibly, Emily accompanied them with *her* child—because where this three-year-old child can have been during Emily's long stay and illness in Switzerland is something far out of our sight now. I conjecture that an agreement was come to by this trio of parents that Emily, unmarried and without an income, should accept the care and protection of Ida's embarrassing little son, both as a playfellow for her own child and as a source of livelihood for herself. I do know, because I learned it long afterwards, that, back in England, Ida nervously but courageously showed to her old mother living in London her 'little Swiss boy'. The old mother, once Sophia Kennicott who had borne ten children to Colonel Calder, seems to have been tolerant, or if not tolerant, loving and forgiving.

And so, some two years later, the little Swiss boy became aware of his small red-and-white home, in Dunsany Road, Brook Green, with an Aunt Emily as his formidable guardian; an Aunt Ida who came visiting frequently and called him her sweetheart, and who sometimes brought with her an enormous boy called Percy Wilkinson, born to her when she was still living with her first husband; another child and playmate in the house, Dorothy Makepeace; and, above everyone and everything else, towering physically as well as mentally, a General Blake, or 'Dum', his 'real guardian'—and the one person he truly and greatly loved in his small world.

6

JAM ABIERAT . . . .

At some date in the months after that grand week-end in Brighton with Dum he left us. Why he left us I do not know. It is one more of the secrets I shall never unravel. He went to live first in some Ebury Street rooms in Westminster near the only temple of which he was really a devotee, the Army and Navy Stores; and afterwards in expensive chambers over a gunsmith's in Pall Mall, near his club, the United Services. I watched him go, my heart heavier than it had ever been in all my eleven years. Not again would I hear his latch-key turning in the hall door and know that I was now free from all danger of slappings by Aunt Emily; not again, from the play-room window, see him coming homeward along Charleville Road and tear down the stairs that an opened door might welcome him before the latch-key touched it. Not again would Dorothy and I, on other than schooldays, walk laughing and skipping on either side of him down Charleville Road to North End Road and West Kensington station, happy to be with him at this first stage of his journey to Town, because he so obviously enjoyed having us with him, and teasing and making fun of us, often pressing coppers into our hands rather furtively 'for suitable purchases at some neighbouring confectioner's'. I was left in Aunt's care, and not again would there be a close season for slaps from evening onwards.

I don't know whether Dum, now that he was no longer a 'boarder' with us, gave her less money for the upkeep of the house in Gledstanes Road, but memory paints her as always in debt after his going. While with us he gave her £600 a year, and this was enough to sustain that large house, pay two servants, and feed us all well. Once Dorothy told her that a schoolfellow had asked, 'Is your auntie very rich?' and Aunt advised Dorothy, 'If anyone asks you that again, you should say, "No. Just comfortably off."'

She was not comfortable now. Dum gone, a great change came over our household in Gledstanes Road. We had no longer a cook at £18 a year and a housemaid at £12. We had one 'general servant' or none at all. Aunt with her quick temper which so easily caught alight and flared out of control could not easily retain a servant who worked alone in a large up-and-down house. She lost one servant after another; and then, on returning from school, or on a holiday, I was made to discharge any one or two—or three—of the following labours: cleaning the brass fittings on the front door, cleaning the brass taps in the bathroom, cleaning the knives on the knife-board in the scullery (this happening long before stainless steel), polishing with black lead and emery paper the huge kitchen range and its fender, dusting the drawing-room (and what a weary task was this with the multiple objects on piano, mantel, bureaux, and tables, how weary and how scamped), sitting at the dining-room table and polishing with a pink powder all the cutlery, cruets and salvers, teapots and other silver. Or I was polishing the endless India brasses and Indian silverware which Dum had brought home, and Aunt had hidden away from his forgetful eyes when he decided to leave us and take 'a few things' with him. Seldom an evening but I was sent on an 'errand' to dairy, baker's, grocer's, or greengrocer's. 1901, and I recall that at the grocer's a pint bottle of Fremlin's ale cost $2\frac{1}{2}$d., a bottle of whisky (for Mr Reay) 2s. 6d., and a packet of twelve full match-boxes $1\frac{1}{2}$d.

Once on being sent to get two bottles of beer for Uncle Edwin who was coming to dinner I felt the bottles, held by their necks one in each hand, to be very like Indian clubs. Now I was an expert with Indian clubs at this time because my current ambition was to be as muscular and powerful as Percy, so as I came up Charleville Road I swung these convenient bottles in proper Indian club fashion, now up in the air and way out to left side and right, now behind my neck and now before my knees. From the breakfast-room window Aunt observed this performance (technically excellent) and waited with a smarting slap in her hand for me when I got back.

'Don't you know that shaking is ruination to beer?' Ruination was a favourite word of hers. 'They might have exploded in the street. All over you. Glass and beer and all.'

I learned my lesson that evening. I have never swung a couple of beer bottles again.

On another occasion Aunt thought she had forgotten to tell me to get cakes at the baker's, and she sent Dorothy fifteen minutes later to get them instead. But at the baker's the pleasant woman behind the counter said, 'Oh, but your brother has just come and got them.' Dorothy said, 'Oh, thank you. Sorry,' and went out to return home. But, half-way up Charleville Road, she stopped and stood still. Just now she was wholly under the influence of Mr Hilliard, whom she worshipped both in church and out of it, and was accordingly convinced that a child must never bear false witness. So she went all the way back to the baker's and said to the pleasant woman, 'I think I ought to tell you that he's not really my brother.'

The woman nodded and smiled; and Dorothy was able to return home, at peace with God and Mr Hilliard.

(Quotation from Dorothy's diary, when aged about fourteen: 'It is many years since I last wrote in my diary which is a pity as I have had an interesting and, under God, happy life.')

Now and again, deep in debt, Aunt would borrow from her generous and hearty brother, our well-loved Uncle Edwin, and when after a time—generally a long time—he suggested a repayment, she would use us as vehicles for the reception of her irritability at such behaviour. 'He with all the money he's got! And he my brother!' All her life she seemed to think that any pressure for the repayment of a loan was one of men's more unattractive habits. Polonius might have had my Aunt Emily in mind when he warned Laertes, 'Neither a borrower nor a lender be; for loan oft loses both itself and friend.'

§

But, whatever her worry with debts or her 'servant trouble', Aunt maintained a brave show in the Gledstanes Road house during these our last months in it, and soon my life in Dum's absence was less unhappy, less unacceptable, than I had foreseen. She loved anything that amounted to a party, whether it was one of her At Home days or a 'Children's Party' at Christmas; and always she devoted herself to entertaining the guests adequately, whether grown-ups or children. Often during an At Home I was called in to recite an uplifting poem to the assembled ladies: Longfellow's 'Village Blacksmith', or his 'Psalm of Life'—'Life is real! Life is earnest! And the grave is not its goal; "Dust thou art, to dust returnest," Was not spoken of the soul'; or Mrs Hemans's 'The Better Land':

> Eye hath not seen it, my gentle boy!
> Ear hath not heard its deep songs of joy;
> Dreams cannot picture a world so fair—
> Sorrow and death may not enter there;
> Time does not breathe on its fadeless bloom
> For beyond the clouds and beyond the tomb—
>   It is there, it is there, my child.

Always there came generous applause for me, and I went back to my homework or my play, reasonably well pleased with myself, though I conceive the performance was pretty inferior.

More than once at a Christmas party she produced in a large bare top-floor room, to which the guests from the drawing-room came crowding up, a costume play acted by us and 'all our little friends'. Here, preserving a soiled existence after sixty years, is a programme of one of these plays, laboriously flowered and elegantly scripted by me. The play was especially written for us by one of Mr Hilliard's sons.

Programme
A visit from Santa Claus
by
Harry Hilliard

———

Santa Claus (King of the Fairies)...........Harry Hilliard
Sunray.........................Miss Majorie [*sic*] Dove
Moonray........................Miss Dorothy Cameron
Starlight...........................Miss Olivia Forrester
Zephyr.........................Miss Evangeline Hilliard
Dawn Light.........................Miss Edythe Blaine
Aurora Borealis.................Miss Dorothy Makepeace
Crooked Sixpence (the evil fairy).........Ernest Raymond

There were also some civilians whom this galaxy of immortals visited—but enough is enough.

Another 'programme', still surviving, though yellowed and split with years, provides perhaps a more universal picture of life in a Kensington home in days long before radio, television and family motoring, when the heart of the home's entertainment was the grand piano in the drawing-room. All movable chairs in the house have been congregated in the drawing-room, some thirty of them, facing two tall screens hired from the Army and Navy Stores. Behind the screens is the 'stage'. Among the chairs is Dr Owen's magic lantern to flood the stage with its light, Dr Owen, kindest of doctors, loving to help any of his 'little patients' with their parties. The programme begins, 'Conjuring . . . Mr. Hoering'; then comes 'Song with violin obligato . . . Mr. Keely [our Uncle Tom] with Mr. Hoering and Mr. Smith accompanying.' (Mr Smith was my late frustrated music master.) Next: 'Song, "Do buy me that" . . . Mr. Smith.' Now come the centre-pieces of the whole programme, the *tableaux vivants*, Aunt's creation and her joy.

1. Daisies and Buttercups. . The Misses Keely and Dorothy Makepeace
2. The United Tea Company. . The Misses Daniel and the Misses Keely
3. Kept In. Sonnie Keely and Ernest Raymond
4. Nancy Lee with song by Mr. Keely. . . . . Dorothy Makepeace
5. Tweedledum and Tweedledee. . . Alan Christie and Ernest Raymond

Here there is an interlude before the tableaux are resumed. 'Tambourine Dance . . . The Misses Daniel; Violin Solo . . . Mr. Hoering. [Mr Hoering seems to have been a talented man.] Song, "Little Brown Jug" . . . Mr. Keely.'

Then the tableaux again for the programme's grand close.

1. Pears' Soap
2. Miss Muffet
3. Great Expectations
4. The Rival Dollies
5. Final Tableau, 'Good Night'.

This last everyone agreed was 'very pretty'. All the incandescent gas-lights in the room had been turned down one after another by the good Dr Owen, and the screens, parting, disclosed all the children in their nightgowns and bare feet, holding lighted candles and facing an imagined stairway which led up to bed. After the magnificent applause which greeted this, and while we children were still standing there, unmoving, since this was a Tableau, Uncle Tom at the grand piano sang the song, 'Good Night'.

But in the course of this fine programme there had been one technical hitch, which we did not know about till afterwards when it was reported to us by Dr Owen who had been working his magic lantern. It was during the tableau 'Tweedledum and Tweedledee . . . Alan Christie and Ernest Raymond'. He flung a beam on to the linked twins, only to perceive that Tweedledee, dressing in a hurry and excitedly and happily, had left all his fly-buttons undone. So he quickly raised the beam above Tweedledee's waist and did not lower it till, to his relief, the tableau was over.

These party days were good days, brightly lit in memory and flushed through with laughter; and we owed them to an ardent, emotional, and restlessly vivacious guardian.

7

AWAKENING

My broken attempts to keep a diary stop jaggedly with the description of the newsboys calling 'Death of Queen Victoria'; three brief statements follow, mere splinters after this breakage; they are 'I did not say yesterday that we went back to school because I was so taken up in writing about the Queen'; then, months later: 'Our pretty servant Lilian was married today at 9 o clock. We went to see her. There were three weddings taking place. The third couple were a very humble set'—(compassion from an Edwardian 'gentleman' of eleven?); and finally for the next day, 'I went to Holiday Class because I am trying to get into St. Paul's School.'

Thereafter nothing; nothing for three years till the September of 1904 when there is an abortive attempt to start the diary again. There are only five pages of it, pages of a facetiousness most regrettable but probably inescapable in a schoolboy just waking up to the whole world around him and to strange new potentials within him. Sixty clean pages of the feint-ruled exercise-book follow; sixty empty pages, browning under the breath of sixty years—and there the end.

The attempt begins in fine style:

Re-Commencement of
My Diary

———

I

Introduction

'Those of you who read these pages will perceive if you can read the somewhat illegible writing, that I have commenced and recommenced them till at last I gave it up in despair and forgot the existence of such a book, but today, discovering it covered with dust, dirt, and cobwebs innumerable I thought I would make a third or fourth attempt to continue the work which I had begun so bravely and proudly, and which was headed by so admirable a title as "Ernest Raymond's Schooldays"—'

If you can bear it, read on.

'Today is the fourth day of the tenth month of the year Anno Domini one thousand nineteen hundred and four and if you are one of those readers who, when they read a book, commence at the name of the owner on the first flyleaf and end at those words which either cause you to shut up the book with a sigh of relief or which you read with a thrill of pain and sorrow, I mean those words "The End"—if you are one of these, I say, you will see that this diary was commenced six years and twenty-three days ago. In those six years many things have happened which would have made this story very interesting but which, most unfortunately, have not been written within the foregoing pages, things which have concerned the world at large, the safety of the British Empire and—'

And further facetiae.

'I will not attempt to relate all these happenings but will tell you such things as concern the welfare of this diary, and which must have been fairly interesting to have impressed themselves on my feeble memory, and these will form the matter of another chapter.

Chapter II
A Retrospect

———

'Almost the last fact remarked upon, in the second attempt to write a journal, was that on September 16th 1901, I attended a holiday class at Colet Court, the school which I graced at that period of my life, to assist and prepare me to enter that ancient and renowned public school, St. Paul's.'

More of Chapter II will come later, but, I promise you, not much of it.

My three years at Colet Court had been neither happy nor unhappy; I see a neutral grey light illuminating them like the light of a cloudy but rainless London day. As I grew from nine years old to twelve I became more and more a shy and dreaming solitary. My only brilliant successes were all in dreams—heroisms, martyrdoms, pyrotechnic displays on the cricket field with crowds applauding, dazzling triumphs on concert platforms, always at a piano, rendering vast bravura passages. None of the other boys seemed plagued with this shyness; they were bold and gregarious, and I found it difficult to establish a friendliness with any of them. I felt alone among them. Sometimes I was an object of ridicule to them.

In the first days of my first term I suffered a withering humiliation among them. It was on a small asphalt football ground, and we were playing 'Sixes' (six a side). Since I was the newest footballer I was inevitably told to keep goal, and there I stood on the asphalt, framed by the white goal-posts. A nimble and fleet boy got the ball somewhere near the centre line and, outrunning all, eluding all, he came with the ball at his foot towards me, unimpeded for about twenty yards. I did not know what one did in these alarming circumstances, so I stayed where I was, framed in the goal-posts but with hands outstretched to receive anything he might offer. And of course he just footed the ball into the goal yards away from where I was standing.

Howls of execration from the members of my side, roars of laughter and delight from the members of the other side, uncontrollable body-racking laughter from all the spectators along the rails.

Though I was less of an incompetent on the playgrounds in later terms (but never good) and far from incompetent in the class-rooms, I still think this early scene on the asphalt is a fair picture of my failure to be anything but a solitary at school. I made my efforts to win some friendships because I craved to be liked, but nearly always my talk with less inhibited boys was like talk through a grating behind which my heart quickened uncomfortably, and a desire swelled to be done with the effort and alone again.

And yet, despite this hampering inferiority in my public relations, despite the poverty of my performances on football or cricket field, despite a feeling that I was unmanly compared with louder and more forceful boys, I had a sure confidence, an exaggerated confidence, that I was the equal of any of them, and superior to many, and that one day the world would know this. I walked alone but with dreams of some triumph that would one day conquer the world.

This sense of inferiority, married so oddly to a dream of greatness hereafter, I must believe was in large part the gift of Aunt's violently slapping hand, and her cane.

Since I was twelve and a half when I exchanged Colet Court for St Paul's, it was natural that my last terms at this junior school should be a period of awakening to the grey dawn-light of manhood. No information about sex had reached me as yet. Perhaps because of my withdrawn and unsocial character no boy visited me with revelations about sex or with an improper invitation. And so the surprises that now caught me were those of a solitary.

A first surprise was my perception that the public caning of a boy before his class-mates stirred a bodily excitement in many of them. Mr Bewsher, our headmaster, was a good and earnest man, desiring only the spiritual welfare of his pupils; and his canings, never frequent, were directed to this end. So also, I have no doubt, was his habit of punishing the offender before his class. The offender was made to kneel before a bench and lean over it while Mr Bewsher turned back his cuff, prepared his pliant cane, and then administered the traditional six, the boy quivering and wilting at each cut. Sometimes the child stretched out his legs full-length behind his kneeling body because of the pain. And meanwhile all of us were excited and staring spellbound at an entertainment which, for many, was stimulating and pleasurable. More than one schoolfellow with whom I have discussed this business in after years has admitted that the excitement could even take the form of an erection. And yet it goes on in schools to this day, sixty years after; some of the schools permitting the senior boys, or prefects, to perform this (often) sexually stimulating duty. When, I never cease to wonder, will headmasters, housemasters, prefects and fagmasters learn a disturbing lesson from the books on flagellation displayed in the pornographic shops along the Charing Cross Road or in the streets of Soho?

Whether Mr Bewsher's caning of a boy in the privacy of his study was sometimes necessary and right I will not argue here. There is a tendency in us all when discussing corporal or capital punishment to warm up into vehemence. All I will say is that when we knew that one of us was to be caned in that room, we gathered outside its closed door, listening excitedly to the cuts of the cane, and were stimulated.

I perceived this curious and secret excitement at twelve years of age but did not yet know enough to relate it to sex.

Then one day I was climbing the rope in the school's empty gymnasium. It was because of my desire to be as muscular as Percy Wilkinson, whom I then hero-worshipped, that I would go so often into the gymnasium, and exercise alone on horizontal bar, parallel bars, bridge ladder, and rope. By now I had developed good arm muscles, and sometimes I would ascend the rope to the very ceiling, using arms alone, my legs extended properly below, toes together and pointing to the floor. But more often I raced as quickly as I could up the long rope with my legs doing their full share around it. And on this day I was more than half-way up when I halted and hung there because of an unexpected pleasure between my loins that stirred breathless delight in throat and heart. I hung there to let it endure, and it endured. . .

There was no emission at this age of twelve, only delight.

Why did I tell no one of this unforeseen experience? What reason was there for something like shame? Did this reasonless doubt and shame come from out of the long tribal past behind my birth?

After this I would sometimes go back to the empty gymnasium in the hope of knowing again this curious, gasping ecstasy that was the gift of the rope. More often than not I failed to find it, but there were times when I succeeded, and then I would hang there for quite a while in the empty gym, while it played its exquisite game upon me.

Thus did the dark gods within me speak to my innocence.

Fitting, perhaps, that this first innocent step on to the threshold of manhood should be contemporary with my final preparation for entry into St Paul's, a senior school, majestic, dignified, and dominating the Hammersmith Road with its red towers, black spire, and green academic grounds exactly opposite the milder red-brick of Colet Court. I must quote again from the facetious 'Chapter II *A Retrospect*' that ends my diary for ever.

'With my heart in my mouth and my books in my hand I left Colet Court and crossed the road to St. Paul's, never to return as a pupil again, in the company of about thirty other boys and led by Mr. Samuel Bewsher, bursar of St. Paul's, like a pack of Sunday School children following their teacher into church. Having escorted us into his room, he arranged us in a row and gazed at us with his scrutinising eye and then smiled and seemed very pleased with what he saw.

'He then escorted us into the Great Hall and we sat down and awaited with anxiety for our examination which we thought was going to be a most ridiculously difficult one. However we were set to do a Greek exercise which we all had done several times before, and then the Venerable and Most Revered Highness, Frederick W. Walker, High Master of St. Paul's School, Honorary Fellow of Corpus Christi College, Oxford, and Member of the Most Worshipful Company of Fishmongers, came over and glanced at my work. He said, "I've seen worse. Let him pass", and Mr. Pantin, the master with him whispered to me, "Go to the Book Room and get your cap."'

Pantin spoke thus softly because all the masters at St Paul's were as afraid as the boys of that terrible old grey-bearded, silk-gowned, mighty-voiced 'High Man', F. W. Walker. His awesome spirit broods over St Paul's to this day.

Now, behind this picture of my crossing the Hammersmith Road and entering into the corridors of St Paul's there hangs another mystery that will never be resolved with any certainty.

The Times of 2 September 1901, a fortnight before my admission into St Paul's, contained this entry under *Deaths*: 'BLAKE.—On Friday 30th August, at 16 Beaumont Street, W, Eliza Gordon Blake, aged 65, wife of Major-General George Frederic Blake, late Royal Marine Light Infantry. Friends will kindly accept this, the only intimation.'

This death of his estranged wife freed Dum to marry again, and after a proper interval he married a Miss Lilian McKellar, daughter of a General McKellar and thirty-eight years younger than he; a magnanimous woman who, in spite of everything—and he had told her everything—remained a generous friend to us till her death.

Well, when more than fifty years after my admission into St Paul's my age qualified me for the State's retirement pension I was asked to produce a birth certificate that would establish that age. There was no such thing. Or there was no hope of finding it, if it existed, in Switzerland or Paris or Argentières. Fully intending to enjoy the pension, I came upon the idea of writing to the Bursar of St Paul's for a statement of the date when I was admitted, and my age at the time. He replied courteously: 'Dear Sir, In reply to your letter I have pleasure in certifying that your date of birth as shewn by the school records is 31.12.1888.' This did not fully meet the State's need, so I asked for a more detailed statement, and he sent me a formal certificate. 'This is to certify that Ernest Raymond entered this school at the Michaelmas Term 1901 and that as no birth certificate was submitted a declaration on oath before a Commissioner of Oaths was accepted in which it was stated that Ernest Raymond was born on 31st December 1888.' Fascinated by the words 'a declaration on oath', I sought further information from this friendly and helpful correspondent, and his next reply runs: 'Dear Sir, Thank you for your letter of June 10th. I am sorry to say I do not think I can produce exactly what you want. Our records show that you were born on December 31st 1888, that you entered the school in September 1901, and that both your parents were dead. That you were a member of the Officers Training Corps and that you served in the Manchester Regiment in the 1914/18 War. This is as far as our information goes, but I am willing to certify that the particulars in this letter are those as they appear in our books.'

This fully satisfied the Ministry of Pensions, but not me, though of course I troubled the good man no more.

'That both your parents were dead.'

Who lied? Apparently on oath. Dum was living comfortably at this time either in Ebury Street or Pall Mall, and wooing, I imagine, Lilian McKellar; Aunt Ida was living in smaller style but comfortably too in a Brook Green flat with her now six-foot-five son, Percy Wilkinson, and her husband, Dr Broenner, our Uncle Franz, whom Percy called 'the Deutscher'.

Who lied? In the very face of the Law. I have little doubt it was Aunt Emily. And, crime or not, it was an illustration of her more benevolent side; and, did she slap me or not, I am grateful to her for her determination to get me into a famous school. A mild unscrupulousness never troubled her, Mr Hilliard and St Andrew's Church notwithstanding; unlike Dorothy ('I think I ought to tell you he's not really my brother'), she would be very ready, since it seemed necessary, for a little perjury. After all, there was nothing wrong with the date of birth which was the important matter; and anything else could be regarded as mere trimmings; as a satisfactory, picturesque, pathetic, and convincing background. Anyway whatever may be the penalty for a false statement on oath, she is now, and has been for thirty years, far out of reach of the Law's indignation. May she rest in peace.

§

It was in my first term at St Paul's that a revelation, unsought, unexpected and quite literally epoch-making, was vouchsafed me. If the dark gods spoke to me on the rope in Colet Court, it was another, and an incorporeal god, who touched me awake now, a god who was to take me captive and rule the rest of my life. It so dedicated me to one idea, one aspiration, that my life thereafter became a single journey, often balked and twisting, often halted and driven back, but ever driving towards its single goal.

This did not happen in any class-room at St Paul's but in the little cramped dining-room of our flat in Charleville Mansions.

Yes, we were now in a little flat, 38 Charleville Mansions, almost opposite and not forty yards away from our old house in Gledstanes Road. One thing was sure: that if we had, in our new impecuniosity, to move from Gledstanes Road, Aunt would not move out of reach of Mr Hilliard or any distance from his church and parish hall. In joking mood she would look from one of the flat's windows towards the old red, up-and-down house across the road and say, 'Well, now we have exchanged the vertical for the horizontal.'

The little flat, once we were in it, seemed beleaguered by the regiment of Aunt's debts. They stood menacingly around. Nowadays there was one 'errand' on which she could not send us but must go herself, quietly, furtively. This was to a pawnbroker's somewhere in Clapham, over the river and safely far away. The objects of silver and brass which Dum had brought from India, the ornate Sèvres vases which had taken his fancy in the Army and Navy Stores disappeared from the drawing-room shelves or tables and went into hibernation at this unknown depository in Clapham. A picture comes into mind to show how straitened Aunt was for money, how greatly 'on the save'. It is her birthday, and visitors are in the drawing-room, having brought her gifts wrapped in tissue paper. We children are there because she has called us to see 'all these lovely presents'. She is seated near a little table, and while talking and talking—and still talking—has picked up a paper-knife so that, after smoothing out a sheet of this convenient white tissue paper, and folding it at right angles again and again, she can cut it absent-mindedly into neat little squares. The destination and ultimate duty of these white squares is all too obvious, and we children in a social agony frown and grimace at her to bring her to a realization of what she is doing so publicly. She smiles and lays aside the knife and her little pile of useful paper.

Still much of a hermit, preferring loneliness to the company of noisy and formidable boys who might at any moment make fun of me, I had inevitably become an habitual reader, an addict to the drug which story books could be. My entrancing drugs at this time were Captain Marryat's sea-stories, *Midshipman Easy* and *Peter Simple* and others, which so transported me that when sorrowfully I reached their end I would turn back to their beginning and start again. I could do the same with Rider Haggard's *King Solomon's Mines*—what a night that was when I read it till four in the morning.

But I was still reading only for a story's excitement; these books were doing nothing to deepen my conception of literature, though may God be thanked for the rapturous pleasure they gave me in my quiet corner chair, or on summer lawns lying prone, or in my bed with the warm clothes almost covering my face and the hand that held the book —and the magic.

It may sound absurd to say that an event quite literally epoch-making, for me, was brought into being by a horse, but so it was.

The horse was helped a little in this task, perhaps, by Shiny Villiam. Here is the tale of the horse.

One morning when I ought to set off for school I had a slight tooth-ache and made it out to be much worse than it was. I acted considerable pain, a fist pressing on my cheek, a foot beating stoically under the torment—actions that almost began to be justified because I was slightly enlarging the pain by making such a show of it; and by begin-ning to believe in the show. So Aunt said I'd better stay at home and, if it got no better, she would take me to the dentist's in the afternoon. 'Lie down a little,' she said. And I lay down on the saddle-bag sofa which had been crammed into that small dining-room.

She went out to the shops, Dorothy to her school, and I was alone. Alone on a sofa with no very severe toothache, nothing that the drug of an exciting book wouldn't expel from mind. But I had no new book and could not think of any old one I'd like to read again. *Midshipman Easy* and *Peter Simple* had been recently read twice—or thrice—and so were temporarily out of the running.

Now, crammed also into that small dining-room was a break-fronted bureau with bookshelves behind the glass. On these shelves were the books you would have expected to see in the year, 1901: Tennyson and Longfellow the only poets, but novels by Rhoda Broughton, Henry Seton-Merriman, John Strange Winter, Hall Caine and a complete set of Dickens, some of its volumes looking shop-new, others abraded and torn. Because these were the novels of grown-ups I could raise no desire to read them. Still, having no boy's book to read, and no one to play with, I scanned these shelves, but was dis-couraged and turned from them. I lay on my couch again and wondered what to do. At last in desperation I rose and snatched at one of the Dickens volumes, carelessly, almost angrily, hoping little. By the grace and favour of God it was *Pickwick Papers*. An unpromising title; a heavy volume. 'Oh, well, open it at any old page and see what is there.'

The book seemed to open itself at pages 58 and 59. These at a glance showed Mr Pickwick, Mr Tracy Tupman, Mr Winkle and Mr Snodgrass at a Rochester inn, taking breakfast, and discussing how to get to Dingley Dell. The comic name 'Snodgrass' I found surprising in an adult's book, and encouraging. I read on.

> 'Post-chaise won't hold more than two,' said Mr. Pickwick.
>
> 'True, sir—beg your pardon, sir—very nice four-wheeled chaise, sir,' said the waiter. 'Seat for two behind, one in front for the gentleman that drives—oh, beg your pardon, sir—that'll only hold three.'
>
> 'What's to be done?' said Mr. Snodgrass.
>
> 'Perhaps one of the gentlemen would like to ride,' suggested the waiter, looking towards Mr. Winkle; 'very good saddle-horses, sir.'
>
> 'The very thing,' said Mr. Pickwick. 'Winkle, will you go on horseback?'
>
> Mr. Winkle did entertain considerable misgivings in the very lowest recesses of his own heart, relative to his equestrian skill; but as he would not have them suspected on any account, he at once replied with great hardihood, 'Certainly. I should enjoy it of all things. . . .'
>
> 'Let them be at the door by eleven,' said Mr. Pickwick.

At eleven they are all on the pavement looking at the chaise.

> It was a curious little green box on four wheels with a low place like a wine-bin for two behind, and an elevated perch for one in front, drawn by an immense brown horse. A hostler stood near, holding the bridle of another immense horse—ready saddled for Mr. Winkle.
>
> 'Bless my soul!' said Mr. Pickwick, as they stood upon the pavement while the coats were being put in. 'Bless my soul, who's going to drive? I never thought of that.'
>
> 'Oh, you, of course,' said Mr. Tupman.
>
> 'Of course,' said Mr. Snodgrass.
>
> 'I!' exclaimed Mr. Pickwick.

'Not the slightest fear, sir,' interposed the hostler. 'Warrant him quiet, sir; a hinfant in arms might drive him.'

'He doesn't shy, does he?' inquired Mr. Pickwick.

'Shy, sir?—He wouldn't shy if he was to meet a vaggin-load of monkeys with their tails burnt off.'

The last recommendation was indisputable. Mr. Tupman and Mr. Snodgrass got into the bin; Mr. Pickwick ascended to his perch. . . .

'Now, Shiny Villiam,' said the hostler to the deputy hostler, 'give the gen'l'man the ribbins.' Shiny Villiam—so called, probably from his sleek hair and oily countenance—placed the reins in Mr. Pickwick's left hand; and the upper hostler thrust a whip into his right.

'Wo-o!' cried Mr. Pickwick, as the tall quadruped evinced a decided inclination to back into the coffee-room window.

'Wo-o!' echoed Mr. Tupman and Mr. Snodgrass from the bin.

'Only his playfulness, gen'l'm'n,' said the head hostler encouragingly; 'jist kitch hold on him, Shiny Villiam.' The deputy restrained the animal's impetuosity, while the principal ran to assist Mr. Winkle in mounting.

'T'other side, sir, if you please.'

'Blowed if the gen'l'm'n worn't a gettin' up on the wrong side,' whispered a grinning post-boy to the inexpressibly gratified waiter.

Mr. Winkle, thus instructed, climbed into his saddle with about as much difficulty as he would have experienced in getting up the side of a first-rate man-of-war.

'All right?' inquired Mr. Pickwick. . . .

'All right,' replied Mr. Winkle faintly.

'Let 'em go,' cried the hostler—'Hold him in, sir,' and away went the chaise and the saddle-horse, with Mr. Pickwick on the box of the one, and Mr. Winkle on the back of the other. . . .

'What makes him go sideways?' said Mr. Snodgrass in the bin to Mr. Winkle in the saddle.

I loosed a bellow of laughter, little to be expected from one suffering from a savage toothache. But the flat was empty.

Strange that such simple words as 'What makes him go sideways?' should have determined a boy's career.

'I can't imagine,' replied Mr. Winkle. His horse was drifting up the street in the most mysterious manner—side first, with his head towards one side of the way and his tail towards the other.

All that day I read on and on, passionately. Alarm sank my heart when Aunt spoke again about my going to the dentist. I assured her that the tooth 'seems to have got better somehow', and read on. At some stage in the reading I knew with a happy breathless certainty that this was what I wanted to do with my life: to write books like this. Dickens was long dead, and it was time this sort of thing was done again. And I would set about doing it. (I need hardly subjoin that it has never been done again.)

If the italicized and capitalized headings in my diary such as '*Ernest Raymond's Schooldays* CHAPTER I' showed the seed of a desire to write books, the desire had been unconscious. This typography was merely imitative, but now—now the seed had burst above ground and was in full flower. It had even by-passed the season of being a bud.

This new ambition was no pure desire to create things which seemed glorious of their kind. A longing to win the applause of the world, and of posterity, was a heavy ingredient in it. And I sometimes wonder if this sudden uprush and flowering of a resolve which contained both the artist's drive to create and an ordinary human's longing for admiration and love had not sprung from a soil broken and fertilized by the departure of Dum. Were the applause and the affection of the world, in this my new dream, a substitute for Dum's merry praise and lively, laughing love? It is difficult after sixty years to speak with any conviction about symptoms in one's childhood, and to diagnose the condition of a young patient so remote in time, but it does seem to me now that this craving for praise had only a small life in me so long as Dum was there, but enlarged with a strange abruptness and took command of my life as soon as he was gone and there was no one else in my home to provide what he had given.

Anyhow, in the service of this new ambition, through succeeding weeks and months, I read all the other novels of Dickens except the unfinished *Edwin Drood*. I could not bear to be left unsatisfied or to read a completion of the story by someone else. I wanted no other hand. I bought Forster's *Life of Charles Dickens* and read its hundreds of pages as devotedly as those of any Dickens novel. Dickens exhausted, I read the three long Thackerays on the bureau's shelf with an ease and a speed I cannot command today. I found the novels of George Eliot and shed streaming tears over the last pages of *The Mill on the Floss*. I even got myself through the dense historical jungle of her *Romola*.

I read without taste or discrimination; I just read. I thought some of the worst parts of Dickens the best. So adhesive is a child's memory that these least tolerable parts stay in my memory word-perfect. The death of Poor Jo in *Bleak House*:

> 'Jo, my poor fellow!'
> 'I hear you, sir, in the dark, but I'm a-gropin'—a'gropin'—let me catch hold of your hand.'
> 'Jo, can you say what I say?'
> 'I'll say anythink you say, sir, fur I know it's good.'
> 'Our Father.'
> 'Our Father!—yes, that's wery good, sir.'
> 'Which art in Heaven.'
> 'Art in Heaven—is the light a-comin', sir?'
> 'It is close at hand. Hallowed be thy Name.'
> 'Hallowed be—thy—'
> The light is come upon the dark benighted way. Dead!
> Dead, your Majesty. Dead, my lords and gentlemen. Dead, Right Reverends and Wrong Reverends of every order. Dead, men and women, born with heavenly compassion in your hearts. And dying thus around us every day.

That this sort of grand appeal is misplaced in a novel I must agree, but I must also honour the man who made it.

I read it to Aunt because of my delight in it, and she thought it quite wonderful too. We wept together.

This vast reading at twelve and thirteen years old enlarged me in many ways and, coincident with it, I encountered at St Paul's a most eccentric master who, in the maddest way, ripened more and more of my mind and set me free from many of the prejudices and limitations that shackled the thoughts of children in these early post-Victorian years. His name seemed to us as strange, even as mad, as he was himself. It was Elam; and if I were to expound all that 'Old Elam' did for us in his dusty class-room it would take a whole book. To tell the truth, the book *has* been written—and by me—in a highly fictional form, under title, *Mr. Olim.* Compton Mackenzie, an Old Pauline equally impressed by Elam, brought him as a character, 'Mr Neech', into his celebrated *Sinister Street,* whose first volume is devoted almost entirely to St Paul's.

Now for a while this record can leave me reading and reading; often when stirred or excited pausing to study how this or that effect was won, how such a word or group of words was placed for the best impact—and so learning something of the narrative art—but seldom attempting any literary achievement myself. My dream would not allow me to doubt that I would do this one day, but I was too lazy as yet to toil up the steep and thorny path of prose composition when I could take the primrose path of dalliance with other people's books. At thirteen and fourteen Time, like some young daughter of Eternity, seemed ready to wait and wait for me.

8

IDA, PERCY AND UNCLE FRANZ

Since Aunt Ida's comfortable flat in Phoenix Lodge Mansions was but five minutes' walk from St Paul's, a pleasing walk between the fine old trees and the fine old houses of Brook Green, she used to have me to lunch on the Mondays of each week, and over the meal she made much of me. I doubt if she still called me, at thirteen, her sweetheart but her language about me was always abloom with affection. 'Bloom' seems a right word for Aunt Ida. Pink bloom. She was seldom fully dressed when I arrived for lunch because, as I've told you, it took her from pre-breakfast till about three in the afternoon to caparison herself fully for the open road and the public gaze; but her most shapely figure ('Few people have a figure like mine') was duly whale-boned and riveted into the best positions, and usually abloom with a pink and frilly tea-gown or peignoir of silk and lace; her beautiful auburn and silver hair ('Few people have hair like mine') was in its final array, and her soft-featured face, even for a boy of thirteen, was all that the skill of a lifetime could make it. The sleeves of tea-gown or house-coat seldom came lower than her elbows, and her bare arms were so round and soft that I would feel, as with no one else, a desire to touch them. Whether or not I exaggerate in calling this seductive appearance 'pink as the petals of a rose', it was certainly enclosed, as a rule, in a fragrance like the scent of roses in June.

Our lunch which she always 'made pretty' with green lettuce, scarlet tomatoes and dainty discs of egg, was the cold joint left over from Sunday; and it was always eaten in a narrow little room that opened off the drawing-room. About that drawing-room there is a surprising memory; it was full of pretty furnishings, for she dressed it as lovingly as her person, but I never once, in my long association with her, saw it used—except by the good 'Deutscher' who was allowed to go into the sanctuary, sit at the Bechstein piano, and play his German dreams away. Doubtless it must have been used occasionally—for an At Home perhaps—but I suspect that on such occasions she suffered lest her beautiful chairs were scratched, the white Indian carpet foot-marked, or a choice Dresden figure broken. She never sat in it herself; she always sat and sewed, or played *Skat* with Uncle Franz and Percy, in an ill-furnished work-room at the other end of the flat; her enjoyment of the drawing-room was in knowing that it was there, beautiful, swept, dusted, and unspoiled.

I want this story to hold to truth and so I must write simply that, while her fondness for me was genuine, it was not of the kind that could do anything at cost to herself—except in the last days and hours of her life. Words were easy and free of cost; the cold post-Sunday meal was daintily prepared for me, but it was easy and cheap. She was delighted to do this much for me; it eased her conscience. A time was to come when, unlike Aunt Emily, who was ready with a little perjury, she refused to produce an official document that would be of help in my career, because it might be of hurt to her. 'General Blake always insisted that I was never to be troubled,' she would say; and it was the kind and scrupulous Deutscher, usually under her thumb, who rose in stern command, as you shall hear, and insisted that she should produce it.

When, at seventeen, I was taken away from school and put to earn ten shillings a week in the Correspondence Office of the Army and Navy Stores, Aunt Emily gave me sixpence a day out of it for my lunch. Aunt Ida heard of this and asked me, 'But does that really get you enough? A big boy like you?' I laughed and said, 'It's not bad. A cut from the joint and two veg.'

'No pudding?'

'No. That costs another penny.'

'For what?'

'Roly-poly, Plum Duff, or Spotted Dog.'

She thought awhile. She overcame a recoil from spending money unnecessarily, and fetched a sixpence out of a purse and put it into my hand, closing my hand over it. 'There!' she said triumphantly, 'I'll do that for you. Each week.' I accepted the coin with a grateful smile and kept my thought to myself. But at seventeen I had entered upon a rebellious and cynical period, and the thought was, 'Thank you for a penny a day.'

Never did she speak of any relationship with Dum. If his name came up in our talk over our meal, her voice went harsh. She never referred to him as other than 'General Blake', and when at sixty-six he married Lilian McKellar, twenty-seven, she called it 'baby-snatching' and ridiculed it, and when this new Mrs Blake produced for him a magnificent boy (all his children were huge) she scoffed, 'A man of his age! Nearly seventy. It must be making people laugh.'

I stayed silent. I didn't dare release my thoughts for fear of hurting her. I didn't even spring to the defence of Dum though in my heart I longed to. I thought I could do it with laughter and gaiety, but I did not. I stayed silent.

I don't wish these words of mine to ring with bitterness. Some persons are capable of conversion, but most people can but be what they are; and if, as with most of us, one is accepting oneself as one is, it is only fair to accept others as they are. I enjoyed the appearance of being loved by her, even if it expressed itself only in words; indeed I needed it in the absence of Dum; and I shall ever remember that she tried to retrieve all—or much—at the end.

§

When she moved from the Brook Green flat to a villa in Barnes, those luncheons with her before afternoon school came to an end. This rather absurd little villa with its seated lions on the piers of its gate and at the corners and point of its gable was Oakdene, Glebe Road, Barnes, and it abutted on the common, with the Beverley Brook running behind it before emptying itself into the Thames at Barn Elms Park. Here I saw almost as much of her as at Brook Green because of my devotion to Percy. Now eighteen to my fourteen, he had reached his six-foot-five, was massive in chest and shoulders, and easily the commander-in-chief of that household, both his mother and stepfather, Uncle Franz, being a little afraid of him. I, so far, found nothing at fault in him; was he not taller than anyone else, adept at all field games, and a past-master with all tools? He could build in an afternoon, with me as his 'mate' entranced, a sun-house for the villa's small garden, a new chest for his bedroom, or a kennel, gabled and weatherproof, for his hideous but charming bulldog, Punch.

Under Hilliard's influence I still said bedside prayers and once— 'Ask, and it shall be given you'—in admiration of Percy's height and breadth, I added to my other suffrages a petition that I might 'grow as tall as Percy'. This in the end was granted me, with only an inch missing, but unfortunately I had omitted to pray for shoulders as broad and square as his, so the final effect has been nothing like as magnificent.

Vain, and delighting in admiration, as was natural at eighteen, Percy was happy with me as an attendant squire, and many and unforgettable were the enterprises we shared together.

Oakdene being no great distance from Wimbledon Common, I would stay the night with him, and we would rise early in the morning and cycle up Roehampton Lane to the common to bathe before breakfast in its Queensmere lake. Better than this, best of all, was the river. Powerful oar that he was—as effective as I was clumsy—he would drive the boat like a racing skiff with the ease of a Diamond sculler at Henley. And often, resting on his oars, he would pause a moment, and then loose his joyous cry, 'She freshens! Ernest, she freshens!' and up went the sail into the freshening wind, Percy as expert in hoisting a sail as in feathering an oar; and away went the prow, I delighting to steer it, up a lovely tidal stretch of lower Thames, past Brentford Ait and Kew Gardens, past the Old Deer Park and Richmond, past Petersham Meadows and Marble Hill Park, and so to where the tide ends its run 'At Tide-end-town which is Teddington'. Is there any joy comparable to being eighteen and fourteen and sailing between green arboreal banks and before a following breeze?

When the rain, pelting down on Barnes Common, denied us the river, we played Table Croquet on the dining-room table, and on this narrow field which brought him down to my level I was his equal and often beat him.

If Hilliard's large and steepled church, St Andrew's, was the chief power-house of Dorothy's youth and mine, it had, across the vicarage garden, a junior partner of almost equal potency, St Andrew's Parish Hall. No ordinary parish hall, this: it was dominated by a high and proper stage, with gas footlights, gas battens overhead, and lime spotlights hidden behind the proscenium arch. Here we children of the Church produced plays and pantomimes under the direction of Hilliard's three children, Stafford, Harry, and Evangeline, who were all to devote their lives to the Theatre. And here, one year, there was a Parish Fancy Dress Ball. Percy, at our invitation, came to it dressed as Mephistopheles, a truly Satanic figure. A figure in scarlet doublet, hose, and cloak, with a single scarlet feather rising from an evil hood and adding two feet to his six-foot-five. What I represented I cannot remember, but nobody turned to look at me. They looked three times at Percy.

Now, he and I, in our long walks and talks on the commons, had often discussed sex, but rather with a fascinated interest than in prurience. Percy, at eighteen, for all his domineering masculinity, was still a virgin. And I, though interested indeed, was seldom excited, my puberty being a tardy growth; my voice did not break till sixteen,

Emily and Ida Calder *c.* 1880

Ossent-Hefti   LAUSANNE.

'The Little Swiss Boy'

Author and Aunt Emily at Boulogne

Framed picture of the Author referred to on page 142

Wounded being brought
off Cape Helles

Cape Helles battlefield, with the grave of Lt.-Col.
Doughty-Wylie, killed leading the conquest of
V Beach. The unconquered Achi Baba on the skyline

V Beach, with remains
of improvised jetty

V Beach (1922) with
French memorial (the
French landed here two
days after the British)

Caricature (after dinner) of the Author by James Bridie, the dramatist
(Dr O. H. Mavor) at Baku, Russia, in 1919

Newman Flower at time of first meeting with Author

Author today

nor my chin need a razor till twenty. But to this Parish Dance, having heard from Percy what a boy might do with a girl in the way of kissing (no more), and seemingly ought to do at the age of fourteen, I brought a secret resolve to show myself more of a man and to have kissed a partner before Sir Roger de Coverley and midnight ended the ball.

In those days we all, whatever our ages, had dance programmes, with little pencils strung on them, and we boys went up to the fluffy girls arrayed along the walls, bowed ungracefully to this one or that, and asked, might we have the pleasure of a dance with her. Waltz? Polka? Barn Dance? Lancers? If the girl said Yes, as she usually did unless she was heavily bespoken—which was rare amongst our 'kiddy sisters'— we exchanged programmes and pencilled our names opposite the selected dance; and if we were the boy, we bowed again, with a jerk, and walked away, probably thinking more of the buffet supper, due downstairs at nine, than of the girl by the wall.

After supper, towards eleven, a late and manly hour to be up and at large like this, I was dancing with a girl of about my own age, and in the long silences between us I decided that the night was growing late, and if ever I was to act on my resolve, this girl, in her white accordion-pleated frock, and almost as tall as myself, had better be the one used for my purpose. So, breaking another long awkward silence, I asked her nervously, but with an effort at gaiety, 'Shall we wander out a bit?'

'I don't mind,' she said.

'It's getting deuced hot,' I submitted, 'deuced' sounding a manly word. I think I'd only heard it recently. Or got it from Thackeray.

'Yes, it is,' she agreed. 'I'm rather hot.'

Knowing every inch of our Parish Hall, after our pantomimes and plays, I led her past dressing-rooms and the Green Room and out through a back door which led into the vicarage garden.

Past eleven and a starry night.

We stood in silence. Mine was no easy part to play; I did not know its opening lines. I could think of only one line, which at least had the merit of coming straight to the point. I said simply, 'I'm going to kiss you now.'

'Oh, no, you're not,' she assured me. 'I'm not that sort of girl.'

'Oh, I see,' I said.

And that was that. Having accepted that I had misinterpreted the situation, I said nothing more.

It was she who broke this silence. 'No, you've got me quite wrong. I'm not that kind of girl.'

'No,' I agreed, as one who would say, 'Of course not. I'm sorry.'

And silence stood between us again, with the starry dark above us.

I don't remember that I was embarrassed on being told that I'd got my facts wrong; I certainly wasn't disappointed. Indeed it would be truer to say that I was relieved. I hadn't really wanted to kiss her or anybody. I had just wanted to do what other, and manly, boys did. And what is more, the maiden, as far as I can remember after sixty years, was lightly pock-marked.

Often I wonder now whether, in fact, she wasn't really that sort of girl, and I surmise that probably she was. Standing there with a fool who didn't know the game.

She being fourteen like me, but five years more mature than I was, suggested, since nothing further seemed likely to emerge out of the dark and the silence, 'Well, shall we go back into the Hall?'

'Yes, we might,' I agreed. 'Yes. . . .'

In the Hall we found that the orchestra had paused and no one was dancing on the floor. I thanked Heaven for this, because I was able to take her back to her chair by the wall, make my jerky bow, and wander off to see if the buffet was still serving lemonade and claret cup, or, better still, ices.

§

One more scene with Percy, though we must leap onward over two more years to encompass it here. In 1906 a famous Harvard crew, having beaten Yale for the first time in seven years, challenged one of Cambridge's most famous eights to a race on their own Thames course, from Putney to Mortlake. This celebrated Cambridge crew would be stroked by D. C. R. Stuart, who had just stroked it to victory against Oxford, and was to do so twice more. Both crews, Harvard and Cambridge, had resounding reputations, and after Harvard had arrived in England on August 6th, its trial rows on the tideway were read about, with a fascinated interest, by the whole of England, for this was an international occasion. Some in England feared that Harvard would win because in a full-course trial on the first day of September they completed the course in 18 minutes 50 seconds, only five seconds short of a record.

Percy, fancying himself as an oar—he had rowed for his college—was enthralled by the coming contest and had convinced himself that no stroke would lead Stuart when the hour came, no matter what Harvard's timing had been on September 1st. Harvard had been helped, he insisted, by a spring tide and a following wind. No, there was no stroke on either side the Atlantic who would beat D. C. R. Stuart. On the day of the race, September 8th, we placed ourselves at the station Percy had chosen: on the Surrey Side bank between Barnes Bridge and Mortlake, 'because,' said he, 'whoever comes first under Barnes Bridge will win. I don't think there's ever been a case when a crew leading under Barnes Bridge has been overtaken before the winning-post at Mortlake. This is the only place to stand.'

So there we stood in the massed crowd, where we could just see the open span of Barnes Bridge and nothing beyond. All that mattered was Barnes Bridge.

'And look, Ernest,' he enjoined, 'don't be an ass and cheer. There's no sense in cheering and yelling. They can't hear you. It's just a waste of breath. I know because I've been in boat races. Just stand and watch, and let the fools cheer. Whichever boat shows us its bow first will win. That's all there is to it. There's a head wind and a slack tide,' he added, speaking with authority, if anxiously. 'It'll be one hell of a race, but I believe in Stuart. I believe in Stuart.'

Up the river came the roaring of the crowd, louder and louder as it swept towards the bridge, but which crew was being cheered, or whether they were cheers at all, or sighs and groans, we did not know, because we could not see. Percy was silent, his eyes held by the bridge; I was silent too, and prepared to go on being so, as instructed. And then—then came the bow of a boat under the bridge—and the flash in the sun of a light blue oar.

I have never forgotten that light blue flash of an oar's blade. First because it was victory, victory; second because Percy seized me and pummelled me on the back, while he bellowed continuously, like the largest and loudest of the bulls of Bashan. To be pummelled in a frenzy by a giant of six-foot-five is painful; I suffered severely as Stuart's eight swept past our eyes with grace and beauty; onward to victory; but never was pain more welcome than on that September day of long ago.

9

FRESHWATER AND THE THIRD HOUSE

Before all this, before my entry into St Paul's, we had acquired a small house in Freshwater, Isle of Wight, for our holidays, a newly built, semi-detached villa with the ridiculous name, 'Eastbourne Villas' high on the wall of the other house. It cost, I think, £18 a year. Impossible to imagine a more commonplace villa, but since it was a home where we spent all our Easter and Summer holidays it would rest in my memory as the third and happiest house of my childhood, were it not for a dark and lacerating hour whose issue ended our tenancy. We called it 'Arnwood'; it was I who gave it this name because of my love for Marryat's *Children of the New Forest*. That name is still on its gate, though spelt wrong; the tenants of today have no knowledge of its source or of the childish zest that once went into its choice.

Oh, the four-wheeler that came to take us and our luggage to Waterloo station for the train that would take us to Lymington Harbour and the smell of the sea! That old cab was our chariot of fire even if its interior smelt of torn leather, dust and the horse's nosebag. How we looked from its windows and pitied all the people on the pavements who were not going on holiday. The paddle-steamer waiting for us against Lymington Pier! It would paddle through the sea-smelling mud-flats and the assorted buoys with masts like skeleton scarecrows; and then, out in the open Solent, carry us across to the Island. The coach at Yarmouth, like one out of Dickens, which would go spanking along the three green miles to Freshwater and drop us, probably off its box-seat, at Arnwood's gate! And that very afternoon, with spades and pails and shrimping nets and bathing dresses, down to the Beloved Bay!

Freshwater Bay, how we loved you! Freshwater Bay with your two towering rocks standing away from their parent cliff and keeping their feet in the waves: the great Arch Rock, and the Stag Rock tall as a church tower, with its plat of green grass on its summit (gone now) on to which the hunted stag leapt from the hounds' pursuit and so saved its life (as the happy ending has it). No hound could have leapt that distance from the white cliff's brink, over the Arch Rock, and on to that green plat, no bigger than a church's hassock.

That small green cap always brought to my mind the closing verse of Wordsworth's 'Hart-leap Well', which Dum, in great form, had read to us, and which fixed in me, for ever, a hatred of all hunting:

> One lesson, shepherd, let us two divide . . .
> Never to blend our pleasure or our pride
> With sorrow of the meanest thing that feels.

Freshwater Bay: here unlike grey Gledstanes Road and grey Charleville Road, romance stretched before us as far as eyes could reach: white cliffs with entrances into deep vaulted caves like apsed cathedral choirs; rocks and rock-pools where the shrimps hid and the limpets clung; great voluted sea-horses galloping in from the Channel; dinghies aslant on the beach, in which Andrew, the fisherman, would take us dragging the sea-bed for mackerel, with the gulls screeching after us; great ships passing by but so far away that they looked like toys in a shop window; and, finally, the long blue line of the horizon which bounded the known world.

There were angry days when the boiling crested rollers came storming in from that horizon to shatter on our rocks and scale the white cliffs; or calm nights when a high moon lit a silvery path on a tremulous sea from horizon almost to sea-wall; a widening pathway which lost itself somewhere among the indolent ripples in the bay.

Not the bay alone; all the country round was paradisal. Opposite the very gate of Arnwood was Blackberry Lane, where we gathered blackberries, full and juicy, which blued our lips and our fingers, and sloes for Aunt to make the sloe gin; Blackberry Lane which led straight to Farringford, Home of the Tennysons, where the old poet used to

> Watch the twilight falling brown
> Around a careless-ordered garden,
> Close to the ridge of a noble down . . .

and where younger Tennysons now lived, Lionel Tennyson, later England's Test cricketer, being our playmate on beach and rocks.

Then, above the Beloved Bay, on its either side, were the lofty downs over which we could wander, never tiring in that high sea-air: to Alum Bay and the Needles or to Brooke and its fossil forest lying at the beach end, lapped by the sea.

In Arnwood's small back garden there was a large spreading apple tree, from which I had attempted many an unripe apple; but it is chiefly memorable to me for a funeral that was conducted beneath it. One morning I had been fishing for shrimps or prawns, with my pail and shrimping net among the rock-pools that at low tide stretched far into the sea. Though I went from pool to pool and overturned stone after stone I found and netted only one shrimp (as I called it) throughout that long, drifting forenoon. Nevertheless there was the shrimp in my pail, and I took it home with some idea of having it for luncheon. But by the time I'd finished the homeward mile it looked very dead in the pail's bottom; it responded not at all to timid touches with the back of a finger-nail. Aunt and Dorothy, called in as second and third opinions, pronounced it dead.

So I decided it should have honourable burial under the apple tree. First I made a wooden cross, only six inches high for so small a deceased, to erect over its grave. On the transverse bar of this monument I printed in ink a poem, a rather priggish little verse, the first line of which, I suspect now, must have been a plagiarism—but the remainder is indubitably mine.

> Fishermen must earn their bread,
>   But that's no reason why
> Little boys should fish for shrimps
>   And cause them agonye.

I was not wholly happy with this pronunciation, 'agonye', and thought of altering the last line into 'And boil them till they die'; but it was already written in ink and would be messy to remove. So I let it stand, and with the cross and my spade in one hand, and my pail in the other, and the shrimp in its hearse (the pail), I went to the bole of the apple tree, where I dug a reasonably deep grave lest in time the animal stank. I stabilized the cross in a little earth-mound above it. Dorothy suggested flowers, but I told her not to be silly, though wishing I had thought of this first, for in that untidy wild garden there were daisies and scabious, hawksweed and hairbell, yarrow and scarlet corn-poppies, all of which would have looked well, arranged as a border, round a grave.

That honourable tomb survived for some weeks maybe; little more; but what matter to a child? Sufficient unto the day is the pleasure thereof.

At Freshwater I learned to ride a bicycle. I hired the machine from a bicycle shop opposite the station (it is there now, though the station is not). I did not tell the shopman I could not ride; I walked the bicycle out of his sight along the curving New Road which, being really new then, was empty of houses, so that I was free from the eyes of men, as the isolationist in me so often liked to be. I messed about with the bicycle trying to ride it. And at last, at last—just as one suddenly finds oneself buoyed up by the water and swimming—I found myself balancing properly—and riding, riding! I was exalted by this remarkable truth. 'For me, I ride,' sang Browning. 'One more day am I deified—who knows but the world may end tonight? For me, I ride.' The farther I rode along, the better I rode. But I didn't dare to stop. I didn't know what would happen if I stopped. I could imagine only a crash. So I rode on—and on—gripping the handlebars tight—tight as if they were my only hold on life. I passed a family of children who played with us on the beach, but I didn't dare move a hand to wave to them, so I just smiled back at them, faintly, like Mr Winkle on his horse. Soon I would be at the end of the New Road and meet traffic—something must be done. I looked at a quickset hedge bordering the road and ran the bicycle and myself into it. A scratchy finish, not without blood. But I could ride, I could ride. I turned the machine round and here we were riding again. But the New Road didn't go on for ever, and soon I must dismount; where—and more disturbing—how? I tried to dismount as I'd seen others do, swinging a leg behind me over the saddle, but I did it while the machine was going too fast, with the result that it went ahead without me, relieved of its burden. Slowing to a halt, it lay down on the same grass verge which had received me as I fell. I walked the machine back to the shop, paid my score, and departed out of view as quickly as was consistent with an innocent manner, lest the shop should begin to brood over scratches. Or blood.

§

But Arnwood, this third and last house of our childhood (how could one call a flat a house?), this plain semi-detached little villa, unlovely and yet greatly loved, turned for a while, like General Février, traitor. It stands there today, as undistinguished as ever, and no one in it, or passing by, knows that it holds the darkest memory of my closing childhood.

Before the summer holiday of 1904 we saw much of Dum. The new and magnanimous Mrs Blake, knowing all and accepting all, invited us often to dinner on Sundays that Dum might see much of us. So we, after church, would take a bus along the Old Brompton Road to

Cranley Gardens, and hurry along to No. 14 and to Dum. To Dum, as to a loadstar rock in Cranley Gardens.

Dum and 'Mrs Blake'—we never called her by any other name— were now living in 14 Cranley Gardens, a large Victorian mansion in a white terrace of the stateliest stucco. It had a fine white-pillared portico and five wide storeys rising above the basement, most of these handsome floors having three ornamental and separate windows. Here in the large double dining-room a full Sunday dinner would await us, served by a German butler whom Dum always called Herr Lippy (or so the name sounded to us) and a parlour maid. We were impressed by Herr Lippy. After this gracious and heavy meal, made lively by Dum's teasing and Lilian Blake's studied friendliness, he would take us, Sabbath or not, along the passage to his tapestried billiard-room, and there instruct us in billiards or snooker, sometimes praising our 'remarkable skill' if by accident we pocketed a ball, or changing his note to one of banter. 'A main object of the game, Koko, is to hit the ball you're aiming at. It's by no means indispensable, of course, if you're not particularly anxious to win. But bear in mind that these are quite strong balls, and you won't hurt them by hitting them.'

If in response to these comments I took a long time about my aiming, he would say, 'I beg you not to hurry. There is the whole afternoon. Perhaps Queenie and I could go for a walk until you're ready. We might go to the Children's Service in church. It's just at the end of the road. St Peter's, Cranley Gardens.'

And I would beg, 'Oh, please shut up. You make me nervous.'

'Nonsense. Nonsense. Koko is never nervous.'

Tea followed with rich cream cakes in the huge drawing-room on the first floor; and then it was upstairs to the large three-windowed nursery on the floor above that we might see, even poke, that champion baby, Martin, whom Lilian Blake had lately produced for Dum. This buxom infant was handled by an impressive nanny, grey-haired and in the cleanest and neatest grey uniform. Dorothy, I thought, was 'a trifle goo-ey' about this infant, but he was certainly a plump and radiant baby.

Then, alas, it became time to go home, and Dum would take us to the door, saying, 'We mustn't trouble Herr Lippy or the maids on a Sunday afternoon. Go quietly home and remember to do all you can for your kind auntie who is so good to you'; possibly adding dreamily, as he recalled past days in Gledstanes Road, 'Always say your prayers and wash your teeth.'

One late July day, knowing that on the morrow we would be setting off for Freshwater, he stood framed in his handsome doorway, and said to us just such a good-bye, and waved.

§

I passed that house the other day and looked up at its worn front door and down at its littered area. Six bell-pushes beside the door showed that it was divided now into six flats or maisonettes. Differing curtains on each of those three-windowed floors spoke of different families in each apartment—six families pigeon-holed in Dum's dining-room and billiard-room floor; in his vast drawing-room which would surely make a flat in itself; in the grey nanny's fine nursery-rooms above; in the servants' dormer-windowed bedrooms higher still; and in Herr Lippy's spacious kitchen premises below.

What did they know of General Blake, R.M.?

§

That August passed by, as happy as any in Freshwater, filled with the usual delights of bathing, fishing, boating or roving over the downs; and then it was the first day of September 1904, and morning. Breakfast was over in Arnwood, Aunt was upstairs in her front bedroom, either tidying the bed or tidying herself; we were downstairs, assembling our gear for beach and rocks and bathing tent.

Then came a telegram. It was received by the woman in the kitchen who was sometimes there for an hour or two to help us, and she carried it upstairs to Aunt in the bedroom.

Coming down to us, she said, 'Your auntie wants you to go up to her.'

A telegram was exciting; it was always possible that it brought hope of something good, and we hurried up the stairs to learn what it was all about. We saw Aunt looking out of the window at the small front garden with its tumbled hedge of sycamore, privet and bay, and at the road beyond. She held the telegram by the fingers of both hands.

She did not speak at once, but at last, turning to us, said, 'This is a telegram from Mrs Blake.'

Perhaps half-apprehending that this foretold nothing good, we answered nothing, but just stared.

And Aunt said, 'It'—she looked down at the telegram again as if she did not remember its exact words—'it says, "General Blake died early this morning, Lilian Blake."'

I was standing by her large bed and, like a child shot, collapsed into a sitting position on the quilt.

'*Get* off that quilt!' cried Aunt angrily. 'Don't you know better than to sit on a quilt? Haven't I told you a hundred times?'

I stood up again. What did a quilt or a little wrong-doing matter when all my world was in pieces?

But Aunt was not only an irritable woman. She had heard a moan from me and, smoothing the crumpled quilt behind me, she said, 'I knew he was ill, but I didn't tell you because I didn't want to spoil your holiday. But I . . . I didn't expect this. It—it was what they call nephritis.'

What mattered what it was? Even if one understood the word. Dum was dead. Nothing had interest or meaning beyond that. He was lying dead in some high bedroom of his big white house (so I imagined, but, in fact, he had died in Berkhamsted and was brought home to Cranley Gardens).

Did Aunt or Dorothy say anything more? I don't know. I don't think I heard. I walked from that room alone and down the stairs. Out of their sight I sobbed a little, but the sobs ceased, except for a tardy straggler now and then which tore its path through me. Standing in the little dining-room, I could not get my mind away from the one dark piece of knowledge. I looked out of the window at garden and gate and roadway, but hardly saw anything there. Nor anything in the room around me. I was tied to one desperate thought. If for a moment I drew away from it, nothing seemed in yesterday's place, or to matter. Nothing stood in tomorrow's place, or mattered. It was as if some Samson had taken hold of the central pillar in my house of life and broken it, and the house had fallen. All memories lay in ruins, and to touch any one of them was pain.

It was certain that Dorothy, after that telegram, would not come down to the beach to play. She was weeping upstairs in that large front room with Aunt. I snatched at my towel and bathing costume—nothing else—and walked out of the house, and out of the gate of Arnwood. As I walked along the road towards the bay—yesterday's

Beloved Bay—I looked up at the window of that front room which had given me the news, and wondered if I would ever see it again.

I was fifteen; nevertheless I was carrying the thought, 'I will swim out to sea, far out, and . . . perhaps . . .' At fifteen that 'perhaps' could hardly have held what I wanted to imagine in it; lying beside it, there must have been a 'probably not'; but I preferred, and walked with, the darker 'perhaps'. Perhaps I would. There was no hope or joy in the 'probably not'; only a desolation commanded by people whom I had not as yet the grace to love—and, where necessary, forgive: Aunt Emily, the fiery-tempered and punishing; Aunt Ida, the slightly uncomfortable 'sweetheart'. Percy and Dorothy had lost all importance. I doubt if I thought of their existence. Still less did I trouble about my other aunts and uncles, though two of them I had liked, the corpulent, generous, and ever welcoming Uncle Edwin, and the mild and gentle Dr Broenner, 'Uncle Franz'. Liked, yes; but I don't think they even appeared in my memory as I walked down to the bay.

One thought only I was loth to leave (if I did what I had a half-mind to do): this was my ambition to write novels, to be a novelist and a great one. Strange that among all those despairing thoughts—thoughts that lay on the bottom of despair—there should still flourish this irrational and baseless confidence that I could do this; that I was destined to do it. But though sorry to abandon this dream (if so I did), to desert it and leave it unachieved, the sorrow was lessened by the thought that Dum was dead and could never know now of my fame. Much of the fun would be gone from it, now that he would not be there.

But yes, there was one other regret walking with me to the bay. At fifteen I was pretty sure what the truth was of my parentage, and of Dorothy's; but no one had spoken yet. Not Dum; not Aunt Emily; and, still less, Aunt Ida. Emily had dropped her careless remarks and told her careless tales, and I would have liked to have had my reading of them confirmed. 'William Bell Raymond.' There had been that talk by Dum of William Bell Raymond who died; a dear friend who left me to him as a ward. Was I right about William Bell Raymond?

Would I never know now?

Though surely, surely what I believed about him must be the truth. What else? What else?

Wondering, I went on. I passed with curious thoughts the people who were happy; children with their pails and nets going down to the beach for the last of their summer holiday; parents or nurses following behind them; tradesmen on their daily rounds; our good friend, the postman, returning to his office, whom sometimes Dorothy and I used to 'hold up' from behind a tree, robbing the Royal Mail; I passed his familiar office high up on a green bank in a stationer's shop; I passed Mr Trevanion's, the grocer's, who kept the keys of Arnwood when we were away, and the terraces of 'Apartment' villas and boarding-houses—was I never to see them again—nor the long hedges that bordered the last of the road to the bay?

Here was the bay. There the incurving white cliffs, the Arch Rock and the Stag Rock out at sea, and the shelving, pebbly beach with the fishermen's boats and the lobster pots. I went far from the happy people seated or playing or bathing. I undressed beneath the white cliff as near as possible to the cave entrances and the Arch Rock. I laid my clothes against the cliff's base—would I see them again? Would I? I didn't know as I walked over the biting shingle into the sea.

I swam out and out. Out and out, and on and on. On and on because I couldn't decide. Tiring, I trod water to rest and breathe, but my eyes were still towards the horizon. Then I made the mistake—it is a mistake in any race, and not less so in a swim towards death—the mistake of turning round and looking behind. God! the people bathing in the sea or at play on the beach, and the villas on the slope of the down, looked far more distant than I expected. I had come out too far, much too far, helped perhaps by a current or undertow. How shallow had been that 'perhaps'—as shallow as the sea was now deep beneath me. Panic. Panic set my heart thumping. Had I come too far to get back? I could swim well but often tired more easily than I cared to show. The sea was choppy out here; had I the strength left to swim the distance through a turmoil of slapping waves? Fathoms beneath me now. Not but what one fathom would be enough if I could not last the distance. I did not hesitate about attempting to get back—back to life. No halting, no treading of water to debate the issue. I struck out hard for that far-away shore. There were deathly moments of doubt when I believed I couldn't do it—couldn't do it. . . . And as I doubted, there before my eyes were the high chalk cliffs, the beached boats on the shingle, the tamarisk field behind the shattered esplanade, the heaving downs, and the road that led to Arnwood and life again. Doubt and desperation buoyed me up like water-wings through the rampant, buffeting waves; and struggling, breathless, panting, I got back—back to the stony beach, to my clothes lying there, and to the sadness of a world without Dum.

§

In the morning our friend and chum, the postman, brought a letter addressed to us children. It was from Mrs Blake. In her unvarying goodness to us she had troubled to sit down and write, on the day which saw her husband die, to two children. From that letter I remember only these few words; they remain unforgettable: 'He loved you both so dearly, and I think you will always be proud to have been loved by so good a man.'

Good? She had had but two years of married life with him, a young wife nearly forty years younger than he; she knew all his sins, for he had not hidden them from her, but 'good' was her chosen word, and I think she wrote it after quiet thought and with sincerity.

Good? Well . . . yes, always so for me; always, whatever sins in the long years before I was born, or during my fifteen years of life, were veiled from my eyes; always so, until this moment as I write.

Always so, for me; or must I, in this, accept that love is blind?

10

TWO CRUCIAL DAYS

They buried him in the old Brompton Cemetery near his home in Cranley Gardens. Neither Dorothy nor I were bidden to the funeral, either because Mrs Blake thought that children should be spared a sorrowful ceremony or, possibly, because we would be difficult to explain.

But Percy and I decided to go to the cemetery and see the last. We would stand well away from the invited mourners, as two outsiders might. You will remember how Percy, as a child of four or five, living with his mother in Switzerland, had loved to play with Dum or to toil up the mountains after him when he was hurt and unhappy. Dorothy did not come with us; nor Aunt Emily, she who as a rule so loved a ceremony, however sad; nor Aunt Ida in whom bitterness still lingered. Besides, there were still traces in those days of the delicate feeling that women, unless they were principal mourners, should leave funerals to the sterner characters of men.

So we two boys, one very tall and one growing tall, arrived at the cemetery while the church service was still in progress. We entered through its great Doric archway in Old Brompton Road and walked down its central avenue between the lime trees and the high monumental tombs. It is a very long straight avenue, more than a quarter-mile of it, between weeping stone angels and tall broken columns, between lofty crosses, proud altar tombs, and pompous mausoleums. It was as if the whole Victorian age lay buried there. One mausoleum especially attracted my notice because it bore the words '*Ex Umbris et Imaginibus in Veritatem*'. As a classical scholar at St Paul's I translated this for Percy, who had little Latin: 'From Shadows and Fancies to the Truth'.

We walked on, wondering where the open grave would be. No one was to be seen anywhere—on the many paths or among the tombs. The whole place, acres and broad acres of it, had the silence proper to death. You could just hear, beyond its grey enclosing walls, the sigh and hum of continuing life. We came to the sweeping colonnades that embrace a large area before the domed chapel, and are said to be an imitation (but a poor imitation) of the vast colonnaded parvis before the front of St Peter's in Rome. Here, on the western side of the avenue, we saw some workmen around a newly dug grave. It was in the second row from the avenue, and Percy inquired of the men if this was for a funeral coming from St Peter's, Cranley Gardens.

'You've got it, mate,' said one of the men, who was cutting with shears the tall autumn grass around the deep cavity, making a place for mourners to stand. 'Here any minute now. It's for a general or something. A big funeral,' he added proudly. 'Some quite famous bloke, I believe.'

'That's what we've come for,' said Percy. 'We'll . . . we'll wait.'

Sixty years ago there were far fewer graves in this part of the cemetery, and he and I were able to place ourselves under a tree on green lawns, some thirty yards from the grave. That tree has long gone, and the lawns also, to make way for the dead of sixty years. The whole area is now a congregation of crosses and table tombs, row behind row, and it is not easy to descry at once the white cross which bears the name 'George Frederic Blake, Major-General, Royal Marine Light Infantry'.

We waited under the tree till we heard the slow steps of horses, coming unseen from the Fulham Road entrance to the cemetery. The cortège came slowly into view, and it was indeed a fine funeral, justifying the grass-cutter's pride. On each side of the hearse marched a guard of honour from the Royal Marines, eight men in the scarlet tunics and white helmets of full 'Review Order'. On the long coffin the Union Jack lay spread among the flowers. Black carriage after carriage followed, and the people, top-hatted, frock-coated directors or brother officers, unknown ladies in long black silk dresses, descending from them crowded round the grave, while the horses tossed their heads or pawed the ground. Our dear Mrs Blake stood at the grave's foot, on the arm of one of Dum's elder sons, born of his first wife, a tall greying man whom I had never seen before or heard of.

Unobserved, unaddressed, Percy and I watched from beneath our tree, and the only strange thing which I have to recount is this: as the priest, lifting his voice, and his eyes to Heaven, for the great moment, said the words of the Committal, 'we therefore commit his body to the ground, earth to earth, ashes to ashes, dust to dust', and the undertaker's men lowered the heavy coffin into the grave and out of our sight, Percy, six foot five, fourteen stone, burst into tears and long shaking sobs. It was an amazement to me, who was crying more quietly. I had never imagined that Percy could cry. And he had seen so little of Dum since those old days in Switzerland, after his mother and Dum had agreed together to bring their long love-story to an end.

§

One thing more remains to be told of the days after Dum's death. Was it three days or four after his funeral—I do not know—but it was a warm September afternoon, and we, Aunt Emily, Aunt Ida, and myself were sitting in the narrow garden of Oakdene, Ida's house that overlooked the stretches of Barnes Common. Percy was at work in another part of the garden, with his bulldog, Punch, in ready and eager, if useless, attendance. The two aunts were talking of the funeral, Emily, as so often, dropping significant sentences, as though I were not there, fifteen years old now, and listening and thinking. Two sisters prattling together in a garden, unmindful of a mere child beside them.

It was quite soon that, in her sentimental way, Emily laid a hand on Ida's knee and said, 'The one woman, my dear, who ought to have been at that graveside was not there.'

This was the first sentence that drew my attention like a magnet to their talk and away from distant people on the common, though I kept my eyes adrift and concealed my straining interest. The significance of these words, spoken sentimentally to Ida, was surely obvious, and it confirmed, yet again, all I had come to believe.

They began to discuss Dum's will, and Emily said, 'It looks as though Ernest will have a little income of his own.'

Ida turned to me, and, speaking as though I were little more than a growing infant, said, 'There now! Just fancy that! Fancy being a man of private means. *Won't* you feel proud?'

Difficult to answer this with anything but a grin. But I was thinking hard. In the eyes of the world this talk would have established little. Dum might have provided for me, not as a son he loved, but only as a ward, the son of his 'lifelong' friend, William Bell Raymond. Whereas . . .

'Just fancy that!' Ida repeated in an upsurge of gratified affection. 'A man of means.'

But while I was certainly trying to fancy it, she turned to Emily and in the old tone of bitterness, said the most notable thing yet. She said, 'I should have thought he might have done more for Percy than leave him a hundred pounds.'

More for Percy? Why? Since those far-off days in Switzerland, what had Dum to do with Percy Wilkinson, son of 'Old Wilkinson', Ida's first husband, the civil servant?

'I suppose he thought Percy was fully provided for,' Emily suggested.

'Well! I *like* that!' This was an indignant ejaculation from Ida.

Just after this, just after an astonishing thought was visiting me, Percy passed by, with Punch at his heels and a trowel in his hand, making his way to a cupboard in the house where he stored all his greatly loved tools. He was wearing an old brown Norfolk jacket, loosely open. Emily's eyes followed that Norfolk jacket, with its belt about the waist and its pleat up the back. And as soon as possible, romantically inclined again, and forgetting my presence, she said to Ida, 'Doesn't he look like Someone Else?'

The impact of this sentence on me was immediate, complete, and astonishing. It made of this afternoon in Oakdene's garden one of my life's crucial days. This 'Someone Else' was surely Dum. Doubtless Dum in Switzerland had often worn the 'Duke of Norfolk's hunting jacket', which had lately become fashionable, with its waist belt and vertical pleat. Heavens above, how blind, how simple, I had been till this moment. Never till this moment had I imagined Percy to be other than 'Old Wilkinson's' son. But now the truth was as clear, as perfectly in focus, as if a flood-light had been swung on to it. That height, that fine figure, the features, the dark hair, those old stories of Switzerland—then look: Percy was full brother to me. Full brother.

If it was an astounding thought, it was also a greatly exhilarating one, because I was still Percy's hero-worshipper, and uncritical of his less amiable qualities, his domineering ways, his impatience with any opinion but his own, his easy and quick rudeness to his mother or Uncle Franz, his huge self-esteem. There could be no doubt of it: Ida's words, Emily's slyly knowing talk, Percy's whole shape and appearance —all underwrote my certainty.

There *was* no doubt of it. Never in her life did Aunt Ida admit it to me, but Aunt Emily did at last, and why not, since in this matter she had nothing to hide? Wilkinson had separated from his wife because he refused to accept Percy as his son. It became a joke among us of the younger generation to say that Mr Wilkinson's habit of noting in his diary the dates on which conception could have occurred was explained by his civil service training.

But all this was long afterwards. In 1904, in that Oakdene garden, I was but fifteen, Percy just twenty; and as with Dum, as with Aunt Emily, as with Aunt Ida, I said no word to Percy for years and years about this sudden revelation; I kept it to myself, speaking of it only to Dorothy who had proved a splendid audience on that very first evening, 'thrilled' to be Percy's half-sister.

Percy might be marvellously clever with his hands but all his life he remained mentally unoriginal and conventional, professing, not without exhibitionism, a stern Victorian morality, so it is likely that my silence over long years was quite as much a fear of stirring a furious indignation in him as a desire not to hurt him. When twenty years afterwards, maybe, we did speak together of this I learned that, for all his cocky superiority, he had been as innocent and simple-minded as I was, and it was not till his late thirties that the truth broke upon him, his mother never having breathed a word of it. Strange to report that, like us, Percy, the assertive, the bossy, the unsparing, never in Ida's lifetime charged her with it, choosing rather to live alone with what he now suspected—or knew. I think he did this to spare her from hurt as well as to spare himself.

He was primly shocked at my joke about the 'civil service training', but I perceived, none the less, that, if the truth had been a surprise, it was also a private pleasure. Because he had been born while Ida and Wilkinson were living together he was safely 'Percy Wilkinson' in the eyes of the Law, and had best remain so, but Percy was nothing if not class-conscious, even the perfect Victorian snob, and in private, as I could very well see, he much preferred being the son of a distinguished Major-General.

II

1

THE TROOPSHIP

It was an early morning in July 1915, when the *Scotian*, an old ship of the Allan Line, but now painted black all over so as to serve as a troopship in war, steamed out of Devonport Harbour. She was instantly followed by two long, low-lying warships which we called 'destroyers', probably in our ignorance. They sped into position abreast of the *Scotian*, one on the port side, one on the starboard. They were to escort us out of the Channel into the wide Atlantic and there—'in somewhat ungentlemanly fashion', as we said—leave us to look after ourselves.

England was now behind us. Our black troopship, so our Secret Embarkation Orders had told us, was off to the Mediterranean, and we knew what 'the Mediterranean' meant. It meant that all aboard, except the ship's company, were being hurried to the Dardanelles—to Mudros in the Island of Lemnos, perhaps, the Intermediate Base for the Gallipoli campaign, or on to the Gallipoli Peninsula itself.

Some of us knew that Winston Churchill, First Lord of the Admiralty, had persuaded the Cabinet to send enough men and guns to 'carry at any cost the few acres of scrub' that lay between our captured beach-heads on the Peninsula and the hill-tops that would command the Dardanelles Straits, a victory which would let the Fleet sail through to the Golden Horn, fire Turkey out of the war, establish contact with our Russian allies, secure the adhesion of all the Balkan states, and enable us to assault in power the Central Empires from the East. 'Through the Narrows of the Dardanelles,' Churchill had proclaimed, 'and across the ridges of the Gallipoli Peninsula lies the shortest path to a triumphant peace.'

Whether the fall of Constantinople under the guns of the Fleet would have won us these immense advantages has been debated for fifty years. For my part I shall always think of it as the one brilliant strategic conception in our First World War.

We went out into the Atlantic, steaming an extraordinary zigzag course, and it was a marvel to us how bare were the seas from sky to sky. The Navy had swept the oceans clear. All that first day we sighted no single ship; only in the evening light, when we were somewhere off Cape Finisterre, did we descry two little ships, and they both flew the British flag.

Among the thousands of soldiers stowed in our trooper there were eight chaplains, and I was one of them. While eight ordinary men among thousands are as nothing, eight parsons seem a swarm; and there was some cheerful grumbling about them. Would they not sink the ship? Were they not proof of something we all suspected: that great things were about to happen on Gallipoli? Great and sinister things, if this rush of padres was necessary. 'It's not so much a rush of parsons,' one young officer complained to me, 'as a bloody rash. A rash of blackheads.'

Among these chaplains, all of them young men then, was the Rev. S. J. Nisbet Wallace, later a canon of Salisbury, and the Rev. W. C. Wand, later Archbishop of Brisbane, Bishop of Bath and Wells, and, finally, Bishop of London.

I shared a state-room with Sidney Nisbet Wallace; it had an upper and a lower berth, and since I was extremely High Church and he Low, I took the upper and he the lower.

There was a Submarine Watch on the ship: a firing party of twenty men in the bows, and another of twenty in the stern. Unaware of what to do with eight parsons, the Adjutant, after thought, decided that they must take their turns on this Submarine Watch. I took my turn at 4.0 a.m. one morning as the daylight broke, and I had not the smallest idea what to do with the twenty men, should they sight a periscope. If I ordered them to fire, which presumably was what they were there for, I should be acting as a combatant officer, a point which had not yet surfaced before the bewildered Adjutant. I was given powerful glasses and scanned the seas with them, hoping that I should stay safely within the Geneva Conventions if, on sighting the enemy, I said, 'Carry on, Sergeant.'

The sergeant, after I had talked with him about it, decided that this would be all right.

No glimmer of light was allowed to show through the ports and windows of that ship as it ploughed onward through the night. Particularly I recall one falling darkness when I leaned over the rail of an upper deck and saw the hundreds of men spread over the open deck below in every variety of recumbence and undress, for the night was hot. One man, seated on a hatch in the midst of them, was playing his mandoline gently, as suited the night. They were mostly men of the 53rd Welsh Division and, being Welsh, they sang. Sang beautifully as the ship went on beneath a sky fretted with stars to the very rims of an empty sea. The mandoline player led them through air after air. 'If you were the only girl in the world', they sang, and 'Abide with Me'; and, of course, 'The Men of Harlech' and 'All through the Night'.

I was now keeping a diary again. Eleven years after my school-time diary had died of inanition, I took up the attempt again. When I embarked on that ship I had been but seven days in the Army, and, like a new broom, I was resolved to sweep all the historic and exciting events ahead of me into a note-book. I did this for about three months, the entries getting steadily smaller, and then the diary lay down and died like its predecessor, never to be picked up again, though I spent four years at war.

In the first pages I find this entry, unskilled in sailing matters, perhaps, but enshrining a memory.

'The sea was gloriously blue and the sky cloudless, and there to our left, like a cloud-bank on the horizon, lay a pale-washed impression of the coast of Spain. There was a long undulation of what seemed to be mountainous coastlands, and a promontory that we learned was Cape Trafalgar. Trafalgar, off which my great-grandfather, Midshipman Kennicott, gathered his forty wounds. This then was the sea into which he had so nearly been thrown and would now be lying, had an officer not passed by. 'Full fathom five thy father lies; Of his bones are coral made. . . .' I should have kept my eyes riveted on this my first view of Spain if there had not been talk of another land looming on the starboard side. Looking that way I made out the grey wraith of a continent and realised that Dark Africa had crept into view. Wonderful this approach at the fall of a glorious day towards the Straits of Gibraltar, that narrow passage between the white and the black continents. We were now steering due east so that the disc of the sun went down behind our stern. The sea maintained a hue of sparkling indigo while the western sky surrounded the sun's face with circles of gold and orange. I turned to see the happy effect of this upon the coast of Spain, and on restoring my glance to the sunset I found that all the yellow radiance was now an apple-pink. Meanwhile I was sensible that my hands and face had been touched by a sticky moisture—the outcome of a damp wind blowing from Africa. And now came the raucous booming of the ship's fog-horn, for the vessel was surrounded by a damp sea-mist—African breath again. The mist continues, the fog-signals persist, lights and flashing messages in Morse come from the Rock which, owing to the opaque darkness we shall not see on this trip through. Let us hope we shall see it on the way home.'

So we left the Atlantic world behind and passed into the heat of the Mediterranean where, at its farther end, among legendary Greek islands, and in sight of Troy, the Gallipoli campaign awaited us. The ship sailed on through this inland sea, calm with summer, the soldiers crowded together on its deck, some singing happily, some playing their game of 'housey-housey', some silent—a ship sailing onward towards the battlefields of Homer.

§

That was July 1915. How came the listening schoolboy whom we last saw in Aunt Ida's garden to be among the officers on this trooper, and in a chaplain's uniform, ten years later?

In the garden Aunt Emily had told Ida that, under Dum's will, it looked as if Ernest would have a small income of his own. But when she saw the words of the will she instantly interpreted them very differently. The will left £3,000 to Aunt and her barrister brother-in-law, Uncle Tom, 'in trust to apply such sum in accordance with any written directions I may leave for them or, failing such written directions, in such manner as they shall think fit, having regard to wishes I have already expressed'.

Surprised and pleased by these words, Aunt decided that they meant the money was left to *her* so that she could 'keep a little home over our heads' while we two children, leaving school, went out to work and earned money so as to contribute towards the 'nice little home'.

'Ernest's little income' evaporated in a night; so did any 'little income' for Dorothy; but before one judges Aunt too harshly for this capture of all the money into her own hands, one must remember that she had a right (though she could not state this in full) to expect that Dum would provide for one who had been his mistress, and had cared twelve years for his children.

Thus I was to leave St Paul's and go out to work.

Strong opposition to this, came, not from her fellow trustee, Uncle Tom, who seemed rather confused by his new obligations, but, splendidly, from Mrs Blake. 'No, no,' she objected. 'That was not what the General would have wished.' Always, with us, she referred to Dum as 'the General'. 'The General wanted him to go to Oxford.' And, nobly, despite this not small bequest, she offered to defray the costs of at least one more term at St Paul's while they considered the matter further. About Dorothy, now sixteen and a girl—and in this year 1904 —she was less exercised.

Aunt Emily, all her life, was quite incapable of turning away money, and I write in bewilderment that she accepted this arrangement.

But—a term takes three months, death and mourning recede, they pale in memory, other interests fill the days, and somehow it came about, with the assent of all, even of Mrs Blake, that I was taken away from St Paul's and put to a cheaper boarding-school for three acutely unhappy terms. This was a pity, and wrong, because at the time I was in the 'Special' at St Paul's, a gathering of boys who, having been assessed as 'scholarship material', worked independently in the Great Hall, receiving individual attention, one by one, and in Greek and Latin only, from special masters—even, oh God, sometimes from the terrible 'Old Man' himself, who would come in, silk-gowned and bearded and awful, and, smelling powerfully of Havana cigars, and sit down beside you to consider your Greek, roaring to Heaven if he found a false sequence or a mismanagement of an 'Unfulfilled Conditional Sentence'. When this deep-throated roar went up through the roof, all the boys turned round in their separate places to look at the victim.

I suspect that this sending me away to the boarding-school was because Aunt wanted me out of the home as much as possible. Sixteen now, and tall and turbulent, I had put an end to her stinging slaps by means of a stinging and resounding one on her own cheek. This slap was of exactly the same pattern as hers. Slosh on her cheek it went. In exactly the right place. And it not only stung, it sang.

The day of that slap was a watershed day in my life. I was never touched again, but I was reported in the worst terms to the other aunts and uncles.

There was some justification for these terms. No further physical slaps were required to keep her in her place, but if she shouted at me in temper, I would administer verbal slaps, and brutal ones, of which, God forgive me, I was proud, such as 'Really, Aunt, your irascibility increases with advancing years.' Considered purely as a verbal sequence, a rapier thrust, I still rather like this. But no one had ever addressed such words to her before. The only excuse I can offer for these studied cruelties is my recurrent unhappiness at the time—an unhappiness not unusual in adolescence but made worse for me, perhaps, by the loss, still recent and still aching, of the one person I'd loved. I remember a day when, after a steaming row with Aunt I rushed madly half-way up the stairs, flung myself down full-length on the treads and lay there sobbing and sobbing. No wonder Aunt wrote to one of her sisters that 'I was in danger of becoming a dangerous lunatic'. But one can still be an infant at sixteen. Or one could in these long past days when manhood came more slowly.

Unhappy and resentful, hating the new school, inert and slack in these years of puberty, I did not do well there, nor get good reports— 'a difficult boy to influence or guide' said one—so Aunt and her fellow trustee agreed that she should be granted her original plan: namely, that I should leave school, go out to work, and earn some money for the home. And where did I get this work? Where else but at the Army and Navy Stores? Once again Mrs Blake, anxious to help me, and bowing to the views of 'the General's' appointed trustees, secured me employment as a clerk in the Correspondence Office of the Stores. The name of General Blake, lately their director, opened all doors to her.

My salary as a letter-writing clerk in the C.O. was ten shillings a week. I stayed at this job for a few months and then rebelled. I inflamed my self-pity by thinking I had been treated somewhat like my hero, Dickens, who, as a boy, was denied education and sent out to work in the blacking factory (no true picture of the Army and Navy Stores) by old Hungerford Stairs.

I wrote to Aunt's fellow trustee, suggesting that I sought a post as a schoolmaster at a private preparatory school, which would at least be an improvement on my present position. This letter did not draw at all well with Uncle Tom. He told Aunt Emily, and she told me, that he had summed it up as 'airing my own views', though what else one is supposed to do in a letter I do not know. But perhaps there were traces of bumptiousness and snobbishness in it. Yes, I feel sure there were.

He invited me to come and see him, and I went to his home and aired my views. Here, roughly, is the dialogue between us in his drawing-room. He was a man of the highest principles, and therefore, I think, a little uneasy in the situation before him; a little defeated by the burden which had been given him.

Uncle Tom: 'You want to be a schoolmaster, you say, but what aptitude have you shown for teaching?'

Ernest: 'Well, none so far—naturally.' (And thinks: 'One must go into the water before one can learn to swim.')

'But what future can there be for you in teaching? You might get a job in an inferior prep school without an university degree, but nowhere else.'

Somewhat defeated by this, I submitted, 'There's not much future as a clerk in the Army and Navy Stores.'

'I don't know about that. I don't know at all.' (And indeed he didn't.) 'There might be if you worked industriously. There might well be. Do you realize that you are speaking to a clerk?' (He was a Commissioner, or something equally high, in the Lunacy Board of Control.) 'And that your good Uncle Edwin is also a clerk?'

It stays a mystery to me, the way adults underestimate and discount the shrewd perceptions of children. The answer was simple. 'Yes, but there are clerks and clerks. A correspondence clerk at the Army and Navy Stores, at ten shillings a week, is not a Commissioner of Lunacy,' but I did not say it aloud; another, far more personal, answer came to me. 'Yes, but I don't really want a future either as a schoolmaster or a clerk.'

'Then what *do* you want?'

'I want to be a writer.'

'A *writer*?' Am I unjust in thinking that his surprise was in the nature of a shock? 'A writer? What sort of writer? A journalist?' How little he knew the overleaping ambition in this raw seventeen-year-old before him. 'A journalist? Is that your idea? A newspaper reporter? Is that it?'

'I meant a writer of books.'

'*Books?*'

'Yes. Perhaps I could begin as a journalist, and then hope to become more than a mere reporter. . . .'

'More. I see. A leader writer perhaps.' This was offered with a smile, not unkind. 'And are you aware, for instance, who are the people who write, say, the leaders in *The Times*?'

'No.'

'Gladstone used to write them sometimes. And Cabinet ministers and university professors.'

This did not alarm me, or 'learn' me, as much as it was designed to do, because my confidence that my destiny was to be a writer had become so strongly rooted—though rooted so far in desire rather than in any successful activity—that I could not believe that, in the business of mere writing, when the time came to do it, Cabinet ministers and professors would be able to surpass me.

I did seek, with Uncle Tom's kindly but palpably dubious consent, a post as a prep school master, and succeeded in obtaining one at a good school, Glengorse, Eastbourne, though very right he had been in assuring me that the stipend would be small. It was '£60 a year, resident'. But 'resident' meant that for nine months of the year I had no living expenses at all. I enjoyed the work. I liked the boys; the holidays were long; and I was greatly improving my Latin and Greek because I had to prepare boys for scholarships of Winchester standard and could do this only by 'swatting' the night before at the Latin and Greek subjects required in the morning, and so keeping one pace—or possibly two—ahead of my pupils. This may have accounted for my successes with them; my understanding of their difficulties had all the fresh bloom on it of a new bud.

From Glengorse I passed on to St Christopher's, Bath, another good school, and since my stipend here was 'a hundred, resident', I had at the end of each term some thirty pounds in my pocket wherewith to hurry off to Paris, holiday after holiday, and stay with Aunt Ida and Uncle Franz, who were now living in a little villa outside the city.

This was the time I saw most of her, and let me make clear that I drew some help and comfort from her daily and gushing words of affection.

Then, suddenly, I caught from a colleague at Bath the splendid fever of Anglo-Catholicity, which at this date was capturing the imagination of so many young men; and after four happy terms at Bath I resolved, like him, to 'become a priest'—the words in which we rejoiced to phrase it. A priest in the dear old C. of E. which, whatever the Romans might say, was the old original Catholic Church in our country. In error, of course, but so was Rome. And so Constantinople. The Roman Catholic Church in England, as we loved to say, was no more than an 'Italian Mission'.

I persuaded Dum's two trustees to provide ('cough up', as I put it) £300, the cost of two years at a theological college, on the understanding that I paid Aunt Emily the dividends she would lose from this loss of capital. Aunt, I am happy to tell, with her perfervid churchmanship embraced the whole plan with excitement and ardour.

But now loomed an obstacle. Chichester Theological College demanded sight of my baptism certificate. Before I could be ordained they must see proof that a child born so far away as Haute Savoie had been safely baptized. But had there been a baptism certificate, and, if so, where was it?

Aunt Ida had it. You may remember from an earlier page that I mentioned this certificate of a private baptism written on the notepaper of a hotel in Argentières, Haute Savoie, and of a fascinated letter accompanying it from the clergyman who had performed the ceremony twenty-three years before.

The certificate is as follows:

Privately Baptized

1889
August } Ernest Raymond, aged 7 months, Son of
14

William and Florence Bell Raymond, of 62 Rue
Pierre Charrons, Paris, Gentleman,
By me at Argentières,
Chamonix, Savoy—
T. C. Davies
Curate of St. Marks, Sheffield.

This was obviously a damning document for Aunt Ida to produce, and she refused to produce it. She reminded Emily that 'General Blake said I was never to be troubled'.

And said the same to Franz. 'General Blake made every provision that I shouldn't be troubled.' Thereupon, remarkably, the good and gentle Uncle Franz rose from beneath her permanent domination, and spoke. Aunt Emily knew this story, and told me all.

Ida loved her Franz well, but rather like a dear and faithful dog on a leash. In the Paris villa, when they had no longer a 'bonne', he was made to do all the cooking ('Nobody cooks like him') and all the household jobs that might spoil her hands ('Nobody cleans the silver like Franz') and all the work in the little fir-tree'd garden ('Nobody can keep a garden nicer than he'). All her possessions had to be perfect in their kind, whether it was her bosom, or her piano, or the backs of her unread books, or her Ernest, or her Franz. When he went into the unused drawing-room to play his heart out on the Bechstein piano, she would say, 'He is a second Schumann.' He was nothing of the sort. When she was dressing herself (throughout the morning and the early afternoon) and needed him to hook her up, she would call over the banisters to him at labour in the kitchen, or piano-playing in the draw-ing-room, 'Sophie, Mary, Em'ly, Clara, Edwin, Mother, Percy, Ernest—oh, drat the man!—what's his name? FRANZ!' And to me at her side she would say, 'Never do I want that man but I see his coat-tails disappearing into the kitchen or the drawing-room. *Franz!*'

It was this contented helot—and he *was* content in his servitude because he loved her—it was he who told her in something like a flaming quarrel, 'You've simply got to produce that certificate. For the boy's sake. Nothing else is thinkable. You can't ruin his career just to save yourself.'

'General Blake said I was never to be troubled.'

'That can't operate now. Don't be absurd. You'd never forgive your-self if you didn't produce it. For *his* sake, and no matter what he thinks about it or what it reveals to him. He would never forgive you. Nor, darling, would I.'

'Franz!'

'It is so. Give it him.'

Through the medium of Aunt Emily she allowed it to appear, hoping, I suppose, with that blind belief of some adults in the worldly simplicity of children, that Emily would serve as a screen behind which she could still hide. But I was twenty-three now, and Emily had long told us the truth about Ida and Dum—though never about herself and Dum. That, as you have heard, she never divulged, even when at eighty-two she lay dying. Nor had Dorothy once broached any hurtful questions. Aunt Emily died silent.

And yet she was as horrified as Franz by her elder sister's unreadiness to suffer for my sake.

I gave the certificate to the college. I told the Principal the whole of my story, as I understood it, and subsequently the Bishop of Chelms-ford; they were the first people, and the last, to whom I told it. Nor did either of them ever disclose it to anyone else. I still could not bring my-self to speak with Aunt Ida of the things it disclosed. We went on with the old relationship, she 'Aunt Ida', I 'Darling Ernest', as though it had never passed beneath my eyes. 'Forget quickly' was her rule. 'Forget what it hurts to remember, and live as before.'

§

I was to discover later that my decision to take Holy Orders was wrong. It was a mistake because, though I had all the uncritical faith of a singularly immature young man, and a lively devotion to the idea of Anglo-Catholicity, the desire to serve the Church as a priest was not my ruling passion; and it was not too long before I perceived that, if this is not a priest's ruling passion, he is lost. He may honour his Orders by striving to do his job as decently as he can, but he will have become a mere professional parson with the Sword of the Spirit blunted in his hand. It is probable too that, had the true ruling passion governed me, it would have saved, as the events were to suggest after many, many years, the simple faith of twenty-three, strengthening it in riper manhood to withstand the assaults of doubt.

I should have accepted that my one ruling passion was to write books and win fame, an aspiration almost wholly self-regarding instead of selfless, as a priest's should be. And, though some of my motives were high enough, mixed up with them was the notion that a parson's life would give me more opportunities to write than any other profession; in rougher words I was disposed to use the Church as a comfortable house in which I could be fed and kept while I wrote.

Further, when I was reading for Holy Orders at Chichester Theological College, I was being driven by another and utterly self-centred aim. There was no merit in this one at all. It can be summed up in my own crude language, 'I'm absolutely determined to flatten out Auntie X.' (Politer to call her X.) One of the Calder girls, she had heard Emily's black reports about my behaviour in my puberty years and she soon showed that her assessment of me was faintly contemptuous. Not without some justification. Her own children were brilliant, winning scholarships and other distinctions, while I had drifted and slacked through that last unhappy year at the hated boarding-school. 'A difficult boy to influence or guide.'

This was relayed to Aunt X, and no doubt she held me but a poor thing compared with her own bright children.

I suspect now that, while I might call that early aspiration 'a need to flatten out Auntie X', the truth was that she and her brilliant children represented the world, the 'Not me', and the real root of it lay in Aunt's slaps and canings in my early childhood. So perhaps, in so far as they built this drive towards success in me, and since the drive in part reached its goal, I ought to be grateful to her for them. But they hurt at the time.

Paradoxically Aunt Emily, while reporting me as 'in danger of becoming a lunatic', admired everything I wrote, especially my poems, and for this I have always, without difficulty, been grateful to her. To Aunt X she would declare, perhaps not knowing whether she was speaking praise or detraction, 'He's as clever as he can stick.' I think the words inclined towards detraction; after all, the lunatics can be clever. All the same, I felt a desire when my first book was published, to inscribe in her copy, 'For One who Believed', which produced a breakdown.

One of my poems she showed with pride—actually pride—to Aunt X who, on reading it, said, 'Yes, he has a talent for stringing rhymes.' Had I been less conceited, I might have accepted this as praise, but no! Stringing rhymes—No. 'Thank you for nothing, my dear Auntie X. I know faint contempt when I see it.'

And now at Chichester Theological College, I nursed this passion to 'flatten her out'—a most untheological attitude. I think no student worked as I did in my bedroom-study at the College hostel; and in each of the course's eight terms I was placed first in the end-of-term exams. I urged Aunt Emily to get these interesting facts through to Auntie X, and when she did so, Aunt X's comment was, 'These theological colleges don't get the best types. Put him up against university men.' Her two bright children were university trained.

All right. The time came for me to take the Universities' Preliminary to Holy Orders (the final examination for non-graduates). I got a first class. And again she said, 'Yes . . . hmm . . . but these are not university men.'

Oh, hell; for God's sake! Damn university men. What more could I do? I had to sit with others for the 'Bishop's Exam' before I could be accepted for ordination as a deacon in his diocese. Every one of the others sitting with me was a university graduate. I passed first, and so was made 'Gospeller' at that year's Ordination Service.

'Now,' I said to Aunt Emily, 'I beg you will submit this fact to my dear Auntie X.'

And, bless her, I think she did so, not without satisfaction.

But I am clear now that this run of successes was largely due, first, to my driving need to win applause, and secondly to the gift of a remarkable visual memory which enabled my mind's eye to see whole pages of our textbooks and then, aglow, to rewrite them in learned and resplendent words for my examiners. It was hardly fair on the other examinees.

None of these were motives, alas, that should have accompanied my approach to Holy Orders, nor would they have been allowed to live in one who was 'giving diligence to making his calling and election sure'.

Nevertheless, I tried to blind myself to this, to pray aright, and to hope much, to hope for the best, when in Chelmsford Cathedral on Trinity Sunday, 1914, I was ordained deacon, and, ahead of the others, performed my first ministerial task, passing through the altar rails, a layman no more, into the Sanctuary, where I read the Gospel.

Three weeks later the young Gavrilo Princip, at Sarajevo, fired his shot at the Archduke Franz Ferdinand of Austria and killed him. All the pillars of the world were about to fall.

§

I was priested on Trinity Sunday of the next year, and immediately offered my services to the Army Chaplain's Department, a step which had been impossible until I was a priest. It was almost an impudent step now, since I had been priested only a few days before. But my vicar, Canon Dormer Pierce, a genial and affectionate man, as enthusiastic as he was portly, consented to the impertinence and promised, should anything come of it, to 'recommend me in the highest terms he could think of'. And further, since my priesting had involved another 'Bishop's Exam', and parish work in the first year of war had been heavy, he told me to go off for a short holiday. With a companion I took train for Falmouth in the Cornish Riviera Express, wondering if there was any chance whatever of getting into the war before it ended, and looking out of the carriage window sadly, while I doubted the possibility, and even assured myself that the hope was ridiculous.

Among Aunt's papers, found after her death, there are letters and postcards written by me to her at this time. Extraordinary that she who had shown little love to me as a child and much disapproval, even venomous disapproval, of me as a youth, should have now crossed the floor, as it were, and become proud of my examination successes and of my activities during this historic, this incredible, first year of the war. Strange too, and nearly unimaginable nowadays, the mood of the young men of 1914–15 which this correspondence reveals. It was written before the Great Disillusion was even as much as a small cloud on the horizon; before, like Elijah's wide thunderous sky and the great rain, it bore down upon so many, sinking their hearts, and souring their words. Written too when it was being said everywhere that the life of a young officer in France or Gallipoli was fourteen days. And yet in our twenties we were restless to be there. As a chaplain my hope of life would be larger for me than for many, but I know that my craving to be 'in it' would have been the same in kind had my rank been a junior subaltern's, the most dangerous of all.

The first card says, 'I last night asked my vicar's permission to offer my services on being priested to the War Office. He was perfectly ripping about it—said he thinks perhaps I ought to go, tho' it will be a blow to him—promised to secure by his influence *foreign* service and not home garrison duty for which he would not release me—promised to keep Prittlewell (our church) open for me and to subsidize my officer's pay. So if nothing goes wrong, a month or two should see me at the front. You can scarcely imagine my joy. I shall insure my life for War Risks, so you need have no fear, should the unlikely thing happen of a chaplain being picked off. Now for the great experience of my life.'

That 'a month or two' was no more than wishful thinking or 'showing off', because I had little real hope.

On the Sunday in Falmouth I went to Matins at the parish church, and the preacher was a chaplain on leave from France. Over his surplice hung the black silk scarf of a chaplain, embroidered with crown and monogram. A man in middle life, he spoke of his 'boys in the trenches' with pride and love, and towards the end, in a perhaps excessive enthusiasm, he leaned over the pulpit and said, 'I know you are all green with envy of me.'

Whether or not this was true of many in that crowded congregation, it was true of one who sat listening. When I came out of the church I saw him emerge from the vestry in his chaplain's khaki uniform with Sam Browne belt and a captain's stars, and had I not been too shy, I would have gone up and told him that here was one green with envy.

A letter from Falmouth follows. 'We have nice rooms overlooking the Channel, both bedrooms and sitting-rooms. At the foot of the garden runs the road, and then, with no front or promenade to intervene, there is the open sea breaking into foam with that wildness which seems inseparable from Cornish seas. On our right as we look out of our front windows there stretch out to sea headland after headland till the furthest which is enveloped in a wet mist.'

It was lying on that Falmouth shore with a wild sea breaking, though the day was golden with July, that I read in my *Times* Sir Ian Hamilton's first despatch from Gallipoli to Kitchener, Secretary of State for War. What a despatch that was! Sir Ian was probably the only great British Commander since Elizabeth's day who was also a poet, unless we put Lord Wavell at his side. I lay on the beach reading it, body, mind, and soul taut.

'My Lord, I have the honour to submit my report on the operations in the Gallipoli Peninsula. . . .

'Generally speaking, the coast is precipitous and good landing places are few. Just south of Tekke Burnu is a small sandy bay (W). Inside Sedd-el-Bahr is a sandy beach (V) about three hundred yards across, facing a semicircle of steeply rising ground, as the flat bottom of a half-saucer faces the rim. . . . A peculiarity to be noted as regards this southern sector is that from the hill Achi Baba to Cape Helles the ground is hollowed out like a spoon, presenting only its outer edges to direct fire from the sea.

'Altogether the result of this and subsequent reconnaissances was to convince me that nothing but a thorough and systematic scheme for flinging the whole of the troops under my command very rapidly ashore could meet with success. . . . The landing of an army upon the theatre of operations I have described—a theatre strongly garrisoned throughout and prepared for any such attempt—involved difficulties for which no precedent was forthcoming in military history, except perhaps in the sinister legends of Xerxes. The beaches were either so well defended by works and guns or else so restricted by nature that it did not seem possible, except by simultaneous landings, to pass the troops ashore quickly enough to enable them to maintain themselves against the rapid concentration and counter-attack which the enemy was bound to attempt. . . .

'W beach consists of a strip of deep powdery sand, some 350 yards wide, situated immediately south of Tekke Burnu where a small gully, running down to the sea, opens out a break in the cliffs. On either flank of the beach the ground rises precipitously, but in the centre a number of sand-dunes afford a more gradual access to the ridge overlooking the sea. Much time and ingenuity had been employed by the Turks in turning this landing place into a death-trap. Close to the water's edge a broad wire entanglement extended the whole length of the shore, and a supplementary barbed network lay concealed under the surface of the sea in the shallows. Land mines and sea mines had been laid. The high ground overlooking the beach was strongly fortified with trenches. . . .

'So strong, in fact, were the defences of W beach that the Turks may well have considered them impregnable, and it is my firm conviction that no finer feat of arms has ever been achieved by the British soldier— or any other soldier—than the storming of these trenches from open boats on the morning of April 25th. . . .

'The landing at W had been entrusted to the 1st Battalion, Lancashire Fusiliers, and it was to the complete lack of the sense of danger or of fear in this daring battalion that we owed our astonishing success. . . . At 6.0 a.m. the whole battalion approached the shore together, towed by eight picket boats in line abreast, each picket boat pulling four ship's cutters. As soon as shallow water was reached the tows were cast off, and the boats were at once rowed to the shore. . . .

'While the troops were approaching the shore no shot had been fired from the enemy's trenches, but as soon as the first boat touched the ground a hurricane of lead swept over the battalion. Gallantly led by their officers the Fusiliers literally hurled themselves ashore and, fired at from right, left, and centre, commenced hacking their way through the wire. A long line of men was at once mowed down as by a scythe, but the remainder were not to be denied. Covered by the fire of the warships, which had now closed right in to the shore, they broke through the entanglements. . . . By 10.0 a.m. three lines of hostile trenches were in our hands and our hold on the beach was assured. . . .

'Throughout the events I have chronicled the Royal Navy has been father and mother to the Army. . . .'

It recalled Homer and his *Iliad* to read, some months later, Admiral de Robeck's despatch listing the battleships and cruisers that stood around the toe of the Peninsula, caring for the Army with their thundering guns, as it battled for footholds on W and V beaches. 'These then were the captains of the fleet,' wrote Homer, 'and these their black ships. . . . The beaked, sea-going, well-found ships that had come across the wine-dark seas of Greece.' De Robeck's ships: Battleships *Swiftsure, Implacable, Cornwallis, Albion, Vengeance, Lord Nelson, Prince George*; Cruisers *Euryalus, Talbot, Dublin, Minerva*.

Back to Sir Ian's despatch, and his words about the landing of the

Australian and New Zealand Army Corps, higher up the Peninsula, which lies like a long drooping finger on the sea.

'The moment the boats touched land the Australians' turn had come. Like lightning they leapt ashore, and each man as he did so went straight as his bayonet at the enemy. So vigorous was the onslaught that the Turks made no attempt to withstand it, and fled from the ridge pursued by the Australian infantry. . . . From 11.0 a.m. to 3.0 p.m. the enemy, now reinforced to a strength of 20,000 men, attacked the whole line. This counter-attack, however, was handsomely repulsed with the help of the guns of His Majesty's ships.'

Lying on that Falmouth beach, I felt that, if I had the good fortune to be commissioned as a chaplain, this was the battlefront I would long to go to. I longed to see those beaches which the British and Australians and New Zealanders had 'stormed from open boats' and the hills above Cape Helles and Anzac which they were about to conquer. Think of that battlefield, the long slim Gallipoli Peninsula, with the Hellespont (or Dardanelles) on one side of it, the Aegean sea on the other, and all the Isles of Greece lying around it. And Troy in the distance. But what hope—what hope had I, whose experience as a priest covered no more than days, of getting there? The idea was but a dream.

Yet only a few days after reading this despatch with a surging interest that amounted almost to an identification with those men on the ridges above their captured beaches, I received a summons to 'report forthwith to the War Office'.

So here, speedily, comes another card to Aunt. 'Just had a joyride— left Cornwall 10.15, arrived Padd. 4.45, taxi'd to War Office and inter- viewed [*sic*] Bishop Taylor Smith, Chaplain General. After confab he sent me to the Doctors—was examined and passed "fit for service at home or abroad"—returned to Chaplain General who said, "It's now six, run down to Southend and ask your vicar's consent to release you at once and I'll send you to the Dardanelles next week." Did you ever see such luck? Captain's pay and allowances amounting to £250 a year.'

An unspiritual close, but I had never known what it was to earn more than £150 a year.

I look back across fifty years to that interview with the Chaplain General in his War Office room. I am standing before him in a suit of dark 'pepper-and-salt', which was the clerical compromise in those days between canonical black and the gay holiday clothes of the less sombre laity. He is standing before me, a heavy man of fifty-five in full episcopal array: black frock-coat, pectoral cross, black sashed apron, and buttoned black gaiters. Behind him stands his chaplain in the khaki, stars, belt and puttees of the Falmouth preacher. I look at that uniform and wonder with a breathless hope if I shall be wearing it soon.

Bishop Taylor Smith, whose manner is brisk and brusque, as though he would say, 'There's a war on, and no time to waste', shoots at me a fusillade of questions. He has been Bishop of Sierra Leone, and I am wondering if this quick, sharp manner has been acquired among the Negroes of that 'White Man's Grave', or from his brother generals all around him in this War Office where he has been Chaplain General for fourteen years. Most of his questions I answer well enough, but the last one foolishly. Thus:

Bishop (a low churchman): 'What would you do if a soldier came to you and said he was tired of his sins and wanted to be a Christian?'

E.R. (determined to be loyal to his high Anglo-Catholicity, even if it cost all): 'I should tell him to come and make his confession.'

Bishop: 'Wouldn't understand what you're talking about. Go down to the M.O.'s and see if you're fit for service abroad. Come back and tell me what they say. John, take him down.'

Chaplain: 'Yessir.'

E.R. (returning after a total overhaul by the R.A.M.C.): 'They say I'm fit, my lord.'

Bishop: 'For service abroad?'

E.R.: 'Yes, sir . . . my lord.'

Bishop: 'Good. It's now six. Run down to Prittlewell and ask your vicar to release you at once, and I'll send you to the Dardanelles next week. He will. Speaks well of you. Kneel down and I'll give you my blessing. You've got a great job in front of you, and you'll want all the help of Almighty God that you can get.'

I knelt, and he, laying a brisk hand on my head, said, 'The Lord bless thee and keep thee. The Lord make his face to shine upon thee and be gracious unto thee. The Lord lift up his countenance upon thee and give thee peace. Now go to a tailor's and get your kit. The List of Requirements, John.'

I went out of the War Office and down its steps into the summer evening, and I have never felt it an exaggeration to say that the long stretch of Whitehall, with its statues and public buildings, lay under a light that never was, on sea or land.

To the Dardanelles next week. Gallipoli. The Peninsula with those beaches. The Hellespont. The Islands. Troy.

I walked a hundred yards northward up Whitehall, and here was a tailor's shop—not a large tailor's, just one small shop. It is there still, and I never look through its door at the small counter, and the small back-room beyond, without thinking incredible what actually happened. I went into it, and now the magic lustre upon the world outside lay upon that brief counter and the gentleman behind it. Proud of my words, I asked, 'Is it possible to supply me with a full uniform and all this tropical kit in a few days? I am going to the East.' This much, but this alone, Security allowed me to say.

'Perfectly possible, sir. We're doing it every day.'

'All of it? From you alone?'

'All of it, sir. From us alone.'

'What? Pith helmet, Sam Browne, sleeping valise, water-bottle. . . ?'

'Certainly. Our men are working all through the night. If you will go in there, Mr Charles will take your measurements.'

'How soon can I have it all?'

'You can come for a fitting tomorrow morning, have it in the afternoon, and take it away. Khaki drill packs light. The only thing that beats us is the camp bed. And the boots. You'll have to get that somewhere else.'

'I'll get it at the Army and Navy Stores,' I said, and thought of Dum and his uniforms.

'Nowhere better, sir.'

Next afternoon I returned to Prittlewell in full uniform and more proud of this new wear, in road, train, and Prittlewell streets, than was fitting in one whose business was spiritual and whose profession was peace.

§

The great new secret event on the Gallipoli Peninsula which all on that troopship, the *Scotian*, were expecting proved to be a Second Landing. In the calm black midnight of August 6th, and in the darkness before dawn on the 7th new divisions were landed at Suvla Bay, to the north of Anzac where the Australians and New Zealanders stood.

Other divisions, or brigades of divisions, stood ready on the islands; on Lemnos, Imbros, and Mytilene.

I was among those held up in Mudros East on the Island of Lemnos. The huge, hill-embraced harbour of Lemnos, as scholars will remember, was the port into which the *Argo*, with Jason and all the young princes of Greece aboard, put in for a long rest, spent mostly in bed with the women of Lemnos, before proceeding on their way to the Hellespont, the Euxine Sea, Colchis, and the Golden Fleece.

Suvla Bay was twenty miles from the beaches of Cape Helles where the first landings had been made, and, like Anzac, was out of touch with them. So there mingled with my excited interest in this new and powerful move, a worry lest I should be sent to Suvla, and never see W Beach and V Beach, which had haunted my mind ever since I read Sir Ian's despatch, lying on a beach at Falmouth.

But it was a curious fact of my four years' war-service that dream after dream was granted to me. In 1915, not only was I sent towards my heart's desire, the Gallipoli campaign, but now, on Lemnos, I was ordered to proceed forthwith to Helles and there join the 42nd Division of East Lancashire territorials. These territorials had been brought from Egypt on to the Peninsula only a few days after that pale April morning when the superb regulars of the 29th Division, through a horizontal storm of bullets, had come so miraculously ashore. An old trawler, late of the North Sea, carried me, if you will only believe it, to W Beach. W Beach! There before my eyes, between its headlands, Tekke Burnu and Cape Helles, was W Beach. Behind it in the distance was the low hill of Achi Baba. It was a moment hardly believable, hardly imaginable. I tried to imagine the eight lines of ship's cutters that brought the Lancashire Fusiliers as far as these shallows and the waiting storm that greeted them from those ridges, but there was all too little time for this, as I stepped ashore on to the Gallipoli Peninsula . . . I was on Gallipoli . . . I was where the Lancashires had been . . . Dying and conquering . . . I was standing on W Beach.

2

GALLIPOLI

Gallipoli. I was to be sent to five other fronts in that First War—Sinai, France, Mesopotamia, Persia, and Russia—but none of them has such a place in my memory as Gallipoli. And this not because it was my first sight of battle—but because the Gallipoli campaign had a glamour, a tragic beauty, all its own.

First, because of the legendary places in which it was conducted, and of the waters that washed them. When sometimes I stood in dreams on the low hill of Helles, above V and W Beaches, I saw across the mouth of the Dardanelles the roadsteads of Asia where Agamemnon moored his thousand ships, and on the rolling Troad plain beyond them, the little hill of Troy. There by Troy was Mount Ida from whose summit Zeus sat watching the Trojan War. If I turned and looked the other way I might see the towering table-topped island of Samothrace whereon, so the legends said, Poseidon, God of the seas, sat to consider the siege of Troy. I used to think of him sitting naked on that high rock with his chin on an opened fist, like Rodin's *Penseur*. South of us, west of us, we could see the fabled Isles of Greece 'lying like shields upon the water' in the wonderful violet sunsets. And had I not loitered, waiting, on the Island of Lemnos, where Vulcan, in his smithy, forged the weapons of Achilles?

Then again, by an extraordinary sequence of chance and circumstance, the Gallipoli campaign assumed the perfect pattern, the Attic shape, of a Greek tragedy. It began in the dawn of a spring morning with the boats running towards the beaches; it ended in a winter midnight with an army of tired men, who had fought well, endured terribly, and failed at last, slipping quietly away. It began with a thunder of guns; it ended in a shuffling silence. On that spring morning thousands died, the sea was laced with blood, and the sandy beaches filtered it away; on that winter midnight, so successful were the evacuation plans, not a man died; the only blood on the beaches and hills was that of our poor mules who had been brought through the scrub to their sacrifice.

§

'The Royal Navy has been father and mother to the Army,' wrote Sir Ian Hamilton.

The aptness of this metaphor was never more exactly shown than when, as sometimes happened, the Turk, after his evening tea perhaps, opened what we called a 'hate'. Or, more peaceably, a 'friendly hate', because 'Johnny Turk' after the first raging battles, became popular with us, and everything suggested that our amiability towards him was reciprocated. But occasionally, for common decency's sake, a formal 'hate' there had to be. Impishly, perhaps, he would open a sudden, savage, and prolonged bombardment of our front line, our support lines, or the beach-heads. Then, out of the diaphanous evening light, so lovely in the Aegean, often flooding the islands, the whole sea-scape and even our dug-outs with a violet hue, would appear the Royal Navy. Here came the long destroyers or the heavy-gunned monitors and, if they were several, placed themselves along the side of the Peninsula like a chain of black rulers. I could never imagine where they came from, or how so quickly and so promptly; but over our heads would fly their roaring message to Johnny Turk, sounding like express trains racing over iron bridges, and bursting and exploding in clouds of black smoke on Achi Baba; a message which amounted, we always thought, to 'There now. That will do. Stop it. Leave our boys alone.'

And the Turk stopped, the Royal Navy's expression of opinion having been extremely loud and blunt. Order restored, the ships put about and went unhurriedly home.

§

In the autumn of 1906 an exceptionally brilliant group of boys came up from Eton to Balliol, Oxford; they included Charles Lister, Patrick Shaw-Stewart, Ronald Knox and Julian Grenfell. In the same year another youth, Rupert Brooke, bringing a high reputation, came from Rugby to King's, Cambridge. Of these scholarly and locally celebrated young men, Charles Lister, Patrick Shaw-Stewart and Rupert Brooke, eight years afterwards, were to meet together in the Royal Naval Division and play their part in the Dardanelles campaign. And two to die in it.

Sir Lawrence Jones, in his admirable picture of Balliol in the first 1900's, *An Edwardian Youth*, portrays Charles Lister, his younger contemporary there, as the most remarkable among these remarkable Eton boys. He writes, 'He had compassion, and a sense of responsibility

to the under-privileged, to a degree unknown to the rest of us, com-
placent and self-centred in our busy occupations. It was these sensi-
bilities that led him when still an Eton boy to join the Labour Party—
the cloth-capped, Keir-Hardie-led, class-ridden party of the 1900's—
and to manage to combine, at Oxford, a First in Greats with sudden
raids into anti-sweating, Fabianism and strikes. He carried himself with
unself-conscious gaiety in all he did. His good humour was invincible;
his conversation, however fantastic or flippant, was salted with thought.
As a human being Charles was in a class by himself in our generation
and, although he had begun a career in the Diplomatic Service when
war broke out, we never doubted that he would, in due course, be
driven by his fiery and undaunted daemon into public life. Into what
party it is impossible to say. He had already broken with doctrinaire
Socialism. With the fervour of a young Gladstone, the imagination of a
young Dizzy, and a selflessness that neither possessed, Charles must
have qualified from the first as statesman, not politician. . . . When his
name is so often coupled with that of Julian Grenfell, it should not be
over-looked that, had both lived to fame and performance, Julian would
have taken, and gladly, his orders from Charles.'

He then tells us how Charles was sent down for the rest of a term for
seizing the junior Dean of Trinity about the waist, after a bump supper,
and waltzing him around a bonfire; and how Patrick Shaw-Stewart
suggested that the proper appeal in mitigation of this sentence would be
'I wist not, brethren, that he was the High Priest'; but, the sentence
standing, he stood too in the Quad and read a funeral oration as Charles
'went down'.

Charles spent his rustication working for an East End mission.

Ronald Knox, his contemporary at Balliol, has insisted that Lister
'created Socialism as a practical force' in the undergraduate Oxford of
their day, multiplying the University branch of the Fabian Society
five-fold.

Lord Ribblesdale, Charles's father, in a memoir of his son, speaks
with touching humour of Charles's conversion at Eton to Socialism,
'this dismal gospel', as he calls it. With a fatherly smile he accepts his
boy's enthusiasm for nationalization of all the raw material of industry,
'including our few family acres' (of which, if we are to be exact, there
were four thousand and eight hundred) and describes delightfully a reception which he himself, in Charles's interest, gave to the Independent
Labour Party at his great house, Gisburne. 'One day a reception

of the I.L.P. and a tea-party took place at Gisburne; speeches were made by leading extremists slightly cramped in style by their courteous reservations in favour of one particular park and one particular proprietor. Mr. Clough, the member for our division made a capital, if unexpected, speech, all but rebuking Charles for having acted hastily in cutting himself off from the traditions to which it had pleased God to call him.'

Many of us on Gallipoli knew all about Charles Lister, Patrick Shaw-Stewart and Rupert Brooke. The Royal Naval Division lay beside us of the 42nd, and the stories, already shaping into legends, of Brooke, Lister and Shaw-Stewart, came drifting towards us across the scrub. We had read Rupert Brooke's '1914' war sonnets, and newspapers had told us how the Dean of St Paul's on Easter Sunday in his pulpit had described them as the enthusiasm of a pure and elevated patriotism which had never found nobler expression. This after reading aloud to the congregation, 'If I should die . . . '. We knew the story of Rupert Brooke's death on a hospital ship less than forty hours before the Royal Naval Division were to take their share in the Gallipoli landings at dawn on April 25th; and how Charles Lister, Patrick Shaw-Stewart, and others had taken his body on to the Island of Skyros, Achilles' island, and there buried it with every honour in an olive grove under those Grecian hills.

In *The Times* shortly after this there had appeared a tribute to Brooke, unsigned, but over the initials, W.S.C. If those famous initials had not been there we might have guessed the authorship from the high oratory of the words. 'A voice had become audible, a note had been struck, more true, more thrilling, more able to do justice to the nobility of our youth in arms engaged in this present war than any other—more able to express their thoughts of self-surrender, and with a power to carry comfort to those who watched them so intently from afar. The voice has been swiftly stilled. Only the echoes and the memory remain; but they will linger.'

A revulsion from Rupert Brooke's attitude to war and its slaughter—'Now God be thanked who has matched us with His hour, And caught our youth'—has come with time, and a parallel depreciation of him as a 'great' poet, the new critics defining the sonnets as stirring but dated rhetoric rather than the ultimate in poetry. They may be right; all I have to say is that for many of us who, at that time, were young and at war, and had some idealism, especially perhaps those of us on Gallipoli, the five sonnets 'caught our youth', and helped us in secret places of the heart.

It was while I was held up in Mudros East on Lemnos Island, awaiting a ship for the Peninsula, that a message came to me from Lord Dudley, the Commandant, Mudros East, that seven bodies from off the hospital ship, *Gascon*, were coming ashore for burial. As burial officer I went down to the little wooden jetty, the 'Egyptian Pier', to receive them. They were lifted from a steam pinnace on to the jetty, each wrapped up in a grey army-blanket which, holding tight to his figure, gave him the shape of an embalmed Egyptian. Each had pinned on to his breast some available scrap of paper, giving his name, regiment and religion, and no more. The corporal in charge of my burial party said, 'One of 'em's an orficer, sir,' and pointed to the longest figure of all; officers having to be buried in a different part of a cemetery from Other Ranks; so retaining their class distinction beyond the grave. With my record book in my hand I went to the officer's body to enter his name. The paper pinned on to his breast chanced to be an envelope snatched in an orderly room or other office; and I read, 'On His Majesty's Service. Lieut. the Hon. Charles Lister.'

This was my meeting with Charles Lister.

He had buried Rupert Brooke among the hills of a legendary Greek island, Achilles' island, and now I must bury him among the dry bare hills of another, the Island of Lemnos, Vulcan's island.

So alike, and so different, was Charles Lister's burial from that of his friend.

Twelve bearers, all petty officers of the Royal Naval Division, carried Rupert Brooke to the olive grove, a guard of honour around them, led by Patrick Shaw-Stewart with drawn sword; following them came his general, his colonel, the captain of his company and many of his brother officers. By the grave, which he had helped to dig and beautify, Lister waited to receive them. Three volleys were fired over the grave, and the Last Post sounded.

For Charles Lister and his companions in death a G.S. wagon drawn by two mules waited by the jetty. I sat with them in the wagon, and so did the corporal and his burial party, as we jolted to the cemetery. We and the dead were the whole company. Our little army cemetery on Mudros East lay far behind the hills that rolled up from the great Lemnos harbour and held the white tented hospitals in line abreast. It was a bare and lonely little acre on a stony plain within a fence of barbed wire.

But there were a few touches of ceremony here. I at least was robed to lead a small procession; the Greek grave-diggers removed their hats if they had any; a tall and turbanned Sikh, whence come I know not, stood smartly at attention. All saluted in some fashion or other as the bodies went down. But of course there was no firing party or Last Post; only a silence among empty hills.

I left Charles Lister there. The G.S. wagon, its freight unloaded, the service over, went rumbling homeward, across a plain of thistles and stones, towards the tented hills by the harbour; myself seated at the driver's side, and the burial party where the freight had been, their morning's task performed.

Whether Charles Lister's dust still lies in that barren Lemnos plain, as Rupert Brooke's does in a mountain vale on Skyros, I do not know.

§

From the moment I left school I had been writing chapters for a story—or more often dreaming of writing them. How many writers have described to us the daily temptation to do *anything* rather than compose sentences on a blank sheet of paper—to clean spots off the desk, to twiddle a pen while they recall the events of yesterday, to stare through the window at the traffic in the street, or, possibly, to choose hymns for their funeral.

But over the years from eighteen to twenty I had contrived to write a shapeless mass of stuff for my First Novel (the capitals are justified because the book was of such capital importance to my dilatory mind). There were only two subjects I could write about, school and youth—what other experience had I?—but was I deterred by the thought that a few hundred other writers had reaped this meadow before me? I was not. I don't think this discouraging thought once visited my mind, so swollen my confidence.

And now came a magnificent excuse for postponing the strains of composition: my resolve to study hard for the next three years and so achieve the academic success which would 'flatten out Auntie X'. And no sooner was this in being than an excuse far more magnificent, far more publishable, stood up before me: War. War when I must obviously occupy my spare time writing descriptive notes of romantic places or heroic, dramatic and tragic events around me.

This I did for the first few months in my war diary. But it was on the

Peninsula that there broke before me a moment of vision. I saw what to do with the massed and untidy chapters of my school story—or with what seemed the best of them: they would form the first half of a two-part novel which would be a study of my own generation of schoolboys who, after their few years of school, happy or unhappy, had been called upon to bleed or die for England. The first half would be called, *Five Gay Years of School*; the second half, *And the Rest—War*. The scene of this second part would be Gallipoli because of its grand classical background among the seas and islands of Greece.

So good the idea seemed that I began to dread lest, with the shells and bullets flying around, and the diseases infecting so many on Helles, I should not survive to write the book. There were adequate reasons for this fear, and, towards the end, a new one more valid than any before.

A tragic fact of the Gallipoli story is that for a few hours the campaign's objective was won—and perhaps the war with it. Speaking very roughly, the position was this: either of two hills, if finally carried, would have commanded the Narrows of the Dardanelles and determined the issue. One was Achi Baba at Helles, a gentle hill of 700 feet behind V and W Beaches; the other was Sari Bair, a tormented ridge of 1,000 feet opposite Anzac Cove and Suvla.

We never carried Achi Baba but on August 9th in the early morning a Major Allanson, with a battalion of Ghurkas and some Lancashire companies, in a splendid dash, seized the summit of Sari Bair. And there across the tumbled waist of the Peninsula (they saw it with a wild surmise) was—not an ocean but a streak of water: the silver prize of the Narrows. 'The Turks turned and fled,' wrote the Major in his report. 'I felt a very proud man: the key of the whole Peninsula was ours. Below I saw the Straits, and the motors and wheeled transport on the roads leading to Achi Baba.'

Allanson and his men held on to their victorious brink by their finger-nails, but they were not supported, and on August 10th, in the early morning, no less a person than Mustafa Kemal, later Kemal Attaturk, creator of modern Turkey, commanded a powerful counter-attack which swept Allanson and his weary water-starved men off the ridge; and the Dardanelles were lost to us. None of us on the Peninsula ever saw the Narrows again.

The great new effort at Suvla had failed, as Helles had failed before it, and after a few tired months Suvla's proud new army was withdrawn, together with the Anzacs at its side who had been there from the beginning, unconquered. To us on Helles came the word: 'Suvla and Anzac successfully evacuated. No casualties.' This was followed by a Special Order of the Day, telling us that we 'were to have the honour of holding Helles for the Empire'.

Now, if ever, did I wonder whether I should survive to write that Schooldays–Wartime book. The whole Turkish army which had opposed our Suvla and Anzac armies was free to come down to us at Helles and perhaps drive us into the sea or massacre and capture us on our narrow tongue of land. The Germans had broken through Serbia and were also coming. Fast.

But you will know the story. That Special Order of the Day was a diplomatic blinder, addressed rather to Turkish and Greek spies than to us. The Helles army, like its brothers at Suvla and Anzac, was successfully evacuated within a few weeks of the lying Order. I was brought off my so-eagerly sought Gallipoli Peninsula one dark midnight, a few days before that last quiet night when the evacuation of Helles was completed without loss. Indeed I used to jest thereafter that the only distinction I achieved on the Peninsula was that of *not* being 'the last man off'. So many were.

I came off it from W Beach—W Beach again—and as in the darkness I stepped on to the lighter which was to take me away, I tried once more to imagine the Lancashire Fusiliers coming towards this shore in their ship's cutters, eight lines abreast, through the early morning, and somehow, Heaven knew how, carrying the beach and the trenches above—'no finer feat of arms ever achieved by the British soldier'. Farewell to that great morning.

Some pages back I spoke of a shuffling silence on the last night of all. But that silence was only on the road to the beaches and on the beaches themselves. Miles behind our departing troops, if you can credit it, our trenches, without a man in them, were still firing. It was almost as if the ghosts of the thousand dead we had left behind were now manning our abandoned lines. *Debout, les morts.* In truth it was a matter of many tricks with clocks, cigarette tins into which sand slowly filtered, petrol tins which received a slow trickle of water, and other such contrivances which after a time, after we were gone, pulled strings and worked gun-triggers, so that our old friend Johnny Turk might rest in peace believing us still there.

3

SINAI AND MESOPOTAMIA

For the rest of the war my inspiration for the Schooldays–Gallipoli book was warm within me, and it was a good inspiration, however inadequately, as I shall argue later, it was accomplished in my first novel, *Tell England*. At present, however, while I kept the idea for *Tell England* simmering in my head, my piety as a chaplain instructed me that I ought to write a religious book, setting forth all that was fine and heroic amid the horrors of war. I decided to call it *God's Wheat* (i.e. the wheat among the tares). The very title is cheap, and the many pencilled notes for it that I assembled in my diary are all too often facile and sentimental, the phrasing of them pretentious and mannered and flowery. When I bring myself to look at them now, they shame me. I had much to learn about writing when I composed these notes for *God's Wheat*, and for many years more.

After our evacuation from Gallipoli we were sent to Sinai and here the campaign, so far as fighting went, was a picture of ease, comfort and success, contrasted with the Goyaesque gallery of *Desastres de la Guerra* that was Gallipoli. Employing a huge and chattering host of Gippy coolies, we took a railway with us, mile by mile, across the north of the Sinai desert, every valley of sand being exalted by the Gippies, and every mountain and hill brought low, so as to make straight in the desert a pathway to Jerusalem. So little had I to do that I was able to spend hours and hours in my bivouac, binding up my sheaves for *God's Wheat*. In this advance through the sand-dunes of the Sinai wilderness we travelled light; we had no tents, and these 'bivvies' were made of conjoined sticks with grey army blanket stretched over them, or if we were halted near an oasis, of nothing but palm-branches full of leaf—and very pretty little desert homes did these leafy palm-branches make. I completed my dutifully religious book in such a green and open-work bivouac when we and our railway were approaching El Arish, and I posted the thick manuscript off to Aunt Emily in Brighton for safe-keeping. It was never heard of more. The ship that carried it homeward was torpedoed in the Mediterranean, and *God's Wheat* sank with it.

It is better at the bottom of the sea.

§

As I have told you, dream after dream was granted me in the course of the war. After Gallipoli the other battlefield I longed to get to was the slaughtered city of Ypres and the deathly 'Salient' that guarded it. From that Ypres Salient, though the city behind was now but ruins and dust, our armies had defended its rubble through year after year, '14, '15, '16, '17, through battle after battle, Ypres I, Ypres II and Ypres III, never suffering it to fall. And in early 1917 our division was moved from Sinai to France where, after turns of duty in various sectors of the old Somme battlefield, all quiet now and enfolded in a comparative peace, we received—to my delight—orders to march north towards the Salient, and play our part in Ypres III. Ypres III was to be Paschendaele.

So we came marching along that famous straight road from Poperinghe through Vlamertinghe to the dead city. We passed through its rubble and fanged ruins in the last of a dusk. I wrote a description of our march through Ypres which does express, and without exaggeration, what I felt that evening and what I suspected that others, marching with me, were feeling too.

'Now it was dusk, and they were marching through the city of Ypres, up towards the murmuring throb of the battle; and in the half-darkness the eyes of all were turning left and right to feed upon the interest around them. It was the first time they had come by these spectral ruins, and, though for two years the world had been showing them its battlefields, they were as interested in this, the war's crowning and immortal desolation, as any civilian sightseer paying the pilgrimage of a day to the scene of war. They were thrilled as they passed the cascaded tower of the Cathedral and the pallid fangs of the Cloth Hall; thrilled to think their feet were tramping the cobbles of the Grande Place of Ypres, and that their eyes were meeting a signpost which pointed right with the words "To the Menin Gate". The Menin Gate! Veterans of Gallipoli and Sinai, they felt much like a school of children who were being led among sacred places; in their deep interest they forgot that they themselves were going forward to do a thing no different from that which all the ghostly battalions had done, who had gone this way before them and given a sanctity to these stones.

'"To the Menin Gate." Why, soon they would be treading the Menin Road. Soon they would be seeing Hell Fire Corner.

'This—this was the Menin Gate! Those piles of bricks, were they the original pillars of the gate? They were clattering over a bridge—

"Break step. Break step, damn you"—then those were the city ramparts and this moat or stream was Yser water. All Britain warring in France had sooner or later come out through that gate and clattered over the bridge and trod this *pavé*. All—for three years now—marching neither to victory nor to defeat, but simply into liquid mud, intensive bombardments, gas and bombs; for the line round Ypres had hardly moved in all the years. Like Verdun, it had held, that was all; and the enemy did not pass.'

So we went over the bridge and into the darkness and mud of the Salient—then the outermost edge of the world.

After about three weeks in the Salient, unforgettable, a season in a grey and dreadful limbo, but not to be written of here, we were relieved and sent north to the Nieuport trenches, whose left flank was the sea, and where there was little to do but rest. While we were there, G.H.Q. issued a request for the names of chaplains who would volunteer for service in Mesopotamia. I volunteered. I had done a year in France and Belgium and was very ready to see more of the war in other parts of the world. Remembering my urgent despatch to 'the Mediterranean', I guessed that this demand for more chaplains meant, as then, that some big thing was about to happen in Mesopotamia. My candidature was accepted, and I was given three weeks' leave to put my affairs in order before I went East again. In the last days of this furlough, before I must leave London for Devonport and the troopship that would take me to India, *en route* for the Persian Gulf, and Mesopotamia, I went to stay with Aunt Ida in her new home at Surbiton that I might bid her good-bye before going farther away than I had ever been yet, and possibly for a time that must be measured in years.

My arrival at her door was a surprise—a postcard had not reached her—and she gasped with delight to see me on the step. 'Oh, but if only I'd known you were coming!' she bewailed as she kissed me in the hall. 'I've no sheets ready.'

'Sheets!' I laughed, after my three years with the 'Poor Bloody Infantry' in their uncomfortable lodgments either behind or in the Line. 'I don't want sheets. I haven't seen a sheet for years.'

'What? Don't you have sheets?' she asked. So little did a woman obsessed by her pretty home, and the pretty things in it, grasp what the three years of war had been, and were.

'No, of course not. All I need is to roll up in a blanket.'

'Oh, but you can't do that. Dear, dear, what are we to do? Oh, why didn't I know you were coming? The posts are wicked. And the laundry hasn't been. You can't imagine what life is like here in England.'

'I'm sure it's ghastly,' I said.

As always, during the three days I stayed with her, she and I and Uncle Franz lived and ate in an upper 'work-room', furnished with odd chairs and a table, while downstairs her beautiful drawing-room and handsomely equipped dining-room were left tidy, polished, sheeted and closed. All was as it had been a dozen years before when, a boy of fourteen, I came to her pretty flat for lunch from St Paul's. No one entered the sheeted drawing-room except Uncle Franz who was allowed to visit the piano and play and play to himself for hours—her 'second Schumann'.

On our last night, while he was down there playing gently, she and I were sitting together in this work-room upstairs while she sewed, and after a time she became very silent, gazing down at the needlework in her hands. Though she was seventy-one now, she looked as pretty and pink as ever in a frilly tea-gown, and I had no fears for her health. To me she seemed one of my vigorous and vital 'Calder Girls', and the Calders lived long.

I did not know what she was hiding, nor did she divulge it. Courageously she hid it for my sake.

But after a rather long silence she spoke. 'It's thousands of miles you're going, isn't it, darling? When do you think you'll get back?'

I shrugged. 'Who can tell? The war will end one day, I suppose, but then there'll probably be months of waiting for demobilization, and after that the long journey home. Could be years, I imagine.'

She looked down at the plying of her needle, and watched it. Then began, 'Darling, I . . .' but could not go on.

'Yes?' I encouraged.

More work with the needle. Then—it was our last night, and she strengthened herself to speak. 'Darling, you do know that I was your mother, don't you?'

I answered with a smile, so that things might be easy for her. 'Of course, my dear. I've known it for years.'

'And that General Blake was your father?'

'Who else?' I covered this with a laugh. 'And am I proud of him?'

To this she faintly objected. 'He was not a good man. Not at all good.'

I shook my head, resisting this. 'To me he seemed good. Never anything but good to me.'

'Yes,' she conceded. 'He loved children.'

'And was wonderful with them.'

'Yes . . . yes, I suppose so. . . .' Was she thinking of Percy, at four years old in Switzerland, climbing resolutely behind Dum on the mountains?

'Children loved him,' I added. 'We all did.'

'Yes,' she agreed vaguely, but with such hidden reservations that I seemed to hear her sister Emily's voice: 'Keep your dreams. Keep your dreams.'

'And you've known this all these years,' she continued, 'without ever saying a word to me. Oh, I think it's been perfectly sweet of you.'

But it had not been 'perfectly' sweet. Certainly there had been in it a desire to spare her discomfort and pain, but perhaps an even larger and wholly selfish longing to keep adrift from the truth and so save myself from embarrassment.

'Oh, why,' she sighed, needling on, 'why haven't I been able to see more of you all this time?'

(Why, my dear, why?)

'General Blake always said I was not to be troubled.'

'I see.'

'He paid Emily well so that I should never be troubled. That was always his idea.'

'I see.'

'You do know, Ernest darling, how terribly I would have liked to . . . but it was so difficult—more difficult all those years ago than you can imagine nowadays.'

'I understand. I quite understand.'

And again, 'You're so sweet.' And again my thought, 'Not always. Far from it at times. Bitter at times,' but never saying this aloud because it was no moment to give her pain.

'We lived together in Paris and Switzerland as William and Florence Bell Raymond.'

'I know. I gathered this from that old baptism certificate written on the hotel notepaper in Argentières.'

'Oh, I'm so glad I was able to send you that.'

'I should have been helpless without it,' I began, but hastened on, lest any reproach lingered here, 'It enormously impressed the old padre, to be asked all about it, more than twenty years after he'd sat in that hotel and jotted it down.'

'Did it? I suppose it did. He was a nice man. I forget his name. Oh, I'm so glad if it helped you.'

And all the time Uncle Franz, downstairs, was playing his gentle incidental music to this first encounter with Truth. *Ex umbris et imaginibus.* . . . While I, hearing that gentle, dreaming pianist could only think, 'Yes, but it was Uncle Franz who made you do it, my dear.' Keeping this within myself.

'It really helped you in your career?'

'Yes. It did. And here I am.'

'I'm so glad it helped. And you look so marvellous in that uniform.'

In veritatem ad extremum.

Round the Cape I went to Bombay, to Basra in the Persian Gulf, up the Tigris to Baghdad, and on to a little Arab village, Deli Abbas, alongside which my new unit, the 9th Worcesters of the 39th Brigade, was encamped.

It was an easy life under E.P. tents in the dry Mesopotamian wilderness, except for the ruthless heat which could mount to 120° even beneath the shade of our doubly-roofed canvas. If the wind stirred on the baked mud outside, it came into the tents like a burning breath. We hung fresh water in water-skins outside the tents, right in the embrace of the sun, with the result that the water stayed cool, the skins sweating all round it and so insulating it from the sun's hot kiss and keeping its temperature even. Deli Abbas was on the thin upper waters of the Diyala, and in the topmost heat of midday we would soak our pyjamas in its stream and wear them wet as we took our siesta on our camp-beds.

We had no fighting to do—indeed I can't remember what the battalion did at Deli Abbas except sweat the days out. All this easy time on my hands I gave to writing my School–Gallipoli book, passionately writing it, because now I was plunged into love of it, having lost all memory of *God's Wheat*, sunk in the sea two years before. I wrote it, quite illegally, in Army Books 152 Field Service, those little brown books issued to officers for records of their correspondence. From where, or by what false pretences, I had possessed myself of these useful manuscript books I do not now recall, from the Orderly Room or the Quartermaster perhaps, but there must have been some jiggery-pokery somewhere, because the War Office did not issue them to junior officers for the writing of novels. As yet I had no title for the book. So naïve and ill-informed was I about the book market, and so foolishly sanguine about my forthcoming commodity for this market, that I imagined it would travel well enough on its own legs, no matter what cap it wore. When one day I thought of a title, I did it carelessly and nonchalantly, thinking 'This'll probably do,' and was unaware that by luck, not judgement, I had come upon a title as nearly perfect as a title could be, both in its fitness for the story told, and in its power to help the sales of a book. I had recently read again the 'eleven immortal words', of Simonides, his Epitaph on the Spartans who fell at Thermopylae, 'Tell the Spartans, stranger, that here we lie, obedient to their laws'—'the noblest group of words,' said Ruskin, 'ever uttered by man.' Stirred, as ever, by them, I thought of the title, *Tell England*.

These long hot undemanding days ended when we received orders to take our part in the advance to Kirkuk. Then, through several nights, we marched the hundred miles to Kirkuk, at that time no more than a hillside village on the upper waters of the Shatt-al-Adhaim. We came to Kirkuk ten years before the development of the oil-fields around; before the coming of the railway from Baghdad, and the piping of the petroleum to Syria and Lebanon. The Turks tried to defend the place, but our superior forces easily dispersed them. I sat watching the battle for Kirkuk (such as it was) on a hillock above the stream-bed, which was now little more than a procession of white dust and dry white stones. At times I was watching the firing and the sorties with my chin at rest on my right hand, just as I had imagined Poseidon on Samothrace watching the battle for Troy.

In the morning I went with other officers into Kirkuk to learn what we could do for the bed-ridden wounded and sick whom the Turks had been compelled to leave behind. The first hospital we entered was filthy beyond full mention, the excrement of those patients who could move at all lying by the side of their beds, the excrement of others lying around their bodies. It stank like the depths of a cesspool. An adequate description of this hospital would be T. E. Lawrence's famous pen-picture of the Turkish hospital at Damascus where an R.A.M.C. officer, disgusted at the filth and the corpses and the stench, slapped his face indignantly, supposing him to be the Arab in charge.

I returned to camp to find a mail had come up with the rations. There was a letter for me in Aunt Ida's hand. Her writing looked as firm and steady as ever, both on the envelope and in the letter as I opened it.

Pleased to have a letter I stood in the searing Arabian sun to read it. And the first line stopped my heart.

'Ernest darling, I have been trying to write but feared to pain you. I must brace myself to tell you the bad account the specialist gave three weeks ago of my condition, there is no hope of a recovery. I have got rapidly weaker and thinner since then and only milk is keeping me alive. I grieve that I shall not see you again, you are so far away. I know that this news will upset you but try to bear up bravely for the sake of all those you can minister to, and you can do so much good in the world. I have thought of our promised visit to Rome. You will think of me when you go there. I think of your happy visits to Paris, the old guide-book I have put your name in, and in my beautiful prayer-book. I bought a frame for your last lovely photograph, it was the last thing I did after leaving the specialist, it cost 11/6 which I wrote on your blank cheque. It was bought at the A. and N. Stores and is silver with a true lover's ornament at the top in the style we liked in Paris. I thought you would like that and I told Uncle F. to give it to you. It stands on the linen cupboard in my room with face turned towards my bed so that I can see it always. Now that I have written this I fear to send it knowing the pain it will give you. There are many things I would like to say and I should have loved to see more of you. You will be in my thoughts to the last, and remember always how dear you were to me.

'God bless and preserve you always and prosper your good work. Be fast friends with dear Percy always. He is so good now and writes beautiful letters of comfort to me. If it is possible I shall look down and bless you both. My darling, good-bye.'

No signature because there was no inch of room for it, but across the address, in vertical lines and in a hand still firm, there is a postscript. 'P.S. I am trying to get your socks done. I fear to send them as the ship might go down, and you will like my last piece of work done for you. I will give them to Aunt Mary for you.'

If ever I have walked far away from the eyes of men to be alone, to sob a little and to think, it was then. Thinking, I told myself that there must be no bitterness any more, but only understanding, a resolve which I have tried to keep—with lapses—ever since.

I will interpose here that after I returned from the war, good Uncle Franz put into my hand the old 1867 Paris guide-book with the initials

'G.F.B.' within, and told me that all the calf-bound poets in which Dum had inscribed 'Ida Calder' were to be mine. He put into my hand also my war-time photograph—in its silver frame surmounted by a true lovers' knot—which had stood on the cupboard by her bed, facing her always as she lay dying. And then another thing: a sealed envelope, which he passed to me with the words, 'She wanted you to have this.' It contained an ancient and staled sheet of paper with letters of the alphabet laboriously pencilled along ruled lines. In Ida's hand, also pencilled, were the words 'Ernest Raymond Aged 4 and 10 months Oct. 24th 1893'. It was the outcome of a first writing lesson in the kindergarten at Brook Green. Folded within this sheet of paper were three small locks of hair, each neatly, prettily, tied with pink or blue baby-ribbon. They were my hair, her hair (auburn and silver as if lately cut) and Dum's. In a separate fold of paper, secured by a now rusting pin, was another tiny lock of hair, prettily tied, with the same delicacy. Inside this paper she had pencilled, 'G.F.B.'s hair at the age of two'.

Later there came to me a large oil-painting of Ida, commissioned by Dum in the eighties, if one may judge from the dress. At a time when, perhaps, their love was at its brightest.

4

THE HUSH HUSH BRIGADE

At Deli Abbas we had been able to look eastward across sixty miles of shimmering desert towards a long swaying shadow on the sky. This was the long, continuous range of the Zagros and Pusht-i-Kuh mountains. It was the broad left shoulder of Persia. Up there Persia lay on its mountains and tablelands, stretching a hundred miles eastward to Afghanistan.

We looked often that way because the whole Mesopotamian Expeditionary Force had heard a great rumour of 'The Hush Hush Brigade' operating in secrecy and mystery up there. What the secret and purpose of this Hush Hush Brigade might be we did not know. The most we knew was that it was commanded by Major-General Dunsterville who had a picturesque reputation as the original of Kipling's Stalky in *Stalky and Co.* and for his activities on the North-West Frontier and in China; and that it was no brigade in the ordinary sense but an extremely odd contingent composed almost entirely of officers and N.C.O.s. Seventy officers and more than a hundred N.C.O.s, the rumour said; picked men from various parts of the Empire who had experience of warfare on strange frontiers, or the gift of languages. *Emigré* Russians were among them, it was whispered mysteriously; men who had fled the Revolution and could speak Russian and Persian. Would-be know-alls declared that the purpose of Dunsterville's singular assembly, long lost from our sight up there, was to raise, train, and officer an army of Armenians in Georgia—at Tiflis or Baku—who would else be massacred by the Turks, and use them to bar the way across the Caspian into Persia, which was not only the right flank of our Mesopotamian army but also a highway towards Afghanistan and India. Cynics suggested that this was a normal British blend of altruism and self-interest: the Hush Hush Brigade was hastening nobly to save the poor Armenians but also to use them for our own ends, protecting our flank, protecting India, and, best of all, saving the Baku oil from rude Turkish hands and shipping it safely across the Caspian.

The whispering cynics and know-alls had most of the truth. The Hush Hush Brigade, or 'Dunsterforce', as it was more officially called, has since been described by historians as the 'strangest mission of the First World War'. It *was* an astonishing and typically British attempt to achieve with one gifted leader (who could speak Russian) and a motley circus of hand-picked men a dozen things which, on the face of them needed an assured line of communications: to protect the Armenian population of Baku; to turn terrified men into a gallant militia; to set up and support an independent republic in Georgia, comprising Armenians, Georgians, and Azerbaijanies; to use them as a buffer state between the Turco-German forces and the Baku oil; to get this oil to our armies; and to have raised an initial barrier across the road to India. We having captured Baghdad, the old German aspiration 'Berlin–Baghdad' might now become 'Berlin–Baku–Afghanistan–India'. So we sent Kipling's Stalky and a hundred and seventy men or so, regardless of the fact that the line of communications from Mesopotamia's ultimate base at Basra to Dunsterville in Baku would be more than a thousand miles over mountains and deserts and a starving, hostile country. A thousand miles from sea to sea—from Persian Gulf to Caspian.

After the battle for Kirkuk our 39th Brigade had dropped again into ease and boredom—here a little training, there a little battle practice, now a route march—when—dream upon dream for me—just when the rumours of the Hush Hush Brigade were fascinating me more and more; just when I was thinking how lucky they were to have some mysterious commission to pursue in the romantic uplands of Persia—or wherever else they had got to; just then the Order came to our brigade—to ours alone of all the brigades in Mesopotamia—that we were to proceed forthwith into Persia and be attached to Dunsterville. Britain had realized at last that if he and his variegated company of officers and N.C.O.s were to achieve their shadowed aims, they would need at least one brigade. And ours was to be the brigade. The 'strangest mission of the war', and we were to be part of it.

So our four battalions, Worcesters, Warwicks, Gloucesters, and North Staffords, were hastily translated, in lorries, vans and cars, over the Zagros Mountains to Kermanshah, Kangavar and Hamadan. This mountain road was bad; indeed it seemed hardly a road at all, and the Sappers had to go ahead of us, repairing it, remaking it; and yet it was one of the greatest roads in the world; perhaps the greatest; the road of the Great Kings, Cyrus, Darius, Xerxes, and of their galloping satraps from their capital, Ecbatana (now Hamadan), to Babylon and the ends of the Persian Empire, which were almost the ends of the known Earth. One night, half-way to Hamadan, we camped or, rather, 'bivouacked', on a hillside. The valley below us was but a fold in the mountains, and when we awoke in the morning we saw on the opposite hill a small forty-pounder tent, obviously of British make, with a makeshift 'bivvy' beside it. Now, when *we* slept, we had to station sentries around us lest the Kurds came—with knives—to steal rifles from this tent or that. Who then, in the name of sense, could be sleeping alone up yonder in a British forty-pounder tent, unafraid of Arabs, Persians, and Kurds; safe among all?

We heard, before we went on, that it was Gertrude Bell, with her bearer or guide.

From Hamadan we marched some hundred and fifty miles along a fairly good posting road to Kasvin, myself marching in comfort on an excellent camel; from Kasvin on its 5,000-foot level we dropped down and down in cars and lorries, through ever greener, damper, and more densely wooded country, to no-feet-at-all; to below sea-level and the rims of the Caspian basin. From the port of Enzeli on the Caspian we were hurried in a good but smelly ship, the *Kruger*, to Dunsterville in Baku, the Russians' chief seaport on the Caspian, and one of the great oil towns of the world. We found ourselves in a fine half-western, half-eastern city, embraced by a curve of dry hills; the gutters of its fine streets, despite the imposing mansions, schools, and luxury hotels, literally ran with oil and water from the neighbouring wells—or so they did in my day.

The story I want to tell here is less a full and detailed narrative of our hush-hush adventures in Baku, than a record of the adventures of a manuscript—those Army Books 152, Field Service, which held, without warranty, several chapters of my Gallipoli novel. They went safely in my valise to Baku. Often on the Persian tableland when we bedded down for the night I had taken them out of the valise and added new paragraphs which I had dreamed up on my camel. These night camps in transit had been inspiring places in which to write a novel, with the tall poplars around us, so different from the palms of Mesopotamia, the mountains always in sight, purple and blue-grey, the stars overhead surely more numerous and sparkling than in any place I'd come to before, and the bells of our baggage-train camels tinkling in the transport lines where they lay couched and camped.

The Army Books 152 that I had brought into Baku were thus nearly full.

§

To understand the Fall of Baku after our desperate fight to save it, a glance at the whole picture is necessary.

It was always Dunsterville's aim to get to Baku, or, better, Tiflis, and there organize the Georgians and Armenians against the Turkish 'Caucasus–Islam' army, covering the oil-fields as he did so, and controlling the Caspian. Who holds Baku holds the Caspian. But he could not get to Baku until in July the anti-British Bolsheviks were overthrown by the 'Social Revolutionaries', who called themselves the 'Central-Caspian Dictatorship' and actually invited our aid. Dunsterville went in at once with such officers and men as he could spare from Persia; our 39th Brigade followed after him in a broken succession of trips across the Caspian.

Once there, the brigade's task was to stiffen with disciplined troops the largely amateur army of Armenians, Georgians and Baku volunteers. These inexperienced and nervous soldiers could have manned an almost perfect defence line along the dry hills and cliffs, with its flanks, left and right (since Baku sits on a narrow peninsula) resting on the sea. Instead they were holding a far inferior line, much too close to the town, and enabling the Turks to bombard city, harbour and ships.

We came, and now the English Midlands, represented by Staffords, Warwicks, Worcesters and Gloucesters, stood at separate stations among these men of Baku to hearten them in their fight, infuse a little discipline into them, and so save their city from capture and the Armenians from massacre. But unfortunately many of the Baku irregulars, now that these splendid professionals had arrived from England, decided that they could safely leave the fighting to them while they took a frequent French leave so as to drink tea with their wives or to visit their girls and their pals in the town. This was not true of all; they were a mixed-up lot, some of them steady men, and brave; and let mention be made of a few Armenian women who stood with their rifles at their husbands' sides. All that will concern my story here is the dawn of September 14th and the whole of that day till midnight. Headquarters knew from an Arab deserter that September 14th was to be the day of the Turks' great assault. On that day, heavily reinforced with men and guns, they intended to take the town.

And, sure enough, at 4 a.m. on that day the bombardment began. I was then in a large school building facing the main street of Baku, with a quartermaster, a doctor, a very young officer with a new draft, some transport men, a few sick, and two cooks. I don't think we were forty in all. The first shells falling on the town awoke me and, on my quickly rising, the Quartermaster, leaping up too, said simply, 'This is it.'

I asked permission to go up to the Line, and the Q.M. who, as an old ranker and senior combatant among us, had assumed command by consent of all, asked H.Q., in the course of a telephone request for emergency orders, if I could have this permission. He put down the phone, grinned, and told me, 'Brigade Major says "For Christ's sake stop him. The situation is critical. The Turks may be here any minute. They're only a few hundred yards away." And I regret to tell you, Padre, he made the usual joke. He said, "God alive, doctors are necessary evils; padres unnecessary ones."'

We had an early breakfast in a small class-room. It was a meal made uneasy by a background of rifle and machine-gun fire drawing closer—or so we imagined. Suddenly a man came in from a front room. 'Come and look, sir,' he said.

We hurried to the windows of the front room and looked. Down the steep street from the hills and the oil derricks the Armenian volunteers were running—running probably none knew whither. Possibly each man was running lest the man behind should run faster than he. A few came tearing down in carts. Some drew donkeys on which were thrown and bumped their wounded, sackwise. Now and then came a lorry, a madman at its wheel, driving down the centre of the road as imperiously as a London fire-engine. At a cross-roads below our windows a few Russian officers were standing with drawn swords, trying to stem the torrent. But their yelling and brandishing were futile. The stream swept past or round them: men, carts, donkeys, lorries.

'What's it all about?' I asked the Q.M.

'Seems the Turks attacked at the strongest point in the Line where, accordingly, we'd left only Armenians. These are the Armenians.'

'Then the Turks should be here at any moment?'

'That's what the Brigade Major said.'

'Well, what do we do?'

'Dunno. This is panic. Ever seen it before?'

But even as we spoke we saw a British soldier hurrying up the hill from the Hotel Metropole at its bottom. As the Metropole was our forward Headquarters, it seemed likely he was a runner with orders. He shot breathless into the school and handed his message to the Q.M.

'H'mmm. . . .' said the Q.M. 'Brief. . . .'

'What does it say?'

'Says "To O.C. School. Arm all and if necessary hold building to last man."'

Read now, these words sound 'corny'. But they were the exact words. Doubtless there were alarm and haste at Headquarters and a man used the first words that came into his head. Traditional words. One had to consider Turks, not clichés.

We armed all, cooks, batmen, sick, transport men; and the Q.M. sent them to the ground-floor front windows, two to each window. With the butts of their rifles they knocked all the glass out of the windows and sent it crashing in shards and splinters on to the pavement below. Then rested their rifles on the sills and waited.

Armenians were still running down the street. It looked as if more and more of the Line had given way. As I watched this rout I heard a voice say, 'Look, sir, look. Here comes Baku's Last Hope.'

I looked the way he was pointing—down the street and past the cathedral. And my heart knocked with pride.

Of the fine scene which I saw I wrote this afterwards: 'Marching *up* the street, and so against the rout, came a body of perhaps a hundred men; they marched in good order, four by four, with rifles slung; men of all classes and all clothes; prosperous men in frock-coats, Russian workmen in smocks, Tartars in their fur hats and sheepskin coats, the braver Armenians in varied dress, street beggars with naked feet. Regular Russian officers marched at their head. And on the pavement walked or ran many of their women, some weeping.

'"Volunteers to man the breach," said a voice. "Then there *are* men in Baku."

'"And here comes the second line," said the Q.M.

'Some five hundred paces behind the first group came just such another: a hundred men of all classes, marching in fours with rifles slung; Russian officers leading them. Women too, on the pavement, some with red-cross brassards now, and one with a rifle slung behind her shoulders.'

Our boys cheered and cheered them till they were out of sight.

The street emptied after this. I suppose there were no more Armenians to come down from the front. All the doors of the large houses were bolted, and the shutters up in the shops. Occasionally a white-faced woman looked out from a high window. We laughed when a little dog came from under an arch and looked up and down the street, surprised. A silence and pause seemed to have settled on the morning.

What had happened was told to me next day by Dunsterville himself. The Turks, after breaking through the Armenians, stood on the hills, hesitating. Our North Staffords had given them so ferocious a fight that their commander, a cautious fellow, sought a safer estimate of the English in the Line. The North Staffords were the heroes of September 14th at Baku. They nearly saved a city.

Meanwhile, apart from sporadic fire up on the hills and a rare shell on the town, silence possessed the long street.

Someone said, 'It doesn't look as though we're going to be slaughtered to the last man just yet. What about some lunch? Shouldn't we demobilize one of the cooks, sir?'

An acceptable idea, and the cook contrived a meal of bully rissoles, rice (of which there was a plentiful supply from the paddy fields around Enzeli) stewed figs and—caviare. Yes, caviare, for was not the Caspian the home of caviare? It was a free issue to our men in Baku, who complained about it wretchedly, calling it 'the sweepings of the fish-market'.

While we were finishing the meal a runner from H.Q. stood in the doorway. He handed a message to the Q.M. who read it to us. 'Well, here's a chit which says, "Abandon all kit and stores and report to H.Q. in full strength at once."'

We surmised that this meant we were to go up to the breach in the Line. But 'abandon all kit'? *Abandon?* It suggested we would never see kit and stores again.

The men were withdrawn from the shattered windows and paraded in the corridor. As we marched out of the school the old white-bearded caretaker and his wife stood with wistful eyes, watching us go. Wondering what their fate would be when the Turks came, we acknowledged with salutes their sad farewells, for the old man was taking off his hat to each officer as he passed, and the old lady curtseying.

Down in the square before the doors of the Metropole a staff officer, selecting a runner, said, 'Follow this guide.' And the guide led us—not up the hill towards the broken line but down towards the quays and the ships.

Evacuation! We were to be allowed to live. It was only after this moment of staggering sweet relief that I remembered I'd left my Army Books 152, the manuscript of *Tell England*, with all the rest of my kit in the school. And now I should never see it again. This sudden memory was a deathly sickness hardly less than the sickness of death itself, from which I was imagining we had just been saved. Two years of ardent labour lost. Could I ever recover the old inspiration and rebuild the story as it had been? *God's Wheat* had gone to the bottom of the Mediterranean, and now its successor lay on a Baku class-room floor, ready to be tossed by a Turk tomorrow on to a general bonfire. When I heard that order, 'Abandon all kit', I had half-suspected that it might mean evacuation and escape from almost certain death, and in that moment of hope I had forgotten all about *Tell England*, all about the desire to be a writer, all about my 'ruling passion'. More than these, obliterating all memory of these, was the sudden readiness to live.

We had not marched a hundred yards towards the ships before a voice shouted, 'Halt those men. There's been a mistake.'

I looked round and saw that the voice came from a staff-colonel, hurrying after us.

'It's a mistake,' he repeated. 'Take 'em back and hold that building. If necessary, you must hold it to the last man.'

'But—' began the Q.M.

'There are no bloody buts about it. Take 'em back.'

A reprieve was cancelled.

The men swung round in slovenly fashion, grumbled, joked, and began to march in loose, unwilling order and out of step, back to the school with its promise of death. A quartermaster-sergeant, who'd joined us from somewhere, turned round to me and said, 'Well, sir, I reckon it's sacrificing good lives for nothing,' and before I could answer, began slanging the men behind him for being out of step. "Ere! Smarten up a bit. You ain't Armenians. And cut that jawing. You didn't join the Army and expect to live, did yer?'

They laughed a loud denial and a blasphemous, and marched back up the street, singing sardonically 'Only one more bloody route march' to the tune of 'What a friend we have in Jesus'.

Back in the school, they laid their rifles on the window-sills again, waiting for—what?

As I look back upon that day, I remember with surprise how little shaken I was by the renewed prospect of death in minutes, perhaps, or before the day darkened. There was fear of pain, certainly, fear of a tearing bullet or, worse, of a bayonet's thrust, but not of the fact of death. The thought came frequently, 'Well, it's come to a few million others during the last four years, and here it is—come for me.' And now and again there came most definitely (as there always does, even

L

till now, when I think of death) a dim hope which had a taste of sweet-ness: 'I may meet Dum again.' Only on that afternoon the thought went on, 'Soon. In an hour, perhaps.' And it helped me.

Still, it is ever strange to me that my strong expectation of death in that Baku class-room was what I can only describe as 'fairly peaceful'.

After about an hour a young officer came from Headquarters to tell us 'what it was all about'; and the substance of his words, so far as they come back to me out of the past, was this. 'It's *some* story. When the Armenians broke on our left, early this morning, Dunsterville went to their general and said "Unless your troops'll fight, I'm not keeping my men here to be scuppered by the Turks. They've done all the fighting so far; they've saved your town half a dozen times, and their reward's not going to be a capture by the Turks. But if you can induce your people to fight, I'll stand with you. The only way to save the town now is by a resolute counter-attack to drive the Turk from the commanding position he's won, and unless you're prepared to help my men in this, out of your town we go." Fine; they all went into committee, as they always do, and after an hour or two of oratory, passed a resolution to fight to the death. That accounts, I imagine, for the bright lads you saw walking up to the Line.'

We asked who held the Turks at bay while the committee-men unburdened their souls in oratory.

'Who? Need you ask?' he said. 'The Staffords and the Worcesters and the Warwicks. Our good old 39th Brigade. They've given Johnny Turk such knocks that the poor fellow is a little confused. At any rate Dunsterville can't understand why he doesn't make one mighty drive and walk in. And now hush! Not a word. All's ready for the evacuation. An hour ago it was almost determined on. That's why that order came to you in error. But Dunsterville swears he'll stand by the Russian officers and the city fathers if they'll make that counter-attack with us. But he hasn't much hope they can persuade any troops to undertake it. So if you get an order like the last you'll know it's all over and we'd best get to the ships as well as we can.'

'But will the Government let us escape and get to the ships?'

A shrug. 'If not, we fight our way to them.'

This second order came a few minutes after four o'clock. It was worded as before: 'Abandon all stores and report to H.Q.' But this time one of us did not abandon quite all of his stores. I hastily rummaged in my valise for those Army Books 152, got hold of them, and stowed them in a slung haversack with a shirt or two and a sock or two. I took one last look at that old sleeping valise which had been with me during three years of war, and at all that it still contained, wondering which Turk, or Turks, would rejoice in those clothes tomorrow. It was with a sigh that I left it, though I was happy thinking of the manuscript books in my bag. Sometimes I even felt for them with my hand. We went down the street again; and this time our march to the ships was not interrupted by Headquarters; nor did it encounter anything more hostile than the scowls of the populace. But we were among the first to be seen marching significantly to the sea. What when we would have to get a thousand men down from the hills and through a hostile town? Walking pleasantly along by the side of the Q.M., I said of a sudden, 'I've done this before.'

He asked what I meant. I said, 'I began the war in 1915 running from the enemy to the ships at Gallipoli, and now, just when the war is palpably ending, I'm at the only spot in the world where we're running to the sea for our lives.'

'But surely, Padre,' he submitted after some meditation, 'you've learned that the one thing the British do extraordinarily well is retreating. Think of Mons, and Suvla and Helles, and now Baku. We do it in such good order; and damned well.'

There was a spice of truth in this, and I had to say for the comfort of us both, 'Yes, but we always win the last battle, which is the one that really matters.'

'Oh, yes,' he agreed.

I need tell no more of the Fall of Baku, except to report that between nine o'clock and midnight we contrived with much difficulty, and amid many doubts and anxieties, to get all our troops, including the sick and wounded, on to our ship, the *Kruger*, which was lying against a jetty. No one molested them, no Armenians, Georgians or revolutionary Russians threatened them with guns. No armed picket halted them at the jetty. Perhaps the reputation of our English Midlanders as fighters came down the streets with them, guarding their flanks, left and right.

A little after midnight, on a smooth sea and in a starry darkness— just as at Gallipoli—the Hush Hush Brigade and the 39th who'd joined it sailed quietly away.

§

Next morning, under bright sunlight, I stood on the promenade deck of the *Kruger*, looking over the Caspian Sea as we sailed back to Enzeli. We were now out of sight of any land. I could see nothing of the Baku peninsula, nothing of Persia to the south or Turkestan to the east. This land-locked sea might have been one of the world's oceans, except for its calm this morning.

The calm sea stirred thoughts of peace—the end of a world at war and the long-forgotten, hardly imaginable peace that was undoubtedly approaching the world again. On the Western Front there was every sign of a German collapse. In Serbia the Franco-Serbian troops, aided by British and Greeks, were driving the Bulgarians before them. In Palestine General Allenby was putting the Turks to rout. Everywhere our enemies were on the run. We were the only British with our backs to the foe.

It was while I was thinking this, leaning on the rail, that a voice behind me said, 'Well, Padre, did you enjoy your stay in Baku?'

I swung round. A general officer speaking to me—no less. A general with red tabs on his lapels, gold oak-leaves on the peak of his cap, strange medals on his breast, and high Russian boots reaching to his knees. A handsome military face with a grey moustache, hair still dark, and eyes that lay among humorous wrinkles. Dunsterville. 'Stalky'. The gold oak-leaves and the high Russian boots told me that.

This was my only meeting with Dunsterville during the war (though I had many happy meetings with him after it), and it is not for me to write my assessment of him here. If you would know General Dunsterville as he was, you must read his humorous and generous book, *The Adventures of Dunsterforce*. The whole man is there with all his military skills, his subtle, laughing diplomacy, his unwearying tolerance of human weaknesses especially among Eastern peoples, and even something like an amused affection for the Persians and Armenians who everywhere failed him. I long for people to read this well-written, exciting, and, above all, gaily humorous book. But it was published in 1920, and I suppose it is dead now. If words of mine could raise it again, I would wish to do so, and to raise with it the honour of General Dunsterville.

As a junior officer (and a chaplain or 'unnecessary evil' withal) speaking with the Commander-in-Chief, I was nervous at first, but not for long; too much laughter began to leap between us.

'Take a look at that flag, Padre,' he said, glancing towards the flag which the *Kruger* was flying. 'What do you think of it?'

'I'm afraid I haven't thought about it at all, sir.'

'Well, you should. It's extremely odd. To me it seems like a flash of light illuminating the ludicrous and somewhat murky events in which we've all been taking part.'

Observing with amusement my incomprehension, he went on, 'It happens to be the old Russian flag flying upside down. When we acquired this ship for ourselves, the local committees, or Soviets, or whatever they are, wanted me to fly the Red flag, but I told them that, while I was perfectly willing to become a Bolshevik, I had no authority to commit my country in this fashion, so they compromised by letting me fly the old Russian flag, provided I flew it upside down. To which I said, "Oh, sure. Most certainly"; and there it is, and none of them know that the Russian flag upside down turns into the Serbian flag, the flag of one of our allies. So here am I, Padre: a British general running a ship on an inland sea which has never known a British keel before—a ship named after a good old Boer President who gave us a hell of a lot of trouble lately—sailing towards a Persian port under the Serbian flag, after a sorry failure to relieve from the Turks an Armenian army in a city governed by Russian revolutionaries. If you can pick your way through that, you'll get some idea of the job we were given to do here.'

I could detect beneath the laughter his sadness that, after all he'd done, his mission *looked* a failure. I was even more sure of this sadness as he stood there telling me (almost the least important unit in his fighting army) of all that he believed he'd achieved in Persia with a handful of handpicked officers and men (*Stalky and Co.*, though he didn't say this; it was only I who thought it) and the thousand rifles we'd brought to him. Such things as these he told me.

'If we'd not been in Persia in April, May, and June the Jangali army with its German leaders and Turkish armament'—the Jangalis were hotly anti-British Persian revolutionaries—'would have met no opposition on their road to Kasvin, Teheran, and Hamadan, and the population of these towns would at once have raised the Jangali banner and joined the Revolution. All North Persia would have been overrun with Bolshevism, and all the British in Persia, the diplomats, the missionaries, the staffs of the Imperial Bank of Persia and of the Indo-European Telegraph might have been lucky to escape with their lives. Then with North Persia in a state of Bolshevism, and the rest of Persia following suit and linking up with Turkestan, the whole of Central Asia and Afghanistan would be thrown into chaos, and the way lie open to India. This is what the Germans were playing for in these parts, and it makes my blood run cold to think how near they were to success. I think it may be fairly claimed that it was our small force which halted all this. After all, we defeated the Jangalis. That's just a little of what I think we arrested—to say nothing of what might have happened to the right flank of our army in Mesopotamia. I hope General Marshall is thinking of this sometimes, as he pushes on merrily to Mosul.'

Possibly all he said was true. I had not then, and have not now, the strategic or political knowledge to endorse his every word. All I know is that Dunsterville knew much about India and Afghanistan and the East. But I have read historians since who argue that his notion of the Germans advancing over the Persian mountains to Afghanistan and India was logistically untenable, and his Quixotic attempt to save Baku with a force of barely a thousand men, and a line of communications a thousand miles long, was strategically and logistically a blunder. Who's right I don't know; but in the last few words of his book there lies a hidden pathos, so abrupt and brief they are.

'The only task now left was to call the roll and assure myself that not a single man had been left behind in Baku. . . . Orders were received for the dispersal of the Force, and their place has since been taken by regular troops. . . . So ends the story of the adventures of Dunsterforce.'

Which, without word of self-justification or self-pity, masks the fact that he had been recalled home as one who had failed in his task.

5

THE VOYAGE HOME

Less than two months after Baku's fall came the Armistice and peace. Under the terms of the Armistice the British were allowed to occupy Baku, and our 39th Brigade, in acknowledgement of their fine effort to save the city, was given its orders to return there and serve as its army of occupation. So we all took ship from Enzeli again, recrossed the Caspian, and sailed into the familiar harbour from which we had slipped away in the dark. Most of us were billeted in a stately block of luxury flats, and from the windows of this ornate building I could look across the main street and see the windows of the school where we'd prepared ourselves for a 'last stand'. That building was now empty and swept, if not garnished, so that my old valise with all my kit in it, except those manuscript books, must have long since been taken from the class-room floor. Some thundering Turk was probably wearing my clothes.

Five months in Baku, largely spent in enjoying ourselves: on football fields, at the Opera House now alive again, on horses galloping over the dry hills where we had fought and failed; or, if we were Other Ranks—officers had to conceal their private engagements—wandering along the streets in the company of Russian or Tartar girls. God alone knew the name of the language in which these loving couples communicated, but they looked happy enough. Five such months, and I received at last my orders to return to England for demobilization.

This long voyage was remarkable for two occurrences, one a sharp surprise, the other deeply poignant.

It was 18 April 1919, Good Friday, that I set my face for home. Both the officers and men in our troop train, leaving Baku on the Caspian for Batoum on the Black Sea, were disappointed at having to entrain on Good Friday; they had hoped to be in Baku, and not in a train, on Easter Day because they understood that on an Easter morning they could kiss every girl they met, provided they first said, 'Christ is risen'.

Actually they were well at sea over this, because they had not yet grasped that the calendar of the Orthodox Church runs differently from ours.

Four days and nights we spent in that train, crossing the whole of Transcaucasia. Caucasia from Baku to Tiflis revealed itself as a drear country, all bleak desolate hills and dry sandy wastes, but after Tiflis it broke into a lovely part of Switzerland, all wooded mountains, luxuriant valleys, and hurrying streams. I suppose we could not have chosen a better time to make this run through Russia's Switzerland. The nearer and lower mountains were dense with fresh green foliage, the orchards in the valleys were a mass of blossom, the rivers were full and impatiently propelled onward by melting snows. They tumbled along in weirs and rapids and cataracts. And it was not too late for the farther and higher peaks of the Caucasus range to be white with snow. In valleys and on hill-slopes stood chalets and log-cabins and ruined medieval castles. A pleasant factor in this journey, but one for which I have no explanation, was a habit of the local pigs to come snorting on to any wayside platform and greet our train as it halted there. And I may say that, being only a troop train, we seemed to be halted at every wayside platform so that more important trains could pass.

Batoum at last; and here happened the first of the remarkable things.

We were delayed two or three days in a rest camp at Batoum while we waited for the *Nile*, a large liner that would take us across the Black Sea to Constantinople and Salonika. In this rest camp a young officer from a local regiment said to me, 'You were in the fall of Baku, weren't you?'

I said yes, and he went on, 'Well, do you know who we've got here?'

'No,' I said, and wondered whom he could mean. 'Who?'

'None other than the C.-in-C. of the Turkish army that captured Baku.'

'But who *was* the C.-in-C.?' I asked. 'I have never till this moment even heard his name.'

'We know him as Noury Pasha—I think his name is probably Nouri or Nury—my Turkish is not good—but he must be quite a thorough sort of bloke, because he's our prisoner awaiting trial for the massacre of 20,000 Armenians—or some such number—which he ordered or permitted directly he got into the town.'

Deeply interested, I begged, unhopefully, was there any chance I could see the old man?

'Do you speak French?' he asked. And I said, 'Pretty badly, but I can make myself understood.'

'Well, the poor old boy's hungry for books to read—'

I interrupted to suggest, mistakenly, that he probably wanted to get his mind off those 20,000 Armenians, but the young man demurred,

'Oh, no. No, no. They don't worry him at all. One of our officers in charge of him, a jolly bloke, was tactless enough to mention these Armenians and ask him what precisely was the point of massacring quite so many; and he just shrugged and said, "They would have harassed my troops." You see, Armenians are just vermin to him. His only trouble at the moment is this hunger for books. He can read English. Got any books you could give him?'

Now, this chanced to be the one thing I could do. As a chaplain, I could get access to Red Cross 'Books for the Troops' and, all said and done, I thought that Noury was a troop in himself and, as the chief of our enemies, provided a top-class opportunity for obeying St Paul's injunction, 'If thine enemy hunger, feed him.'

I was given the books very readily, and the same young officer escorted me to a pretty little villa, standing in its own grounds, where Noury was incarcerated in an upper room. Sentries with fixed bayonets stood about the house, and we had to pass two more inside it: one in the entrance passage and one outside the door of his room.

We entered, and I saw not at all what I had half expected, which was some heavy old bashaw with a forked blue beard, a turban on his head and a scimitar in his sash, but a youthful slender man, exquisitely tailored in a grey suit which might have come—not from Savile Row, for it had a continental look—but from one of the best tailors in Paris. He rose courteously and bowed. The C.-in-C. of the Caucasus–Islam Army, the conqueror of Baku, bowing to me.

On the colour-washed walls of his bare room there were many large drawings—in charcoal, I think—some in the quick, fluent style of Toulouse Lautrec; others of appetizing girls in the manner of *La Vie Parisienne*. Some had the swirling and seductive lines of Beardsley.

After I had shown him the books and discussed them, my escort told me these pictures were Noury's own work. They were the ways he eased the dullness and, no doubt, the anxiety, and, possibly, the sexual frustrations of this imprisonment.

I complimented him on them, and they were worth my compliments; he was a gifted cartoonist.

'Sit down,' he said, pointing to a chair, 'and allow me to do a little picture of you.'

One suspected that in his present hazardous situation he was ready to enlist the goodwill of any British officer. A chaplain's uniform to the ignorant is not unimpressive, with its black shoulder stars, black stock, and black crosses, so perhaps Noury, Turk and infidel, had no notion of the impotence it signified.

Saying I should be happy to have his picture of me, I sat down, and this dapper young man pulled up the only other chair in the room for himself and, perched on it, drew and drew, glancing at me, while I thought, 'If only I could have known, when Baku was falling about my ears that the general then ordering my capture or my slaughter, would, six months hence, be drawing my picture in his prison room.'

With a bow he gave me the picture, signed in both Turkish and English characters. It was a skilful piece of work, if not a good likeness (I hope). We exchanged farewell bows, and I came away thinking, 'This is the most interesting souvenir I've brought out of the war'; and I've since lost it.

What happened to Noury I've never known. Did somebody once tell me that this awkward prisoner escaped from a gaol? If so, I often wonder if his door was left ajar.

§

Westward across the Black Sea; southward into the Bosphorus, and there before us, aglow in the morning sunlight, was Constantinople, on its seven hills like Rome. All its mosques and towers and monuments and palaces were looped (like the 'Sultan's turret') in nooses of light. We dropped anchor off the Golden Horn—I don't know why—and none of us was allowed ashore, but, at least, here we were—at Constantinople. Those who had hitherto known this city of Constantine pointed out for us the more famous places: the Seraglio Palace just there on our starboard side, the column of Theodosius, the Tower of Christ in the old Genoese and Venetian trading quarter, and the many mosques—Sultan Ahmed's, Sultan Suleiman's, Mahomet the Second's —with, of course the great dome, the semi-domes, and the minarets of St Sophia dominating all; St Sophia, the Emperor Justinian's church, a Christian church for nine hundred years till the capture of Constantinople by the Turks who made it their greatest mosque of all. The legend goes that as the Turks entered the town in 1453 a priest, celebrating Mass at the High Altar of St Sophia, picked up chalice, paten, and consecrated elements and walked straight into the eastern wall, which opened to receive him; and that neither he nor his sacred vessels, nor the Host, were ever seen again.

As I gazed at Constantinople, I remembered bidding good-bye to my Vicar at his Prittlewell vicarage and saying, 'Good-bye, Vicar. I'm off to Constantinople, and I'll send you a picture postcard of St Sophia when I get there. I only hope I'll be there when Sir Ian marches in.'

Well, I'd got there in the end, four years too late and only by a route half-way round the world—across the Atlantic, round the Cape, across the Indian Ocean, up the Persian Gulf and the Tigris, over the Persian mountains, across the Caspian and Caucasia and the Black Sea—but here we were. There was Constantinople aglow in the sun.

Yes, we do tend to win the last battle of all.

I got that postcard from a bum-boat and managed to get it posted from Constantinople, with its apologies for four years' delay. On the other, Asiatic, side of our anchored ship was the town of Scutari where Florence Nightingale set up her hospital and walked round with her lamp, but which for fifteen hundred years has been the plague of all theological students because it (or part of it) was the old Chalcedon where the Fourth General Council of the Church in A.D. 451, condemning the Monophysites, promulgated (and may God help us to comprehend it) the only orthodox interpretation of Christ as both God and man.

The last I saw of Constantinople was the sun setting behind the Golden Horn and turning it, aptly enough, into a golden streak of water shaped like the horn of a ram. Darkness enclosed us as we crossed the Sea of Marmara, heading south-west for the Dardanelles.

The Dardanelles. Since that day I have often declared that my most emotional moment in the war was *after* the war. The sun, coming up as the Sea of Marmara narrowed, and as we steamed into the Dardanelles Straits, opened for me the day that was to hold this moment. The day was April 29th, 1919, four years and four days since the 29th Division, Dublins, Munsters, Lancashires, Worcesters, with the aid of that old collier, the *River Clyde*, our Trojan Horse laden with men, stormed W Beach and V Beach under Cape Helles, in their opening attempt to reach the heights that commanded the Narrows of the Dardanelles.

You will remember that Major Allanson with his Ghurkas and Lancashires caught a glimpse of the Narrows when they seized the ridge of Sari Bair, but that they were driven off in the morning by Kemal Attaturk; and that no one else on Gallipoli, whether at Suvla, Anzac or Helles ever saw the Narrows again. And now I stood on a deck, my eyes aching to see at last these Narrows. We had passed the

town of Gallipoli which gave its name to the Peninsula and, yes, the
Straits were narrowing and narrowing till at last we went into what was
a strait indeed, with Chanak in Asia on one side of it and Kilid Bahr in
Europe on the other. These two clasp the neck of the Narrows. I was
looking down on the Narrows.

That this was where Leander swam across the Hellespont to Hero his
love; that this was where Byron in imitation swam too; that this was
where the Argonauts came sailing in search of the Golden Fleece—all
this I forgot. All that mattered to me now was that there on the
European side, in the lovely pellucid Grecian air, lay the long shape of
the Gallipoli Peninsula. There were the empty dug-outs of the Turks
and Germans; and worming its way among the hills went the road
down which their reinforcements and guns poured for the defence of
Cape Helles. My heart nearly stood still as we came in sight of the
Allies' sector beneath old Achi Baba—Achi Baba no more than a
gentle swell—and the scrubby ground, the 'few acres of scrub', where I
had so often ridden, dodging shells from Achi Baba or Asiatic Annie.

I was proud to be the only one among the men around me who had
been on the Peninsula and to be pointing out the places of interest to an
audience enthralled: Achi Baba, the French dug-outs, the Boyau de la
Plage beneath the cliff, De Tott's Battery, Sedd-el-Bahr, the redoubt
above Cape Helles, and then—suddenly—red with rust, listing, empty,
abandoned, the *River Clyde*, still grounded off V Beach, where we had
left her in that midnight darkness four years before. And not the *River
Clyde* alone: a cable's length away, green with weed, lapped by idle
waves, but motionless like the back of a dead whale, lay the long keel
of the *Majestic*, oldest battleship of all, which, torpedoed in the sunrise
of a May morning, had turned turtle and now rested, deck-downward
and defeated, on the bed of the Aegean Sea.

ADVENTURES OF A MANUSCRIPT

Demobilized, I rejoined my vicar, but not at Prittlewell. He was now Vicar of Brighton, and I found myself one of three curates on the staff of Brighton Parish Church. Welcoming me, the Vicar said with obvious pride and pleasure, 'We have resolved to give all our curates a stipend of £200 a year'; and I said, 'Oh, thank you, Vicar,' not dissatisfied; my stipend before had been only £150. Looked back on now, this Brighton stipend seems small after five years' experience in Orders, four of them in the war; but it provided a living of sorts for a young man in 1919. These were perhaps the last few years in which the Church of England reigned in some assurance and power, especially over a preponderantly middle-class and residential parish like Brighton; our church was large and usually filled; we might have as many as a thousand at Evensong on Sundays; so the work on the curates was extensive and exacting. But I have to write here, guiltily, that I snatched more time than I should have done from parochial duties to give it to the reassembling of those Army Books 152 into a proper manuscript, and then to typing it for a publisher. I bought a portable typewriter and taught myself to type, not with two forefingers and two thumbs, I insist proudly, but with all the fingers of both hands. This reconstruction of my book, because the hours for it were only stolen, took me a whole year; and it was in mid-1920 when the typescript was there before my eyes, complete. I took it to a book-binder and had it bound in half-calf with its title *Tell England* in gold lettering on the spine, thinking that this would encourage a publisher. I knew so little about publishers, my thoughts having dwelt always on the writing of a book rather than on its marketing, that I had no notion as yet that publishers could differ, some preferring to publish one kind of book, some another. Any publisher would do for me. So I turned the pages of *The Times Literary Supplement* and picked on one whose advertisement was conspicuous because of its heavy type. It was 'Hutchinson and Co., Ltd'.

Lovingly, caressingly, neatly, I wrapped up my heavy parcel and carried it to the post office, not without memories of Dickens's description of himself setting out on the like mission, dropping his first manuscript 'stealthily one evening at twilight, with fear and trembling, into a dark letter-box in a dark office up a dark court in Fleet Street'.

My large package went over the counter of a Brighton post office, where the clerk, when I'd stamped it, took it from me and flung it, indifferently and rather disturbingly, on to a pile of ordinary parcels.

A week went by, two weeks, three weeks, a fourth week, till I decided in my ignorance that this 'wasn't good enough', and wrote a courteous but well-phrased letter to Messrs Hutchinson and Co., Ltd, asking if they had safely received my manuscript and were prepared to consider publishing it. Two mornings later the postman rat-tatted on the door of the house where I lodged, and my landlady brought in to me at breakfast a bulky parcel of shape all too familiar. Enclosed with the large and heavy manuscript was nothing more than the usual rejection slip, about three inches square.

Hutchinson and Co., I imagine, met peremptoriness with peremptoriness.

Not lightly hurt, indeed extremely sad, I turned again the pages of the *T.L.S.*, wondering whom to approach next. Before I could decide, I chanced to meet at a party a woman who had actually had a book published, and I sought her advice. She said, 'Why not try a literary agent?'

'What are they?' I asked, never having known that such people existed.

She explained, and I inquired who were the best agents.

'A. P. Watt and Son,' she said. 'They are the oldest, and if they accept your book for negotiation, it'll at least be a few steps on the way home because any publisher they offer it to will know that it has been carefully read by Watt's readers, and they consider it worth handling.'

A. P. Watt and Son. I scribbled down the address, rushed home, re-packed my large parcel, not hopefully but sadly and more wisely than before, and sent it off again.

One week, two weeks, three weeks . . . six weeks . . . and only silence. But I wrote no letter of inquiry. I didn't want the book back in forty-eight hours. Silence. Silence from A. P. Watt and Son. Silence from me. And more clouded, lowering weeks went by.

Then a letter, cold, stately, and formal. In effect it said that, having received a favourable report of my manuscript, *Tell England*, they were prepared to offer it on my behalf; and that their terms were ten per cent of all moneys that might be received by me as a result of their negotiations on my behalf. And that they could not be held responsible for its accidental loss by fire or any other cause while in their offices, in transit, or on offer to publishers. It was signed 'W. P. Watt'.

This was encouragement, and hope lived again—nay, more than just lived; it flourished like a blossoming tree in the pride of spring.

But now it was not a procession of weeks that went grimly by; it was a procession of months, each greyer and chillier than the last. Sometimes I picture the many weeks of those months as a column of grey-habited, hooded, ruthlessly silent monks; Trappists, maybe. I wrote no letters, asking someone to speak. Instead I saw my handsome volume lying forgotten somewhere, or lost, or stowed away and gathering dust in a pigeon-hole—except that few pigeon-holes would have been large enough to hold it.

At last a letter in the long stately envelope of A. P. Watt and Son, its flap embossed with the helmeted head of Athene, goddess of wisdom, dignity, and the arts. It began by saying that Messrs Constable and Co., Ltd, were interested in my book and would like me to go and see them—which was pleasing; but then it subjoined, in tabular form, a list of six publishers to whom the book had already been offered, and who had declined it. It also said that Mr W. P. Watt would like me to come and see him at their office before I went to Messrs Constable's office in Orange Street. I did so, and this was my first meeting with Mr W. P. Watt.

I saw a tall man who seemed to me at first as cold, formal, and stately as his long envelopes, his prose, or as the head of Athene, goddess of wisdom, dignity, and the arts—whom, in features, he somewhat resembled. But there was humour hidden behind the apparent coldness; for example he almost smiled as he said, 'I don't know what Constable's want to see you for. Tell them anything they want to know but, for mercy's sake, don't discuss terms.' He told me gloomily that the six publishers who had so far declined my book had all said much the same thing: that no one wanted to read about the war, and the book, accordingly, was unmarketable. That he had formed a different opinion he did not tell me then. He kept this behind a suitably comfortless mask. I learned later that he was a Balliol man, and I thought that I had never seen a better example of the traditional Balliol product, calm, dignified, undemonstrative, but humorous—even richly humorous, so long as the humour was not spoiled by laughter or other exaggerated demonstrations. And all this enclosed, as someone has said, in a natural consciousness of effortless superiority.

Of my interview with Constable's directors I need give no description because it issued in nothing but an astonishing revelation for me.

M

The two directors whom I met in their Orange Street office were Michael Sadleir and his chairman, O. Kyllman, whom he addressed always as 'O.K.'; and the only noteworthy fact about our hour of talk was that Michael Sadleir spent nine tenths of it lying supine on the divan in his chairman's room with his hands clasped behind his head. They liked the book—in parts only—but like all those who had gone before them were clearly wallowing in a doubt about its 'marketability' and the wisdom of publishing it. They agreed, however, to 'discuss the matter further with Mr Watt'. I went home to Brighton sitting in a train and staring out of the window, not greatly heartened, but hoping, hoping.

Then happened the astonishing thing. I received a letter from W. P. Watt in which he stated with his usual calm formality that he had received from Messrs Constable an offer for the publication of my book which in his estimation was insufficiently satisfactory and which he did not feel prepared to accept on my behalf. Subject to my consent he proposed to decline it.

This to an author who had never had a book published before; whose book had already been rejected by seven publishers (if you add Hutchinson to Mr Watt's six); and concerning an offer from one of the most distinguished houses in the country.

I wanted to rush out to the post office and wire something like, 'For the love of Heaven accept'—preferring in my heart yet more blasphemous words—though I wouldn't have dared address in these frivolous terms so imposing a man. After an hour of pacing up and down, my thoughts a chaos, and after a visit to a wise man, of great business acumen, who pointed out that this oddly haughty action by A. P. Watt and Son could bear no meaning but that they had faith in the book, I went home, sat down sadly, and wrote a letter to Mr Watt in which, compelled to vent my feelings, I said, 'For my part I should have accepted but, on thinking it over, I have decided to leave everything to your discretion.' And sadly I posted this.

His reply came thanking me and stating that he had withdrawn the book.

From Messrs Constable. Lord, lord. . . .

And then another six months. Of silence. Of myself abusing my weakness, with stamps of a foot, for not having courageously instructed that awesome yet friendly man to accept at once. Constable's, publishers of Scott, Meredith, Shaw, Havelock Ellis! Six more months, progressing ever more slowly like a funeral march towards a grave.

Every post of every day equalled Nothing. Or only a blow on the heart at seeing the emptiness. I would walk the streets of Brighton practising a silly custom that has been with me since childhood. I would say to myself, 'If no car overtakes me before I pass that lamp-post the book will be a success.' Or 'If that dog in the distance barks again before I reach the pillar-box, it will be a failure. I shall hear no more from W. P. Watt except when he returns the book like Hutchinsons.' Why one persevered with this childish divination, who knows? —since sometimes the auguries foretold success, and sometimes failure: more often success because one arranged a time-scheme that would be favourable; or one hurried one's steps to the lamp-post. At home it was, 'If no one speaks before I get to the bottom of this page, everything will be all right.' Lord's and the Oval were fine grounds for this game: 'If he hits the next ball good and proper, all will be well. . . . No, he's let it go by. . . . Well, off the next then. . . .'

Hove Cricket Ground was nearer to me than Lord's or the Oval, and I was often there—indeed many clerical collars would be dotted about the Pavilion, parsons being among the few who could steal week-days off—and there were times when I sat there and wondered if watching first-class cricket wasn't the perfect training for accepting disappointment after disappointment, and adjusting thereto, as is so often required of us during our journey through life. One sat there hoping that every next ball would produce an excitement, but it didn't—and again it didn't—and again—and at length one knew, with arms folded and mouth yawning, that one was learning patience and stoicism and all the long littleness of life; *hoping* still of course, but no longer *expecting*. On the contrary, accepting the overwhelming probability that ball after ball would produce only disappointment through the long dreamy afternoon.

So with post after post through six succeeding months—never a boundary from Mr Watt—and at last the shrugging adjustment. Expecting nothing any more.

§

About this time I came to what I now perceive was the third great decision of my life.

The first and master decision was something that sprang to life of itself, independent of my will. It determined my will instead of being driven by it; and it was master of me from twelve years old and onward. This was my desire to write. The second decision, which should not have taken second place, but did so, was my resolve to take Holy Orders. In this, along with a sincere but simple-minded devotion to the Anglo-Catholic Movement, with all its beauties of ceremonial and worship, there was, as I have confessed on a previous page, the less than worthy plan of finding in the Church a profession which would provide me with a livelihood while I took every legitimate opportunity—and a few others—to write. Indeed, was not this just what I was doing now in my service at Brighton of a good vicar and an important church? All through my career at a Theological College, and through my ordinations as deacon and priest, though I had done well in exams, my mind remained naïve and uncritical. I wanted to be loyal to the Catholic creeds, not to think about them. This was a Party Line to me, and I loved it. But a mind grows up, even if abnormally slowly, and at some point after the war I began to think.

My position at this time is best stated as I have phrased it elsewhere. 'But then I began to think. It was strangely late in my life when this happened. I had been happy for twelve years and more in an uncritical loyalty, but now – I was thirty, and I began to think, and it all fell away from me. Not my love of the enrapturing beauty of it all, the colour, the music, the singing, the tapers glimmering and the incense drifting— these live with me for ever—but my faith in the miraculous story which alone gave heart and meaning to it all. From virgin birth to resurrection there was hardly a miracle recorded that I could easily accept any more. ... There were even sayings and deeds of Christ which I could no longer love. They overturned and flung down my worship of him.

'But enough of these doubts. Their rightness or wrongness has been thrashed out in a thousand volumes; they have been ploughed up and raked over for all of two hundred and fifty years, ever since the German sceptics really got going; and only the fact of them has any place in this story of a sad doubter's search; only the loss of a joyous allegiance and an engrossing love.'

Or in a sentence: while not *firmly* doubting the dogmas and miracles I could not longer say in the words of Newman's hymn, 'Firmly I believe and truly. . . .'.

This greatly disturbed and, in secret, sickened me, because it infused an element of hypocrisy into my preaching and teaching; and in my first years at Brighton Parish Church the worry swelled up into a volume of distress that I could no longer bear. I was now intellectually insolvent, I told myself, and in a priest who has to preach to large congregations and to teach young confirmation candidates, a hidden intellectual insolvency is bound to produce spiritual insolvency. And spiritual insolvency, in a parson, weakening the moral system, begins to deal in moral breakdowns. Or so with me.

So I came to my decision. I must resign from Holy Orders. I will put it more harshly, 'I must relinquish Orders,' the point being that the Church does not allow that this is possible, while the State does. The Church says, 'Once a priest, always a priest'; the *charisma* given in Ordination cannot be undone. But this statement depends, of course, on a firm and true belief that a miraculous grace is injected by the laying-on of a bishop's hands; what if one has no longer any such belief? The State, on the other hand (as with divorce) provides the means of relinquishing Orders; it is known as Filing a Deed of Relinquishment. So rarely has it been used, most priests whose faith tumbles being content merely to withdraw from ministry, that my solicitors had difficulty in discovering all about it, and the Chancellor of Chichester Diocese, the bishop's lay judge and legal adviser, when they offered my Deed of Relinquishment to him, had never heard of such an instrument. I believe it is true to say that in all our Church's history no more than some eighteen priests have made use of it.

The Bishop of Chichester, Winfrid Burrows (more charmingly 'Winfrid Cicestr') called me at once to his lovely palace under his Cathedral towers, and could not have been more understanding and sympathetic, as we sat in his study, looking across a lawn at the Roman and medieval walls of Chichester.

'Don't do this, my dear boy,' he said. 'I beg you not to. Just withdraw for a time. For a long time, if you like. Surely this is too final and desperate a step. Why, I've been an archdeacon and a bishop for more than sixteen years and I've never heard of anyone doing this.'

I told him about my longing to write, and how I wanted my mind to swing absolutely free, so that I was writing exactly what I was moved to write, which might mean that I would write things tolerable in a layman, but wholly unacceptable from a priest; even, possibly actionable. With a laugh I said I didn't want to lay myself open, some day, to disciplinary action. (We were sitting in the nineteen-twenties, not in this amply permissive age of the sixties.)

He put a fatherly hand on mine as he said, 'My dear boy, I promise here and now that I will never in any circumstances take disciplinary action against you.'

This was gentleness itself, but I could not help thinking, though not saying, 'But, my lord, you are approaching seventy, and you cannot speak for your successors.'

He added, 'You do know, don't you, that if you do this thing, you can never come back?'

I did not know this, and it shocked me, but instead of shaking my resolution it strengthened it. It seemed to me stupid and vindictive and wrong. Who would make a better priest than one who had gone into the wilderness and learned at last, and with joy, the way home again? Long afterwards, Dr Winnington Ingram, Bishop of London, when pleading with characteristic generosity for the repeal of this stern rule, argued, 'The Church exists to teach forgiveness; surely she should practise it'; and I thought, 'My lord, there are ten hundred sins and more in my life that need forgiveness, but this is not one of them. It has always seemed to me one of the cleaner things I have done, and I know that, after taking this step, I experienced a spiritual peace; more, I felt, though still very imperfect, conscious of a spiritual strengthening that seemed to spring from recovery and better health.'

To respond to my bishop's kindness, and to evade the rudeness of a refusal, I said I would think over it further, though I knew well enough that the thinking would only stabilize my purpose.

'That's right,' he said, 'and I will be praying for you. And now let me give you my blessing.'

I knelt down and he pronounced his blessing over me; which was difficult to take, knowing as I did that I would abide by my determination and would have to hurt him.

The Deed of Relinquishment went through. There was no means by which Bishop or Chancellor could halt it.

Before leaving this matter I want to fly far into a future, much farther than this book can compass, almost as far as this time when I am writing it, more than forty years after my Deed was filed. These forty years I spent in my own private wilderness of doubts and wonderings, going to church no more because I could no longer pray the prayers, sing the hymns, or recite the creeds since they were all based on the Trinitarian doctrine and the deity (as distinct from the divinity) of the Carpenter of Nazareth; and in neither case could I yet say with Newman, 'Firmly I

believe and truly God is Three and God is One' or 'And I next acknowledge duly Manhood taken by the Son'.

But, rather than this story of my withdrawal from the Church should
be left incomplete, let me briefly report that there was a return in the
end. Not as a teaching priest but as a learning layman, still bearing a
burden of unresolved doubts, but attending church again and taking
the Sacrament.

To tell how this return came about after forty years of self-exile
would require a book to itself. If I am to touch upon it in a page or two
of sentences, I will tell it thus.

Never in all the forty years did my heart lose its love for the old
historic Ecclesia Anglicana, especially in its Anglo-Catholic dress; it
was my head which had travelled miles away. My head would not and
could not, from its distance now, accept what the heart so desired.

Secondly, never in all my life have I not preferred a blind belief in an
unknown God to a blind denial of his existence. So my retirement from
Orders sprang from no disbelief in the Deity of God, but only from
bewildering doubts about the deity of Jesus. My attitude after retirement amounted to Theism in respect of a Creator and Agnosticism in
respect of the Trinitarian exposition of his nature. When will people
cease to think that 'agnostic' and 'atheist' mean the same thing?
Agnosticism means simply, 'I do not know and therefore dare not
affirm or deny'; Atheism means, 'I deny'. Thus they are opposites.
The former is a completely intellectual attitude; the latter is not; it can
only be an assumption, a guess, a prejudging, as much a matter of
faith, and as dogmatic, as any article in a Christian creed.

Thirdly, I have never, since I have been capable of proper reasoning,
doubted that the Christian ethic, *applied* Christianity as distinct from
dogmatic Christianity, is the whole Truth and the only way of raising
humans to their noblest potential. By applied Christianity I mean, in a
sentence, the abandonment of all vindictiveness and vengeance and the
clear perception that evil can never be overcome by anything that
savours of itself, but only by its opposite, love in some form. Correction
and controls and incarceration—and even violence in the protection of
others—may often be legitimate, but never retributive violence; never
retaliation in kind. It looks to me as if in the hearts of us all there lies the
seed that can, and with favourable environment does, grow into the
clear vision that applied Christianity is the dazzling Truth—else how is
it that no man, not even the most confident and assertive 'infidel', can

fail to bow down before any reported story of great compassion, great forgiveness, great self-sacrifice? We can but worship love, compassion, and a selflessness even unto death. We can but bow down before 'Father, forgive them' as the nails went in.

So it came about that in the end, thanks largely to a wind of change that blew through the churches in the last decade, pronouncing that a partially agnostic Christianity, though sounding paradoxical, is possible, admissible, and even inevitable, I realized that since all the 'goodnesses' which I had never ceased to worship, however feebly I had performed them, were simply what the young man from Nazareth had taught, then the only thing to do was (if I may turn again to what I have written elsewhere) 'to give oneself to a love one feels and leave all else with the God unknown'. To range oneself with so true a teacher and, further, to range oneself by the side of all the others who had chosen to range themselves with him. After all—all said and done—all the world is mystery and who so mysterious as he? All 'being' is miracle, past understanding; he no less; he more mysterious than any. To go back to his Church in a kind of blind love and trust, asking help for a faith still unsure; 'believing much, if less than all; while hoping all'. Approaching the Sacrament with this humility and reverence, certainly, but, also, not without a kind of gaiety, the Christian *hilaritas*, as I feel all sacramental mysteries, including the Church itself, should be approached, since in the heart of thanks there is always joy.

One word more. A remarkable thing about this return, after an absence of forty years, was that all the words in the old Book of Common Prayer were like new words, and charged with deeper meanings than ever before. Too much familiarity with them in childhood and youth had produced, not indifference, but a blunted impact. Now, unexpectedly, they were, so to speak, both remembered and forgotten; and in so far as they were forgotten, they were new; it was as if they were addressing themselves to a virgin mind and striking upon it with the impact of first-hand things. From boyhood I had responded to their verbal grandeur when Hilliard spoke them, but not to the wonderful meanings within them. As with the words so with the actual church building into which I returned. It had a new look too, a new face, with its flagstones in the pavement covering the Christian faithful long dead, its lights and vestments enshrining the traditions of two thousand years, its thundering organ in its high ornamental loft, and the loyal devotion around me of the remnant of the faithful, all too few in these secular days. One felt embraced within a poem—the great poem of the Church in a devastated world. Sometimes I felt it as a throb of happiness, to be back again with the trusting remnant. They showed me how surely my heart had always loved the Church, no matter how long and how firmly my head had refused a surrender. From the few around me whose devotion was plainly sincere and whose faith seemed untroubled there came towards me an encouragement, a breath of spiritual support—let me call it a happy infection. Maybe their faith was not so untroubled as it seemed—whose ever is?—but sometimes as I saw their heads bowed deep in prayers, I would think, with more confidence than King Agrippa showed to Paul, 'Thou persuadest me to be a Christian.'

Anyhow, I felt love for them, and longed to be one of them.

This happiness in fellowship could sometimes be a pleasing hope that these strangers, nameless and unknown but familiar, because so often kneeling in the same pews near me at a quiet Communion Service attended by the few, were possibly helped, like me, by a sense that I was at one with them.

Christ himself, though I still did not know how to define him, had this new face too. Parable after parable, saying after saying, struck upon me with the new impact. He was so obviously the New Man, who had put away for all of us the violent and vindictive Old Man of the Old Testament, and taught, practised, and died in the service of compassion, forgiveness, and love. In some sense I could but worship him. To me he spoke the Word whereby alone men can save themselves.

§

Those second six months after Mr Watt's refusal of Constable's offer drew their slow length along. It was somewhere in the fifth of them that, as a small amelioration of my day-long anxieties, I composed a ballade addressed to Mr Watt, though assuredly never delivered to him. It was a most irregular ballade, because the refrain closing each stanza and closing the envoi was technically intolerable; a kind of Alexandrine, and not a good one at that. I know of no ballades whose refrains were Alexandrines instead of decasyllabic or octosyllabic, but mine was such, and here it is: 'All my clothes are wearing out, and fame no further near'. 'Further near'—good heaven!—but I kept this abomination because I liked it: it expressed exactly the objectionable and cocky snobbishness with which Fame kept its distance from me. The envoi began in the old tradition 'Prince'—and 'Prince' was no bad title in which to clothe Mr W. P. Watt.

> Prince, why this shocking silence dost thou keep
> When knowing well the things I long to hear?
> Pray hearken, if not dead or fast asleep:
> All my clothes are wearing out, and fame no
> > further near.

And then in the sixth or seventh month, out of the silence, a silence now of twelve months, broken only once by the Constable occasion, came Mr Watt's voice again. In a letter which ran, 'Mr. Newman Flower of Cassell and Co., Ltd., has expressed an interest in your book, and I would like you to go and see him at his office in La Belle Sauvage, Ludgate Hill, London, E.C.4. Since writing to you last I have offered your book to—' and here followed, in a tabular column as before, the names of five more famous publishers who had declined the book as unsaleable, making eleven refusals in all—twelve if you add Hutchinson's.

Before going to La Belle Sauvage, I visited Mr Watt who went so far—though gloomily—as to say, 'Mr Flower is enthusiastic about your book. He effervesced about it'—this said as from one who didn't hold with effervescence—'so there is no doubt he will take and probably pay well for it. But for mercy's sake don't discuss terms.'

Naturally I shall never forget that first interview with Newman Flower. Nothing from his lips but enthusiasm. There on his big table between us, where it had come to rest after rejection by twelve of his brother publishers, lay my unwieldy leather-bound volume, dishevelled and tattered with much travel. It made me think of some tired and mangy old dog. He knew of its many rejections. What an opportunity, then, for an astute publisher to do a little depreciation of the book's chances and a little bargaining. Nothing of the sort. Only the effervescence which had slightly grieved Mr Watt—that perhaps over-effervescent optimism of which I was soon to learn he was always capable. Only 'We will do our best with the book if you will trust it to us'. Trust! Only, when I said, Of course I would trust it to them, a 'Splendid! Splendid!' Followed by 'And I should like an option on your next two books.' My next two books. Shaken – with happiness – bewildered by it, and knowing that I had no more books on my desk, I said, more in a social politeness, I fancy, than in a true diffidence, 'But

I don't know that I have anything more to say'; to which, with a laugh, he replied, 'Nonsense, my dear boy, I want many more books from you.' Many! While I stared at this glorious word, he went on 'Wonderful title you've got. How did you think of it?'

I said, 'I don't think I thought of it as anything very wonderful. It just seemed to fit. The Spartans who fell at Thermopylae. The English who fell at Gallipoli. Tell Sparta. Tell England.'

'But it's a selling title. Didn't you realize that?'

'No, I don't think I knew there were such things as "selling titles".'

'Well, I can assure you there are. And you found one.'

'Do you really think it will sell?' I asked, excited by that word.

He smiled. 'I'll promise nothing. Books play the craziest tricks on us. Sometimes those we expect to get away from the start just lie down and refuse to move. Others that we half fear will be still-born, get up and run away so that we're caught unprepared and have to run after them with our pants down. All I'll say is that it'll be one of the surprises of my life if this book of yours isn't a run-away seller. Anyhow, we'll do all we can for it. You can be sure of that. October now; we'll go straight ahead and hope to have it out late in January.'

So rapid was gestation of a book in the twenties; nowadays it usually takes, as in another field, the full nine months—from seduction by the author to parturition by the publisher.

I thanked him in a voice unstable, and he said, 'Not at all. I'll now get down to arranging an agreement with Bill Watt.'

'Bill' of that august personage!

Laughingly, almost affectionately, he spoke of the Watt brothers— there were three of them, A. S. Watt, Hansard Watt, and W. P.—as 'the Robbers', which promised well. And then, 'Good-bye, my dear boy, I hope we're going to see much of you. I hope this is the beginning of a long connexion.'

Do you remember La Belle Sauvage on Ludgate Hill, that old inn-yard of coaching days? Its buildings, old or new, were all intact when I came to Newman's office in 1921. But the Germans destroyed them all, together with so much of the City, in the great fire-raid of May 10th, 1941. Then all Cassell's buildings burned for a night and a day. This was the last desperate throw of the 1940–41 Blitz, and so the home of Cassell's went down, beneath a sickening spite, with the last of London's victims—the last till three years later when the V–bombs came.

Of my coming away from Newman's office in 1921 and stepping

into the long coach-yard I can only use again the words I used about Whitehall when I came out of the War Office, knowing that I was to be sent to the Dardanelles: that over its cobbles, its many windows, and its archway, lay a light that never was, on sea or land. The poet's dream.

2

COMMENT ON THE BOOK

While three months pass and the book awaits its public appearance and its fortune good or bad, let me appear again out of the distant future and, after forty-seven years gone by, offer a few comments on this production of my youth.

If I read it now, which I find difficult to do because parts of it make me shiver, I am hardly able to believe that I am the same person as the young man who wrote it. Reading one's first book after nearly fifty years one can feel a little like its author's father—or even his grandfather. Between the shivers, the stabs, and the shocks there are parts of it that can still please me: these are the comic scenes, the dramatic scenes on Gallipoli, one or two shrewdly satirical scenes that get full fun out of army absurdities; and some examples of a narrative skill not unremarkable in a first effort. *But*—the naïve romanticisms, the pieties, the too facile heroics and too uncritical patriotism—at these I can almost cry aloud in distress. How, I ask myself, could this shrewd young satirist and merry comedian canter in the same harness as an exceptionally unripe Victorian sentimentalist? Perhaps the one thing that saves the book and allows it to live on quietly is the fact that it purports to be the work of a naïve and guileless youth just fresh from school and tossed into war, and it may be that people reading the book now will think that its *naïvetés* were slyly intentional and clever; but, alas, they were not; they were the author at that time.

The overspill of pieties and 'spiritual uplift' I can understand. When they were written I was in Orders and not ready yet to shake myself free of what I have already styled 'my impossible loyalties'. Only when I shed these did I begin to be my real self, striving to be obstinately and fearlessly individual; which is the prime need of a writer. In the comic scenes, the satirical scenes, and the dramatic scenes, which had nothing to do with a loyal churchmanship, I was already free and myself; in the pious and religiose chapters I was writing for my Party Line. I had allowed myself to grow little further than when, at about fourteen, I wrote an essay on Intemperance for Mr Hilliard, who had asked all the members of his Church of England Temperance Society to do this. You will detect in its opening paragraphs a desire to be a truly fine writer but also a diplomatic intention to provide exactly what was expected of me; exactly what was desired by Mr Hilliard. Its date must be about 1903, and the essay smells of it.

Essay on Intemperance

'To slay the omnivorous and apparently undying germ of Intemperance which is for ever creeping about, bringing death, disease and misery to the home of the working man, and to rid the country of a national degradation are objects as yet unattained, and which command the interest and aid, however small, of every loyal Englishman who would wish to remove a stain from the pages of British [a concession in this field to the Scots?] history.

'Great is the suffering, and deadly and far-reaching are the evils which the propagation of this sin has brought about, as with a destroying hand, it has crushed love, romance, domestic happiness, and all the things which tend to alleviate the poverty and hardship our poorer fellow-creatures are destined to undergo.

'The romantic and cheery old inns which afforded a welcome to rich and poor alike, the merry ostlers, the jovial landlord [echo of "Pickwick"?], all topics which great authors have loved to dwell upon, have disappeared and in their place has arisen the massive and flaring building, the present-day publick house, universally an object of pity and contempt. . . .'

Oh dear, oh dear. And I so enjoy a visit to one of these abominable places now.

Tell England, at its most high-minded, echoes a little less the Georgians and their clergy than this, but not much, or not enough.

Another thing that is a cause of wonder to me as I re-read the book is the indubitable but wholly unconscious homosexuality in it. The earlier part was written when I was eighteen or nineteen; the latter part in my twenties, and in those far-off days 'homosexuality' was a word which—absurd as this may seem now—I had never heard. It was not then the daily topic in newspapers and converse that it is today. But naturally I knew all the rude words like 'buggery' and 'sods'. And these described practices that, so far from having any appeal to me, produced a grim recoil and a surprise that such things could be. I did not know that homosexuality could exist in embryo without even knowing itself for what it was, or desiring the least physical satisfaction, till the time came for it to die and be transcended by full and normal manhood. Its presence in the book is one more evidence of its author's unusually slow progress towards maturity. A fellow clubman, a witty Irishman, who, though fifty or sixty now, persists in loving *Tell England* always delights me when he says, as he has more than once, 'I have just read that damned book again, and as usual I've been surprised that your Radley [the hero schoolmaster in the first part] does not reappear in the Gallipoli chapters, but then, of course, I suddenly remember that he'd have been doing his five years in jug.'

3

THE EVENT

Cassell's could not, after all, produce the book in January, and they postponed publication till February 16th, 1922.

The first signs of something good about to happen, the first raindrops bespeaking a shower, were small paragraphs appearing here and there in February's first weeks. The *Sunday Times* noted, 'From all one hears about it, *Tell England* to be published by Cassell's on Thursday week promises to be one of the big successes of the season.' The *Daily News* reported, 'Mr. Newman Flower thinks he has alighted on a Cassell novel which will be a good selling book. It is called *Tell England*, the author is a new hand, Mr. Ernest Raymond, who is young, was a padre in the war, and the novel has grown from his experiences.' *The National Newsagent* seized upon the Baku story. 'This is Mr. Raymond's first appearance as a novelist, and the manuscript of his story had a narrow escape from being lost when he and his comrades were flying for their lives from Baku, after a trek across Persian mountains to the relief of Armenians. His notes, in fact, were the only things of all his kit that he was able to save.'

Then arrived—what an experience for a new author—the six presentation copies of his first book. And in what a dust-jacket. How typical of its date. Above the title ran the words 'A Great Romance of Glorious Youth', and the brilliantly coloured picture showed the petals of the Red Rose of England falling one by one into the flames of war.

February 16th, and, lavishly advertised by Cassell's, the book was out. A few days of joy beyond belief, and of excitement and hope because of this far-flung advertising—and then the critics got to work.

I can assure you that it was no small experience for a young author who had an innocent admiration for his first book, and could remember many joyous years of struggling to make it in his simple view better and better, to be reviewed by Rose Macaulay. *Daily News*: Rose Macaulay writing: '*Tell England* is apparently by a rather illiterate and commonplace sentimentalist. . . . Some schoolboys are highly civilised persons of good literary taste; others may like *Tell England* and the novels of Mrs. Barclay (you could, by the way, transfer whole sentences and paragraphs from one to the other of these two last contributions to literature without detection). *Tell England* has no beauty, and its silliness and bad taste are not the work of a writer. It is difficult to say which is the more sloppy, sentimental, and illiterate, the school section of the book or the war section. . . . It need only be added that the young men compose verse just about as bad as Mr. Raymond's prose, and that all die beautifully. The recent war is a great godsend to writers of this type; it provides a vent for their worst tendencies. It can only be hoped that one venting will be enough.'

'Sentimentality' I willingly concede, but of 'illiteracy' I am less confident.

S. P. B. Mais was brief: 'A quite unreadable novel about public school life and the war. It is being much boomed, so I warn you. "Dear, me, how annoying!" is typical, to Mr. Raymond's mind, of schoolboy phraseology. Alas, where was he educated?'

The schoolboy, of course, was being facetious, but this had eluded Mr Mais.

Alec Waugh, whose main interest in life, apart from his excellent story-telling, has always appeared to be cricket, concentrated largely in the *Sunday Times* on the cricket match in the book, and thereafter drew stumps, omitting all reference to Gallipoli—which one would have thought the more important topic. '*Tell England* comes to us in the raiment of modernity, but its heart is with the sixties. To read the first half of it is to be transferred to our preparatory school, to the days when we wore Eton collars and devoured "Eric" and "St. Winifred's". . . . The story hurries on past probability, past possibility, to the inevitable cricket match that is the curtain for every school story that has ever been written. Of course Ray distinguishes himself. He gets the important wicket at the important moment. It was a strange match, though; the description of it displays, I am inclined to think, the most profound ignorance of the game I have yet encountered.'

The *Evening Standard* had headlines which stabbed and killed the heart: 'The Sentimental Schoolboy. Eric Outdone'; and among its comments were 'Whether Mr. Raymond has tried to draw his schoolboys from life or from his own imagination, the result is laughable—when it is not revolting by reason of the sentimentality with which the autobiography of Rupert Ray is sticky from cover to cover. . . . When the bully (in a bullying scene), moved by the noble behaviour of his victim, offers to own up, he does so with the remark, "My colleagues and I are determined to do the right thing." Only at Kensingtowe, the curious school created out of Mr. Raymond's imagination, do the boys (one hopes and believes) speak of their "colleagues". It should hardly be necessary to add that one of the favourite amusements of the boys of Kensingtowe is the "ragging" of the French master. But Mr. Raymond, so far as recollection serves, has forgotten one ingredient of the complete school story—there is no Fat Boy.'

As regards that word 'colleagues', it was designed as a deliberate ridiculing of a prefect's pomposity, but either I had failed to establish this or the reviewer had rather skimmed the book. They have to sometimes.

Gerald Gould in the *Saturday Review* stated that the most one could do was to forgive these schoolboys their existence and, having done this freely, to desire to hear no more of them.

Francis Birrell (but this was later) broadcast over the air that it 'was the most nauseating book to come out of the war'.

I was almost beginning to feel as if I'd committed a criminal offence by writing it. It began to look like one more disgrace to humanity. I feared for a few hours to show my face in the Brighton streets.

The *Daily Telegraph*, however (may its name be blest), mixed a little mercy with its condemnation. 'A first novel invites indulgence and encouragement, and we shall hope to meet Mr. Ernest Raymond upon some other occasion which will justify our congratulations. It would, however, be a poor compliment to himself and scant service to his readers, if we let good nature persuade him that *Tell England* displays much of the necessary quality of a novelist.'

On the other side of an extraordinarily wide chasm Mr Hannen Swaffer in the *Daily Graphic* provided banner headlines, '*Tell England* a Great Book', 'The Epic of the Youth of England', and spoke loud. 'Every now and then comes a book of penetrating analysis, a volume that illumines the souls of thousands. *Tell England* is such a book. . . . In the shape of a story which contains many passages of moving beauty, in English that is Biblical in its simplicity, and in the form of fiction which is eternally fact, an unknown parson has written a book that will be read proudly wherever English people live. It is a book which will live as long as our spoken tongue.'

Thank you, Mr Swaffer, but this was really saying a packet.

The *Birmingham Post* said, 'The thesis is not shaped into a novel of plot but in a lively and episodic chronicle of friendship and youthful development which interests because it is literature. The charm of the author's writing is not the neat sparkle of the artificial fountain; it is a charm akin to that of the ocean—a beauty of proud movement, of foam-roses carelessly tossing, of a sudden sail, of winged colours.'

Here was balm indeed, if maybe a little richly applied, for that open and aching sore left by Rose Macaulay's 'illiterate' and 'bad as Mr. Raymond's prose' and 'not the work of a writer'.

But it would be unbecoming to reproduce here more of the reviews that applauded the book (greatly as I am wishing to) but I must be allowed one more, from the *Teacher's World* because it opened with a column attack on Alec Waugh instead of on me—which was a change. 'The immediate cause of this adventure among books,' it said, 'was a review of a new book in a Sunday paper by one of the cleverest of our younger novelists, and one gathered from it that the book had not pleased him. He attacked it with fervour and ability; tore it to pieces, so to speak, with bill and claw and then stood up and flapped his wings and crowed. . . .' Turning to the book, the reviewer proceeded, 'It is obviously a first book and it has a good many obvious faults, but they are as nothing beside its great, its transcendent merits. I am a fairly seasoned novel reader, but *Tell England* held me tranced for hour after hour, and it was not until my eyes could hardly see that I could make up my mind to switch off the light.'

In subsequent years Rose Macaulay, Gerald Gould, and Alec Waugh were all my friends. Gerald Gould was kind and sometimes very kind to my later novels. Rose Macaulay and I were both active Liberals, and on that somewhat thin and trackless pasture we met often. We once broadcast together, not very successfully, in the old B.B.C. studio on Savoy Hill. The last time I saw Dame Rose was in her late seventies just before she died. It was at a Bank Holiday fair on Hampstead Heath, and she was standing in the long queue, waiting her chance for a ride on the Big Wheel. Attracted perhaps by the multi-coloured legends painted on the Wheel's tower-like piers: 'Get into Space', 'One Way to the Stars', and 'Hold Tight, Girls'.

Of course this wide divergence between attacks and acclamations, between saying that the book was terrible and saying that it was good, acted like the bellows in a smithy, blowing up the smoulder into fine dancing flames. I could not pass a station in London's Underground without seeing double-crown posters advertising 'A Great Romance of Glorious Youth' and showing the Red Rose of England dropping its petals into the red conflagration of war. The *Financial Times*, of all papers—how could a junior curate in Brighton be of interest to the tycoons of finance—but here was their organ reporting, 'It is announced by the House of Cassell that the fourth impression of Mr. Ernest Raymond's wonderfully successful novel, *Tell England*, is almost exhausted, and the fifth impression is now in the press.' A telegram came to me from Newman Flower: 'Passed the ten thousand mark.' A Brighton bookseller rang me up to say, 'Just sold my hundredth copy.' Cassell's followed up Newman's telegram with an advertisement stretching the whole width of a newspaper's page: 'The fifth impression of this remarkable romance is exhausted. The publisher's regret any delays in filling orders due to the enormous demand and have made provision to ensure adequate supplies in future.'

Good reading in a Brighton lodging.

A vulgar moment must be recounted. It was undoubtedly vulgar, but I cannot, to this day, repent of it or do other than delight in it. As a schoolmaster I had never earned more than £100 a year; as a curate never more than £200, so I sometimes wondered why a bank consented to accept me as a customer, I who could never pass across its counter more than £50 four times a year. However, the bank clerk to whom I usually handed this exiguous offering, always treated it as a pleasant and normal occurrence, requiring no murmurs of disapproval. My 'advance on account of royalties' for *Tell England*, had been the customary £25, but now came my first cheque for royalties in excess of this advance on publication. It was a cheque for £990-odd. Did I go speedily to the bank and there await my chance to offer it to my usual friend, the bank clerk? I did. He man-handled it inattentively at first, then looked at it, then stared at it, and then—may I so put it?—lost his usual calm. He recovered quickly, smiled, and asked quietly, 'Do tell me how it is done.'

'I don't know,' I said. 'All I can suggest is that you write a book which so upsets the critics that they savage it without mercy.'

'I shall set about it at once,' he said. 'Thank you.'

Yes, a vulgar moment, but good.

Another moment that lies sweet in memory was when Newman in his Belle Sauvage office told me that Walter Hutchinson, Chairman and Managing Director of Hutchinson and Co., had just rung him up, and that this was their colloquy over the telephone.

'Look here, Newman, is all this stuff that you are putting out about this book true, or is it a lot of lies? Why, dammit, the book was offered to us first. Long before you.'

'Of course it's not lies, Walter. Cassell's don't tell lies.'

'Bloody hell.'

Forty-five years can produce a detachment, almost impersonal from one's earliest work, even though, once upon a time, it was the whole of life within one's heart; and I learned yesterday, when for the sake of this chapter I read again all the old Press-cuttings, that I enjoyed the rude ones most; though I confess that their hurt at the time was like a death. And I was able to acknowledge that, while some of them were over-heated and uncontrolled they dealt with things about the book that were unhappily true. Having accepted this with a sigh, I could only hope that the eulogistic ones—if a little overdone too—did no less. There must, I thought, be some better qualities in the book than the all-in, no-holds-barred reviewers allowed, or how came it that the book had never ceased to sell in forty-five years and needed only recently a fortieth edition? I think I discerned two factors that have helped to keep it alive: the first is that it is a school story followed at once by the ex-citements of war, and so appeals to children, who are uncritical so long as they are excited and, intermittently, made to laugh; the second is that, after nearly half a century, it has acquired a kind of period patina, its sentimentalities and heroics belonging so plainly to Edwardian and early Georgian years, and when people regard a book they are reading as a 'period piece', they forgive much.

Way back in 1922 the book's roaring career as a seller, and the acclaim of the kindlier critics seemed a hardly credible culmination to two decades of dreaming and four years of effort—but I did not yet know that a double price has to be paid for a lottery success like this (and it *was* a lottery success because, while a book must have some qualities of its own to capture a public, it requires extraneous and fortuitous pressures if it is to drive ahead of competitors).

One part of the double price is this, that a monumental success throws its grey and baleful shadow over the books that follow it. Book after book is accorded the faint and therefore damning praise of 'Yes; quite good, but not a *So-and-so*'. Conan Doyle's fine adventure stories simply couldn't flourish beneath the mighty shadow of Sherlock Holmes, and that's why he so hated that picturesque and engaging gentleman; R. D. Blackmore's quite excellent romances could not meet the challenge of *Lorna Doone* and were gently killed by that lovely girl.

In my own case I have always said that not for thirteen years did I remove the threat to my next books—or partly remove it—of *Tell England*; not till 1935 when, having learned far more of what a writer ought to be, and having gathered some sophistication, I published a book called *We, the Accused*. It was a book as grim and unsparing as *Tell England* was softened, maybe, and sweetened; it had a far wider and less mixed critical reception, and has been a persistent seller over thirty years, though never attaining the freakish sales of its predecessor.

The other half of the price is the label which a successful book, universally read, hangs round your neck, possibly for ever. In the nature of things a first book is likely to be immature and sentimental (though the sentimentality may take the form of ugliness in excess rather than of too much 'beauty') and there you are: with a label on your breast, a rude label, 'Popular Sentimentalist', which puts you out of court with all serious-minded critics. That this label was doing its damnedest among critics up to the appearance of *We, the Accused* was shown by one reviewer who opened his remarks with the words, 'Mr. Raymond has surprised the critics by producing a book harshly and sternly true.' He approved of the book (in his state of bewildered surprise) and asked, incidentally if the title *We, the Accused* was meant to apply to the murderer and his mistress who are the protagonists in the story, or to the readers and Society generally who must stand in a dock too, as partly responsible for the dark happenings narrated. The answer is simple. This title was designed to apply to either or both. Just as a reader cares to take it.

I thought for a year or so that *We, the Accused* had destroyed the damning label; but no; only for a while; these labels are generally indestructible, and I soon learned that it was safely back on my breast again, there to stay.

Then, over and above this disconcerting truth that in all fields of life if people get labelled they stay labelled, there is an extra trouble in the case of a book that goes on selling for years. It is this: who among its readers of today know that it was a first book and the product of immaturity, published forty or fifty years ago? They may think that you wrote it only yesterday, or only a year or two since, and imagine that it expresses your mind at the moment.

From which interpretation may Heaven withhold its readers.

But whatever the disadvantages of an early best-seller, they are small compared with the joys that were mine in 1922, and the enduring pleasures which the success of a first book opened before me. There was the possibility of a new career, which I needed now, having withdrawn from the profession in which all my capital, and eight years of experience, had been sunk. There was the start of a forty-years friendship with Sir Newman Flower who, as I would put it, was to act as midwife to some fifty books of mine—and this after I had said to him at that first interview, 'But I don't know that I have anything more to say.' With Newman as a friend of the years was Aubrey Gentry, his second-in-command. There stretched before me also a forty-years friendship with the austere and dignified but humorous W. P. Watt, so tall, grave, and handsome, who was to be my agent till his death. Friends though he and I were, I could never, never strengthen myself to the point of calling him 'Bill'. I once said to his son, Peter Watt, 'I'd love to call your father "Bill", but I simply daren't.' He told this to W.P. and later reported to me that his father had said, 'There's nothing I'd like better than for Ernest Raymond to call me "Bill"'; but it was no good; I couldn't get round to naming such quiet dignity 'Bill'.

A charming story that portrays W.P., with his reserved and often unsmiling manner, better than any words I am using, is that of a small boy who with the untroubled ease of children experienced no difficulty in calling him 'Uncle Bill'. At the breakfast table one morning he suddenly explained to the family, 'When I grow up I'm not going to be jolly like Daddy; I'm going to be nice and gloomy like Uncle Bill.'

Once I sent two women, who needed an agent to negotiate a play for them, to W.P. with a letter of introduction. On my asking them afterwards how the business had prospered, one of them said something that could have come only, so I conceive, from the lips of a woman. 'Well, Penelope did most of the talking to Mr Watt, while I sat there all the time thinking what a pretty baby he must have been.'

Then, in after years, was to come an enduring friendship with the sons of these famous bookmen; with Desmond Flower and Bryen Gentry, the present directors of the House of Cassell, who have been so faithful to me, though it was to the offices of their fathers in old Belle Sauvage Yard that I first came so humbly and hopefully; and with Peter Watt, W.P.'s son, who to the distress of all London's bookworld died at the age of fifty. He left an endearing memory. And I think of others who have served in the Houses of Cassell and Watt, and gone, or are there still, to whose skilled labour I owe much.

As I bring this story to a close I think inevitably of one particular scene soon after the publication of *Tell England*. Like most young authors who can hardly believe that they've had a book published, which is now on display in the market, I would meander from bookshop to bookshop to see my book in its window (with the petals dropping from the Rose of England) and on its counter inside. This spying was safe enough because I was a new and unrecognizable figure in the book-world. Hatchard's in Piccadilly must have seen without disturbance a tall young man wandering into their shop and in due course wandering out again, without having bought anything; Bumpus's too, and the Times Bookshop, and Harrod's book department, and Selfridge's, and of course the old familiar book department of the Army and Navy Stores. None of them knew that this anonymous and straying visitor was always in some fear lest an assistant should approach and ask him what book he was seeking. This happened at times.

'Can I help you, sir?'

'No . . . no, thank you. . . . I was just . . . just looking around.'

'Was there any special title you were interested in?'

'Well, no. . . . I was just looking around.'

Whereafter I would slip out and far away as inconspicuously as possible.

On one occasion I went thus furtively into a bookshop and, to my surprise, saw no single copy of my book anywhere. Other newly published novels were there, some heaped up into pyramids, but not mine. Instantly my emotions changed: furtiveness became indignation, and, when not indignation, anxiety; diffidence became courage, invincible courage. Were they deliberately not stocking my book and displaying it? Had they read Rose Macaulay, Alec Waugh, and S. P. B. Mais, and concluded that it was bad and not for the best people? If so, why had they not read Hannen Swaffer, the *Yorkshire Observer* and other papers which had said it was fine? Or could it be that the book had quickly finished its run and was now dead? I had to ease these anxieties; an assistant was near; I asked her (such courage does indignation coupled with anxiety give you): 'Have you a book called *Tell England*? By Ernest Raymond?' Yes, I even uttered my own name, all weaknesses blown away by a great wind of care.

'We've had it, sir, but it's sold out.'

'It's a new book. Just published by Cassell's,' I told her, lest her words had been the usual mendacious excuse for not having a title in stock. Or, if it was the truth, to encourage them to buy some more copies quickly, and instruct them where to go for supplies.

I have learned since that this was a mistake on my part because in the bookselling trade there is a firm suspicion that if a visitor comes into a bookshop and inquires about a book of which he knows the exact title, the correct name of its author and of its publisher, he is the author himself.

Appropriately enough it was in the book department of the Army and Navy Stores that the scene with which I close was enacted. I had wandered in for a second or third appreciation of the state of the market, in relation to one book, at this good focal centre. Well, naught for my discomfort here. There on a table, all to itself, was a big and shapely pyramid of the book, perhaps fifty copies of it, with a large card above, saying, 'The Book of the Season'. Standing to look at this display was a small slight woman whose figure seemed familiar. My movements here being of a prowling and stealthy nature, I worked myself towards her and stole a sidelong look at her profile. Lilian Blake. Mrs Blake who had always been so good to us. Where else should she be but in the Army and Navy Stores? I went up to her at once and confessed to my guiltily secret behaviour in this place. After laughing and saying kindly, 'I can well understand it. What more natural?' she seized both my hands and pressed them in wordless congratulation. Dropping them, she turned to look again at that pyramid of books and the card above it. And when, after a little, she turned to speak with me again, it was with a trace of tears in her eyes and a shaking of the head as if to drive them back. Her words, as she glanced once again at that high stack of books, were, 'Oh, if only the General could have lived to see this.'

FAR